The Dundee Whaling Fleet: Ships, Masters and Men

THE DUNDEE WHALING FLEET
Ships, Masters and Men

Malcolm Archibald

Dundee University Press

First published in Great Britain in 2013 by
Dundee University Press

University of Dundee
Dundee DD1 4HN

http://www.dup.dundee.ac.uk/

ISBN 978 1 84586 159 9

British Library Cataloguing-in-Publication Data
A catalogue record for this book is available on request
from the British Library

Typeset in Warnock by
Koinonia, Manchester
Printed and bound by CPI Group (UK) Ltd, Croydon, CR0 4YY

For Cathy

Contents

Acknowledgements

This book would not have been written without the help of the following people. Rhona Rodger and Fiona Sinclair, The McManus: Dundee's Museum and Art Gallery; Iain Flett and Richard Cullen, Dundee City Archives; Caroline Brown and Michael Bolik of the University of Dundee Archive Services and the staff of the Local History Department, Central Library, Dundee.

I also wish to thank my wife Cathy for her patience as I once again lived my life in the Arctic seas, albeit mainly through the aegis of centuries-old books, documents and memoirs, augmented by the hypnotic flicker of the computer screen.

I would also like to thank Sarah Campbell for her incredible patience and dedication in editing what was a very rough manuscript. It is entirely due to her skill that it is now a book.

Introduction

In 2004 I wrote *Whalehunters: Dundee and the Arctic Whalers*, concentrating on the 'Greenlandmen', the seamen who manned the whaling ships that left from Dundee. I wrote about the whaling industry from their perspective, attempting to build up a picture of life as they knew it. I investigated their experiences on land and sea, their superstitions and beliefs and the lifestyle they lived. This book is intended to complement *Whalehunters* by looking at the history of Scottish and, in particular, Dundee Arctic whaling from the angle of the ships. The idea came from my participation in the Dundee Whaling History Project run by Dundee Museums and Art Galleries and involving a partnership of various Dundee institutions. The book is based on information unearthed by the project, including logbooks, journals, and Customs and Excise records, contemporary newspapers, accounts and wages books from whaling companies, certificates of discharge and memoirs. The Ingram Records held in the Central Library in Dundee and a number of secondary sources, in particular Gordon Jackson's *The British Whaling Trade*, together with hundreds of fascinating photographs from the Dundee collections, helped piece together a vivid picture of a unique industry.

The two opening chapters give a brief historical overview of the British whaling industry and describe the process of whaling and sealing in the Arctic. Chapter 3 concentrates on the fortunes of the whaling trade through the wars of the eighteenth and early nineteenth centuries and shows how warfare helped the British ports rise to supremacy in the Arctic. Chapter 4 follows the rise of the industry in Dundee from its one-ship beginning in 1753 to its position as the largest whaling fleet in Britain by 1860, while Chapter 5 details what the whaling men hunted and why.

Chapter 6 provides an introduction to the development of whaling ships and the conditions in which they worked. A description of each vessel that worked as part of the Dundee whaling fleet is given in Appendix 1, The descriptions have been built up from a wide range of source material and

Volume (for oil)

Imperial measures		*Metric measures*
Tun	252 gallons	1,145.45 litres
Butt or pipe	126 gallons	575.50 litres
Hogshead	63 gallons	287.77 litres
Barrel	34 gallons	154.54 litres
Gallon	4.54 litres	

Mass (for blubber or baleen)

Imperial measures		*Metric measures*
Ton	20 hundredweights (cwt)	1,016.00 kg
Hundredweight (cwt)	112 pounds	50.80 kg

include, where available, technical information about each ship and details of the ships' masters, owners and best catches. The notes draw a pen picture of the life of each of the vessels. Chapter 7 explains the business side of whaling, the real reason men ventured into the ice to kill whales, while Chapter 8 concentrates on the whaling masters, with thumbnail sketches of some of the more prominent provided in Appendix 2. Chapter 9 examines the lives of the Greenlandmen, both at sea and on land, and Appendix 3 gives brief but illuminating details of 250 men who sailed aboard Dundee whaling ships in the century and a half of the industry's existence.

Chapter 10 gives an account of what may be Dundee whaling's most famous exploit, the voyage of four ships to the Antarctic in 1892. Chapter 11 looks back at the Arctic whaling industry in Dundee and ties together the threads, while the final chapter gives a very brief description of Scottish whaling in the twentieth century, when Dundee was no longer involved.

Readers will find that the appendices help to fill out the detail in the sketches drawn in the chapters of this book of the ships, masters and men of the Dundee whaling fleet. They provide a wealth of information on the Dundee whaling industry for researchers and family historians.

For the sake of historical flavour and continuity, the measurements used throughout the book to quantify the volumes of blubber, baleen, whale and seal oil brought back by the Greenlandmen are those used in the original source materials. However, the units of measurement quoted from the source materials are often used inconsistently and the volume of whale oil can be given in tuns or tons. A tun was originally a measurement of wine equivalent to the volume of the largest barrels which was 252 gallons. Ships were measured by the number of tuns they could carry and from 1694, this was described as 'tonnage'. Measurements of a ship's tonnage altered on several occasions, with gross tonnage being the total space between decks and net tonnage the total space minus allowances for crews quarters, food and fuel. A ton is a measurement of weight ashore but a measurement of capacity at sea, and they are roughly equivalent, so that, over time, the terms have been used interchangeably in measuring the volume of oil.

The table across gives the imperial measures used in the whaling industry together with their metric equivalents.

1

The Progress of British Arctic Whaling

The Greenland Trade is at all times a trade of the greatest uncertainty
Gazetteer and New Daily Advertiser, 2 January 1765

It started with the Basques, who hunted the stormy waters of the Bay of Biscay for the North Atlantic right whales. As the Basques became more expert, the whale stocks reduced and the hunt had to expand further afield. They formed whaling stations on what is now Eastern Canada, and the seas off Labrador were stained red with the blood of harpooned whales. The English were next on the whale trail, following the scent of blubber and profit to hunt around Spitsbergen, otherwise known as East Greenland. Dutch, French and Danes followed and Scotland eventually joined the hunt. For the 'Greenlandmen', the professional whale hunters of eighteenth and nineteenth century Dundee, the bowhead was the 'right' whale to catch. They called it the Greenland right whale to differentiate it from the related North Atlantic right whale and, in their turn, they decimated the stocks to light and fuel homes, towns and industry throughout the country. Dundonians were not the first to hunt whales in Arctic waters, but they were among the last.

In 1577 the English Muscovy Company gained a twenty year monopoly on whaling which led to minor disputes with rival Hull seamen but no recorded whales. Although their expedition to Spitsbergen in 1611 aboard the 160-ton vessel *Margaret* was unsuccessful, they paved the way for an influx of whalers from across Europe. In the resulting mayhem, nations clashed over whaling rights and Londoners fought men from Hull under the perpetual summer daylight of the north. In 1613 the English Muscovy Company claimed the Svalbard archipelago, including Spitsbergen; the Danes made a counter claim three years later, and all the time the blubber boats butchered the whales. King James VI and I of Scotland and England backed the Muscovy Company, but as the English squabbled amongst themselves, the Dutch proved the better whale hunters and gained gradual ascendancy. The Dutch Republic was Europe's maritime powerhouse at that time, while King James VI and I curbed England's piratical economy and guided his

United Kingdom toward the more legitimate, and ultimately more profitable, pursuit of steady trade.[1]

At that period the whales were hunted by small boats but towed to a suitable bay for processing. With the English eventually relegated to the bays south of Kongsfjorden in Spitsbergen, the Dutch donned the blubber-hunting mantle of the north. They dominated European whaling so that much of the terminology they used was later transferred to the British ships. Nineteenth century whaling men from Hull, Peterhead and Dundee became as familiar with terms such as 'specktioneer' or 'a fall' as the old Dutch masters had been. Well into the eighteenth century, British ships used the expertise of Dutch professionals, with, for instance, Aryan Volckerts commanding the Aberdeen whaling ship *St Ann* in 1755.[2] The clutch of the Netherlands stretched northward from the maritime towns of the Low Countries to encompass much of the Arctic, with summer colonies on Spitsbergen dedicated to hunting and processing whales. The name of Smeerenburg, which translates as Blubbertown, together with makeshift graves and rubble, remains as a haunting reminder of raucous times and bloody profit.

The Dutch seemed destined to be the supreme whale fishers; they were technically more skilful, with better vessels and experience that grew with each season. As the focus shifted from shore-based bay whaling to hunting in the open seas, Dutch ships became as familiar among the drifting bergs as they were at the Cape of Storms and around the gilded seas of the East. The Dutch hunting technique was also superior, if very simple. They sailed north to the edge of the pack ice and allowed the current to take them south; as the migrating whales followed the same route, the Dutch could not help but be successful.[3] But, although the English gave grudging best to the Dutch, they remained, with their Muscovy Company retaining a national monopoly of whale fins and whale oil.[4] By the second decade of the eighteenth century, when the Greenland seas yielded less profit, the Dutch braved the fogs off Cape Farewell and probed the Davis Straits in the quest for whales.

Although Scotland was a maritime nation, Scottish involvement in the early whaling industry was minimal. An Act of Parliament in 1154, which granted a tenth of all whales captured in the Forth and Tay to the king, proved at least recognition of the benefits of whaling[5], but certainly commercial interest was slow in arriving. Nevertheless, King David 1 was able to give the King of France a present of a narwhal tusk,[6] although the provenance is unfortunately unknown. Scotland also had a minimal part in seventeenth century whaling. In 1618 King James granted a 35-year patent to the Leith-based Scottish East India and Greenland Company and at least one ship returned with whale oil. However, in an action that foreshadowed the later tragedy of Darien, the English Muscovy Company complained their monopoly was being compromised and the Scots were forced to withdraw. There were further attempts in 1625, 1670 and 1682. The latter was the most hopeful with two ships – one with Scots, the other with Dutch harpooners – but all failed to make a profit. Scotland seemed doomed to be a maritime nation without a whaling industry.

By the latter decades of the seventeenth century the maritime peoples of the North American colonies joined in the whaling industry and with their superb nautical skills and access to seemingly unlimited supplies of timber, they made a big impact. Long Island was said to be the first to venture into whaling, with Nantucket following in around 1690. The early American vessels were small at around 50 tons, and the crews included Native Americans. Despite ugly prejudice on land, whaling crews seem to have been fairly egalitarian. Although colonial whaling vessels followed the Dutch lead and thrust into the Davis Straits as early as the 1730s, their main expansion occurred in the years between the Seven Years War (1757–63) and the American War of Independence (1775–83)[7] when Massachusetts alone sent 183 vessels to the Arctic.[8] It is possible that the larger government bounty from 1766 onward helped encourage the colonial trade; the British government paid a sum of money to whaling ships over a certain size and the colonial Americans were able to claim the money as well as home-based ships.[9] The North American colonials also joined the Dutch in exporting their catch to Great Britain, stifling native endeavour in the whaling industry and draining the British economy of gold in return for baleen and oil. A government Act of 1764 that removed duty on colonial baleen also encouraged American exports.[10] Ultimately the whaling industry of New England was a magnificent thing, although the whales may have disagreed, and the sea road between Nantucket, New Bedford and London was perfumed with the scent of boiled blubber.

It was in the eighteenth century that Scotland properly entered the whaling trade, but it was not until the nineteenth that Scottish ports dominated European whaling, first with Peterhead and then Dundee. The latent interest was apparent in 1711 when the Convention of Scottish Burghs mentioned: 'the whale fishing is another branch of the fishing which . . . begins from the Orcades and extends northward . . . there are people here very well inclined to set it agoing.'[11] However, another four decades passed before any Scottish ship ventured toward the whaling grounds.

By the 1730s the government realised that Britain was trailing in the whaling trade and tried to create interest by offering incentives, or bounties, for whaling ships. The bounty system was fairly common in the eighteenth century. The government paid companies a bonus if they participated in a certain industry, for instance linen, fishing or whaling. The idea was to encourage a particular enterprise by removing some of the element of financial risk until the industry was sufficiently established to stand on its own feet. The bounty system for whaling was slow to make an impact despite a temporary rise from twenty to thirty shillings a ton during the War of the Austrian Succession in 1740.[12] Not until 1750, when the government doubled their stake to £2 a ton for whaling ships of over 200 tons burthen, did Scottish adventurers accept the challenge. England, and in particular London, had kept her nautical toe dipped in whaling waters since the seventeenth century, but with the increase of bounty payments, whaling companies sprang up all around the British coast. Only two whaling vessels sailed from Great Britain in 1749; by 1756 there were 83.[13] The whaling companies were not being hoodwinked by a simple handout; there were sound commercial reasons for whaling with a growing market for oil in the textile trade and for street lighting, while the female fashion industry required baleen; the merchant adventurers were assured of a strong market.[14]

However, the bounty system was not set in stone. The government periodically reviewed the amount it paid out. An increase in the early 1770s, at a time of increased Dutch and Colonial competition, led to 22 more vessels sailing from London,[15] but, perhaps surprisingly, a corresponding decrease in 1787 had no apparent detrimental effect; the numbers of British whaling vessels again increased.[16] It is possible that by that year the industry was firmly established and the demand for whale oil was enough to counteract the lesser bounty. It is equally possible that, with weaker competition from the Dutch and the recent collapse of colonial competition, the British whaling companies knew there was profit to be made despite a lesser bounty.[17] Even with the reduced payouts, the government still handed an annual £100,000 to the whaling companies, while retaining duties on imported foreign whale oil. In an age of protectionism, the Dutch also levied a 12 per cent tax on British oil. In the 53 years from the start of the bounty system in 1733, the government paid over £202,158 to Scottish whaling firms and £1,064,271 to English firms.[18] Nevertheless, there was constant speculation about the ending of bounties and in 1824 they stopped completely. However, the industry continued with the significant ports now much further north than London.

As well as bringing home blubber and baleen, the Arctic whaling trade was considered an excellent method of training men in seamanship. To receive the bounty, each whaling vessel had to carry a number of apprentices, known as 'greenmen', so when the next war came along there would be large numbers of seamen trained and ready to join the Royal Navy. There was one instance in 1790 when a greenman deserted so the ship master replaced him with a more experienced man. The bounty was refused.[19] Although the whaling companies benefited from the bounty, when drumbeats called young men to the colours all across Europe and the Admiralty stretched predatory hands to clutch at seamen, they still demanded protections so their crews would not be pressed into the Royal Navy. While masters and mates were automatically protected and specialists such as harpooners and line managers were relatively safe, ordinary seamen could only obtain a protection from voyage to voyage. Even so, the Royal Navy frequently stretched the laws to suit themselves so even at sea the 'Greenlandmen', as seamen who worked in Arctic whaling and the whaling ships themselves were known, were at risk of impressment.

The whaling masters had to follow strict regulations to obtain the bounty, including a requirement to keep a logbook with a record of the bearings whenever land or a whale was sighted.[20] The customs officials were quick to note omissions, for example in this extract of a customs entry in 1807:[21]

Honorable Sirs
In perusing the Log Book kept of the Transactions of the ship Advice of this Port James Webster Master from the Whale Fishery at Davis Streights cleared outward under the Act 26 Geo 3 Cap 41 and Subsequent Acts we found the Instances following where land was discovered and no Soundings taken and Humbly Submit the same to your Honors for Consideration and Directions in regard to forwarding the necessary papers for obtaining the Bounty viz:

That upon 4th April last Cape Elizabeth bore N by W dist 5 Leagues Ob 62.21 no soundings is stated 'no opportunity of Sounding as they were beating to windward thro Bay Ice

That upon 14th April last Resolution Isle bore NW dist 10 Leagues no Soundings taken, it is said they were beating to windward.

That upon 16th of said April Resolution Isles bore NW by N dist 15 Leagues no soundings taken nor is there any reason given why this was not done

That upon 12th of May last Queen Ann's Cape bore S by W distance 8 or 9 Leagues no Soundings taken owing it is said to the Ship having so much way through the water

That upon 13th of May at 8 Poll Disco Isle bore SE distant 6 leagues at noon same day the said isle SSW dist 3 leagues no soundings as they were doing what they could to get up to the Fishing ground.[22]

The first Scottish whaling company of this period was the Leith-based

Edinburgh Whale Fishery Company in 1749[23], which sent out the aptly named *Tryal* of Leith commanded by Captain Whitehead,[24] but her initial voyage was a disaster. She left Leith on 12 April, took 40 days to reach the whaling grounds rather than the customary 14, was trapped in the ice and caught only 'a few sea horses'.[25] However, despite this initial failure, the owners financed two ships the following year[26], beginning a fairly successful relationship between Leith and the Arctic. As a comparison London had 40 whaling vessels.[27] That same year Glasgow sent out a vessel commanded by Captain Fisher[28], but Scotland's share in the 350 whales brought back to the United Kingdom in 1751 was painfully small[29]. True to her motto, Leith persevered and in 1752 her three vessels brought back 13 whales; a ship from Dunbar captured 4; vessels from the Bogle family's Glasgow Whale Fishing Company caught 9; and the ships of Bo'ness and Campbeltown, 2 between them. That same year, Scotland, using a system of business partnerships, sent a healthy total of 9 ships north, while England floated 23, Denmark 5, and there were 2 French, 13 Hamburgers and an impressive 117 from the Dutch Republic.[30] The Glasgow merchants soon altered their whaling ship base to Bo'ness, a sign that the East Coast was more favoured for the whaling industry.[31]

Veteran Dutchmen frequently aided the initial Scottish whaling ships, such as Jurgan Brueri and Symon Cornelius who sailed in *Dundee* of Dundee in 1754,[32] but by the 1770s Scottish Greenlanders were claimed to be the equal of any other nation.[33] The Dutch may not have agreed. The Scottish whaling industry grew steadily – never spectacular but gaining experience and bringing home sufficient whale oil and baleen to keep the companies alive – although in the early years, probably only the certainty of a government bounty guaranteed financial viability.[34] The country remained a minor player compared with the Dutch who fielded 159 ships in 1758,[35] 132 in 1759,[36] 137 in 1760[37] and 154 in 1762.[38] In the latter year, the Seven Years War was raging and there were just 25 English and 16 Scots ships at the whaling, catching a total of 21 whales between them.[39] The bounty was a lifeline to British whaling at a time when the Dutch were consistently more successful (see Table 1.1).[40] Those British ships that did make a profit usually carried professional Dutch whaling men, which tended to argue that the British, despite press claims, were not yet particularly skilful. Indeed in the decade following the Seven Years War, the colonial ships once again dominated British whaling.[41]

In 1763 there were 157 Dutch ships and 167 in the following year[42] but bad weather curtailed the catches, with 'not above three days good weather'.[43] By 1768 there were 240 Dutch ships whaling,[44] and with the North

Table 1.1 Comparison of selected British and Dutch whaling ports, 1773

British			Dutch		
Port	*Ships*	*Whales*	*Port*	*Ships*	*Whales*
London	28	45	Amsterdam	47	84
Hull	8	10	Zaandam	19	43
Whitby	5	7	Rotterdam	7	17
Leith	4	1	Harlingen	5	2
Dundee	3	1	Zandijk	2	3.5
Other	12	20	Other	14	39
Total	61	84	Total	94	186.5

American colonies also expanding their fleet, Britain struggled to stay in touch. However, there were also ships from Hamburg,[45] Denmark, France,[46] Portugal,[47] Bremen[48] and the Channel Islands[49] hunting along the Arctic ice, so even with financial incentives, it is hardly surprising that 85 per cent of the whale oil in Britain came from non-British sources. Until the American War of Independence, the New England ports alone provided nearly half the oil sold in Britain. Even at a time of protectionism, the need for whale oil was so acute and the demand so great, particularly in London,[50] that Britain continued to import from elsewhere. Other nations were not so willing to compromise, with Denmark prohibiting the import of oil into Schleswig, Holstein and other Danish territories except in ships from Danish ports.[51]

Despite the British whaling bounty, the Dutch Republic remained the most important Arctic whaling nation, but Great Britain was closing the gap and some of the German states were also heavily involved. Table 1.2 gives further details of purely British catches in the Greenland fishery for 1776.

The importance of London is obvious while ports such as Liverpool and Exeter, which do not figure in whaling in the later years, are also involved. In this year Dunbar was the most significant of the Scottish ports: Bo'ness had lost both her whaling vessels the previous year and was temporarily out of the trade while Dundee stubbornly sent a single vessel north. However, although the various states competed for trade and calculated the amount of ships sent by their rivals, once at sea there seemed little animosity between different nationalities, at least in peacetime. For example, in 1756 *Dundee* of Dundee rescued the crew of a shipwrecked Dutch vessel[52] and in 1762 Dutch vessels carried home the crew of *Hawke* of Anstruther, which was lost while

Table 1.2 Greenland fishery, 1776

Port	Ships	Whales
London	32	85
Whitby	10	15
Liverpool	20	45.5
Hull	5	10
Dunbar	3	15
Leith	3	10
Newcastle	3	8
Lynn	2	6
Exeter	1	7
Dartmouth	1	3
Dundee	1	1
Sunderland	1	0
Scarborough	1	0
Total	83	206.5

in the act of catching a whale.[53]

Wartime was always a different story. The American War of Independence was a strange transatlantic civil war in which the British won many of the battles but lost the campaigns, possibly due in part to a reluctance to fight their own blood, to the nature of the conflict and also to the sheer number of states that combined against Britain. The French carried out maritime and land based campaigns as allies of the Americans and expended a great amount of treasure for an end that benefited them hardly at all. However, despite Britain losing the war and many of its colonies, its whaling trade did ultimately benefit. As early as 1775 British whaling companies exploited colonial difficulties by floating more vessels, while the government introduced a bounty for the Labrador and St Lawrence fisheries. The colonial whaler men lost ground.[54] In winning independence, the maritime states of the new republic lost the trading advantages with Britain they had once enjoyed; they could no longer depend on a steady market. Many American vessels, for example *Little Fanny,* joined the British whaling fleet, and some slipped free of port and plunged into the Southern Fishery, based on the Falkland Islands.[55] Whaling in American Greenland and the Davis Straits never reached the same level as it had in pre-revolutionary years.

The Southern Fishery, comprising anywhere south of 59 degrees 30 minutes north, did not qualify for the whaling bounty. After the American War, numbers of ex-colonial whaling men crossed the Atlantic to London and virtually established this new whale fishing area, operating chiefly in the South Atlantic between Brazil and the Cape Verde Islands. The whalers in the Southern Fishery hunted the sperm whale rather than the bowhead and made much longer voyages, eventually penetrating into the Pacific, the coasts of Australasia and the fringes of the Antarctic. There was no intercourse between the northern and southern whaling communities and, save for the fact both hunted whales, very little similarity.[56]

With the American competition removed from the Arctic, British whaling companies eased into the gap and increased their share of the home market. Despite the difficulties of the war years, there were some impressive catches, with the 1779 Arctic fishing season particularly successful at a time when the Southern Fishery was badly hit by Spanish privateers.[57] 1781 was even better, so that Captain White of the London vessel *Young Eagle* called it 'the greatest fishing ever known; not one clean ship'.[58] But when peace broke out, even with the American Arctic ships removed from the equation, the Dutch remained a significant force in Artic whaling.

The British seemed to use the Dutch whaling industry as a yardstick against which to measure the success of their own, for instance in 1763 the London Press spoke of the Dutch whaling industry making £100,000 annually and suggested the British make more of their whaling.[59] There are also frequent comparisons between British and Dutch performance, as if the British were pupils learning from their master. According to the British press, the Dutch were better disciplined, with daily prayers, a lack of drunkenness and penalties for fighting.[60] However, as the Dutch sided with the Americans during the war, their ships were fair game for British privateers and the Royal Navy so that by 1782, the Dutch whaling fleet mustered a mere 30 vessels that caught only 50 whales[61] compared to a catch of 336 in 1753.[62] As well as the material loss in shipping and revenue, the drop in the importation of whale oil must have pushed up oil prices in the Dutch Republic, leading to discontent among the population. In contrast, 1783 was perhaps the most successful year yet for the British whaling trade.

London's continued domination of the domestic whaling trade, with over a third of all British whaling ships, is revealed in Table 1.3. Not too much significance should be attached to Dundee's position as second amongst the Scottish whaling ports, as the number of whaling ships in any port was liable to fluctuation over short periods. The fall in overall numbers was presum-

Table 1.3 British whale catches, 1783[63]

Port	Ships	Whales
London	19	107
Leith	6	34
Bristol	5	27
Newcastle	5	26
Dundee	3	29
Liverpool	3	19
Aberdeen	2	16
Bo'ness	2	12
Orkney	2	11
Hull	2	11
Lancaster	1	9
Port Glasgow	1	9
Isle of Man	1	8
Other	2	12
Total	54	339

ably due to the demands of an unsuccessful war.

The immediate post war period saw a surge in the number of British Arctic whaling ships, with more than 70 from London in 1784[64] and a reported 16 from Newcastle the following year.[65] The boom was sustained until 1787, when a high demand for oil in London[66] encouraged whaling companies to send a massive 253 ships to the Arctic, employing around 10,000 men compared with 6,400 the previous year.[67] After a mediocre beginning, Hull immersed herself in the whaling trade in the mid 1760s when a merchant named Samuel Standidge revived the Hull Fishery Company and from that time, the port never looked back.[68] After the American war, Hull had 31 ships[69] but the 1787 season that started with high hopes ended in disaster with at least 11 and possibly as many as 14 English ships lost in the ice, although there seem to have been few lives lost.[70] There was irony in the losses, for fifteen of the ships were waiting to return home, but the new bounty regulations stipulated they must wait in the ice until 10 August. As they waited, the ice crushed them with a reported 700 men shipwrecked.[71] That year of peacetime saw more ships lost than were taken by the French

Table 1.4 The Scottish whaling fleet, 1787

Ship	Master	Port	Seals	Whales	Butts blubber
Royal Bounty	Paton	Leith	9	8.5	130
Raith	Young	Leith	1430	5	140
Grampus	Balfour	Leith	15	5	45
Six Brothers	Ferguson	Leith	1	1	35
Princess of Wales	Muirhead	Dunbar	9	6	140
Endeavour	Dawson	Dunbar	22	6	140
Caledonia	Pottinger	Bo'ness	260	1	
Leviathan	Mason	Bo'ness	19	1	
Ocean		Bo'ness	0	1	
Peace and Plenty	Steel	?Greenock		4	88
Neptune	Stein	Kincardine	0	1	
Dundee	Souter	Dundee	1500	5	150
Tay	Webster	Dundee	1400	0	
Dempster	Cunningham	Montrose	500	0	
Latona	Storie	Aberdeen		6	110
Hercules	McLarin	Aberdeen	330	3	90
Perseverance	Lawrie	Greenock		1	40
Satisfaction	Chapman	Greenock	3	5	75
Paisley	Boyd	Port Glasgow		5	140
Christian	Law	Aberdeen	1341	0	

Source: General Evening Post, 1 July 1787

during the war. Despite the English losses, all the Scottish ships returned safely with *Neptune* of Kincardine the only one with serious damage.[72] That was a bad year but not the worst; in 1758, 17 ships had been lost in the ice.[73]

Table 1.4 shows both the extent of whaling in Scotland and catches of whales and seals. The number of whaling ports had increased, with Dundee sitting firmly in the middle ranks, while the types of catches reveal the diversification from purely whaling to sealing as well. After the disaster of 1787, fewer ships sailed from London, but Hull, Whitby and Newcastle increased the size of their fleet.[74] In 1789 the figures were as follows:

London still dominated with nearly a third of the total number of vessels,

Table 1.5 British whaling ports, 1789

Port	Number of ships	Port	Number of ships
London	52	Dunbar	4
Hull	29	Ipswich	3
Liverpool	17	Montrose	3
Whitby	15	Whitehaven	2

Source: Whitehall Evening Post, 9 August 1789

but the overall focus of the industry showed signs of moving north as Hull continued to increase her fleet, while Liverpool, Whitby and Newcastle were now significant players. The Scottish ports were small-scale in comparison, but retained their steady, unspectacular presence. Leith retained the top Scottish spot while four ports including Dundee vied for second place. Overall, however, Scottish ports still played a poor second best to those in England.

As Europe uneasily watched France rip herself apart with revolutionary turmoil, the whaling season of 1791 was not a success. Many of the Scottish ships returned *clean*, i.e., devoid of whales. War returned to Britain in January 1793 but despite inevitable setbacks and hardships, the outcome was ultimately favourable for the British whaling industry. When the French annexed the Dutch Republic in 1794, the Dutch automatically became enemies and the Royal Navy virtually annihilated their whaling fleet. For example, in one short period in May 1798, the Royal Navy captured nine Dutch whaling vessels and convoyed them to Yarmouth.[75] Nevertheless, wartime created hazardous conditions for the whaling and the number of British vessels fluctuated from year to year. In 1800, after seven years of war, there were 72 British ships, including 26 from Hull[76] and ten from Scotland.[77] That was a drop of more than a hundred since the beginning of the war and another sign of the northward swing in whaling. Despite the hostilities, Hull continued to expand its fleet, with 36 vessels in 1802[78] and 40 in 1804.[79]

There was a major dip in 1808 when all trade suffered as Bonaparte's Continental System, which from late 1806 had imposed an embargo on trade between mainland Europe and Britain, began to bite. With the dawning of peace in 1815 and major opposition all but removed from the whaling grounds, Great Britain dominated whaling in the Greenland Seas and the Davis Straits. This situation continued throughout the nineteenth century. Notwithstanding their local dominance, Britain was not the largest whaling nation in the world. After losses in the Revolutionary War and the war of 1812, the United States built up their whaling fleet until they floated more vessels than the rest of the world combined. For instance, in 1856 New Bedford alone possessed around 320 whaling ships: that same year Dundee had 4. However the American ships concentrated on the Southern Fishery, leaving Britain to dominate and capitalise on the Northern Fishery until Arctic whaling collapsed in the early twentieth century. However, as rival nations disappeared, there were other threats. In 1821 oil prices slumped in the face of more affordable rapeseed oil, and in 1824 the government ended bounty payments.[80] Shortly afterwards, another and even more formidable enemy appeared: the commercial adoption of gas for lighting in the early nineteenth century was a serious blow to the demand for whale oil.

Gas lighting was nothing new. The Chinese had used skins full of natural gas for centuries, but in 1792 the Scotsman William Murdoch was the first person in Britain to use gas to light his home. He worked for Boulton and Watt, the Birmingham based steam engine manufacturer, and around the turn of the nineteenth century, the firm also began to build gas works for industrial premises. In 1807 Pall Mall in London was lit by gas. As gas was created from coal, a substance Britain had in abundance, there was no need to import.[81] Lighting gas cost about a quarter of the price of oil. In 1816 whaling ship owners presented a petition against the Gas Light Bill,[82] which threatened to spread the use of gas. The petition failed and gas was here to stay. From that date the whaling industry faced an uphill struggle.

As the London fleet diminished and died in the early nineteenth century, the Hull fleet grew, with 56 vessels in the Arctic in 1817. The ice continued to take its toll with a reported 10 ships lost in 1819[83] but even so, there were 6,000 men and 159 British ships in 1821, including 10 from Dundee. That year another 13 ships were sunk. The number of ships fluctuated wildly, so in 1824 there were only 94 British whalers in the Arctic with 4,000 men, but the pendulum of ascendancy continued to shift northward. In 1823 Hull had 41 of the 115 British ships; Peterhead had 15, Dundee 10, Whitby 10 and the rest were in single figures. London, once so dominant, had three ships.[84] Hull had assumed the crown of king of British whaling ports but the 1830s was a grim decade for the whaling trade. In the disastrous year of 1830, 19 British ships were sunk crossing Melville Bay to fish in the West Water and another 21 came back clean. Some were trapped in the ice from June until September: so many vessels were crushed and sank that a thousand men were camped out on the ice. The shipowners could not continue with such losses, and when more ships and men were lost in 1835 and 1836, even the Hull shipowners began to lose interest in whaling. Her trade diverted to the Baltic and North America and her merchants looked elsewhere for profit.[85]

Nevertheless, Hull's connection with whaling limped on for nearly three decades. The British whaling fleet diminished year on year, from 91 vessels and 4,120 men in 1830 to 25 ships and 1,146 men in 1843.[86]

In the 1850s, experiments in the USA uncovered a process of distilling kerosene from petroleum, while a commercial oil well was sunk in Poland. From small beginnings, the petroleum industry grew rapidly, dealing another major blow to the demand for whale oil. For the next half century the British Arctic whale fishery was slowly, irrevocably dying, but it fought back with every technique and ounce of ingenuity it could muster. The industry tried steam ships, new types of whaling guns, searched for new whaling grounds and diversified the products it brought back from the Arctic, but the odds were stacked against success. As well as facing gas and petroleum products, the industry had diminishing resources.

As long as whales could breed as fast as the hunters could capture them, the whaling ships were virtually assured of some success. However, as soon as the number of whales killed outnumbered births, the industry was on a downward spiral. By the early nineteenth century, every decade saw whaling ships probing into more dangerous seas. Despite the increasing difficulties in catching sufficient whales, Scottish ports continued in the trade. Peterhead had surged to dominance while the newcomer Fraserburgh enjoyed a bright, brilliant few years before concentrating on the herring industry. By the middle of the nineteenth century, Peterhead had by far the largest whaling fleet, although they were as likely to catch seals as whales. Dundee continued, unspectacular but dogged. In 1853 The numbers of whaling ships

Table 1.6 Whaling and sealing ships, 1853

Port	Number of vessels
Peterhead	27
Hull	13
Dundee	4
Aberdeen	3
Fraserburgh	3
Banff	2
Kirkcaldy	2
Bo'ness	1
Nairn	1
Total	56

sailing from British ports in 1853 are shown in Table 1.6.

The total of 56 vessels compares with 47 in 1852, 38 in 1851 and 32 in 1850. The reason for the increase was not due to higher numbers of whales but the general movement toward sealing.

Hull's star continued to fade. In 1866 the Hull steamer *Diana* was trapped in the ice for six months and many of her crew died of scurvy. Three years later *Diana* was wrecked, but ironically on the Donna Nook Sands on the Lincolnshire coast rather than in the Arctic. Her loss signalled the end of Hull's participation in whaling.

By the end of the 1830s the hunters had already noticed a scarcity of whales, but there were incalculable numbers of seals. Sealing had been important for decades, with, for example *Hawke* of London bringing home 250 seals in 1765,[87] *Weymouth* of London catching 3,300 seals in 1767,[88] and *Duke of York* bringing home 5,500 in 1774,[89] but it became ever more vital as whale stocks decreased. Scottish ships had also hunted seals with *Princess of Wales* of Dunbar catching 'a great many seals' in 1775[90] and *North Star* of Dunbar 850 seals in 1783.[91] In 1803 *Hope* of Peterhead made a profit from her catch, or, euphemistically, 'capture', of 180 seals and other vessels followed her lead in concentrating on sealing rather than whaling. In 1819 *Active* of Peterhead brought home 2,500 seals and by the 1850s seal hunting was as lively an activity as whaling, with better returns for the investment. However, the prime quarry for the industry ostensibly remained the Greenland right whales.

Arctic whaling and sealing was a dynamic industry, a constant search for improved hunting techniques. Possibly the most bizarre was in 1832 when the Leith ship *William Young* carried harpoons laced with Prussic acid, a procedure invented by the Edinburgh University toxicologist Robert Christison. Perhaps fortunately for the whales, the ice claimed *William Young* before she could use the harpoons, but there were other more traditional attempts to improve the science of whale killing. The first known attempt to create a harpoon gun was in 1731. Contemporary technology only allowed a flintlock firing mechanism, where a fast moving spring propelled a flint toward a block of shaped steel; the impact threw a shower of sparks into a pan of gunpowder. The resulting explosion sent a harpoon hurtling forward toward the whale. However, a flintlock is unreliable at the best of times, and anything but suitable for use in a small boat, bucking in sometimes tempestuous seas and spattered with spray. However, there was another, vaguely mysterious device sent north with Captain Murray of the Leith ship *Tryal* in 1751. Invented by a student from Edinburgh University with the evocative name of Bond, this was described as 'a very curious machine for throwing harpoons'.[92] The experiment does not seem to have been repeated, so presumably it was not successful. In 1772 the Society of Arts, Manufacturers and Commerce awarded 20 guineas for improvements to the whaling gun and ordered 24 swivel guns to be fitted with locks and sent north in the whaling ship *Leviathan*.[93] In 1790 a cover was invented to keep the flintlock dry and sometime before 1844, William Greener replaced the flintlock with Forsyth's percussion cap, which became a fixture in the Arctic fishery.[94]

Dundee was not backward with the new techniques and in 1817 the Dundee Whaling Company paid £39 6s for a whaling gun for *Active*.[95] When in 1859, Edmund Balchin created the exploding bomb lance,[96] and then the Norwegian Svend Foyn invented a swivel-mounted explosive whaling gun, the days of hand thrown harpoons had ended forever. Scottish vessels frequently used locally made weapons, with Dundee's David Neave of King William Dock producing whaling guns from at least 1861 until 1877:[97] the whaling ship *Erik* carried a Neave-made gun.[98] However the English Greener model was also popular, and was carried on *Narwhal* in 1876, when Thomas Macklin, the surgeon, mentioned 'one of the ship's guns, a Greener'.[99] Arguably even more important than the actual hunting machine, toward the close of the 1850s, Dundee and Hull both fitted whaling ships with auxiliary steam engines, and the whole concept of Arctic whaling altered.

Steam powered vessels had the advantage of being able to sail against the wind, so could leave harbour at a specified time. They could also sail on two voyages a year; an early one for sealing, then return to port, refit, coal up and steam out for the longer whaling trip. The extra power provided by coal also enabled a steam ship to penetrate ice fields closed to purely sail-powered vessels, so they could hunt for whales deeper in the ice. The old whaling men had a saying that 'frost nips the wind', which suggested there were many calm days in the Arctic when sailing ships were either static or had to be towed; steam alleviated that problem.

There were drawbacks, of course. Steam ships were more expensive to build and required a constant supply of coal, which cost money, while a set of sails could last years if properly maintained. The engine room and coal bunkers also took up space, thus reducing cargo carrying capacity. Even when the ships had steam, the engines might be low powered, as Vannet's journal recorded on SS *Morning* in 1910: 'could not steam against the wind; had to set fore lower topsail and run in again before the wind blowing very hard'.[100] After the 1860s, steam ships became the norm in the Arctic and purely sail powered vessels, such as *Chieftain* of Dundee, became scarce.

Nevertheless, not every innovation was successful. There was disaster when whaling ship owners tried to substitute iron or steel hulled vessels for the traditional wood. There was a small number of such vessels, with *Empress of India* sailing north in 1859 and *River Tay* in the mid 1860s. Both were lost on their maiden voyage. When the Aberdeen-registered *Empress of India* sank, the Dundee *Narwhal* was close by. Usually when a ship sank, the crew rescued all they could of their personal belongings and scrambled clear. In the case of *Empress of India*, the crew of *Narwhal* boarded the sinking ship to 'save as much as possible from the wreck'.[101] However the crew of *Empress of India* was still on board and there were angry scuffles and the exchange of 'the most obscene oaths'.[102] There were no more experiments with iron among the ice and wooden hulled vessels powered by sails and steam dominated the Scottish whaling and sealing industry until its demise in 1914. By that time only Dundee was left.

The latter part of the nineteenth century saw the inevitable death of British Arctic whaling. Only Dundee's unique position as the jute capital of the world plus periodic rises in the price of baleen, made the now-anachronistic industry tenable. Jute required copious amounts of whale oil to make the raw material pliable while baleen was in demand as a flexible material for a host of products. The Peterhead fleet shifted its focus from whaling to sealing in the middle decades of the century before competition from Dundee and the use of larger steam vessels forced her to follow London and Hull into decline.[103] Dundee fought hard, opening bases in St John's, Newfoundland, building superb steam-powered vessels that could make two voyages a year, and branching out into the leather trade with seal skins, but in the face of declining stocks of whales and seals and no desire to adopt more modern hunting techniques, Dundee's old Arctic trade faded away. There was neither fanfare nor funeral as the city bade a quiet farewell to the whales.

2

The Hunting Process

According to an agreement entered into by the captains of the fleet killing was delayed until the 27th and even then many of the young seals were very small and not worth killing

Dundee Advertiser, 23 April 1872

From a haphazard process of bay whaling in the early seventeenth century, whaling and sealing evolved into established routines by the latter decades of the eighteenth, when bounty payments and the Arctic weather helped dictate their timetable. Around the middle of January, the vessels were fitted out and prepared for the voyage. Vessels sailing to the sealing grounds of the Greenland Sea left port in February and those bound for the whaling in the Davis Straits in March. Not until the advent of steam power at the end of the 1850s did the procedure alter, for steam ships could regularly manage two voyages rather than the normal single trip of wind-powered craft.

There were always celebrations as the fleet left port, with wives and families and girlfriends waving a heartsick farewell to their men, for voyages in the Arctic were dangerous. The journals and diaries of the whaling men frequently mention the protracted farewell with passages such as: 'We did not get up steam . . . till 12.30 PM as our crew were not all on board, they being mostly engaged in taking their leave of their families and bidding them adieu. In one case this took about an hour.'[1] The intense emotion cannot be wondered at, for augmenting the routine maritime dangers of storm and accident, there was always the possibility of being trapped in the ice or having one's whaleboat smashed by the swing of a whale's tail. Once out of the Tay, the ships would sail to Orkney or Shetland to fill up with supplies and recruit more men. The island seamen were skilful, particularly in the small boat work so essential in whaling and sealing, and contemporary reports indicate they were paid less than men from the mainland ports: 'their labour, while it is of course cheap, is at the same time valuable.'[2] Prior to 1793 the law banned whaling ships from recruiting Shetlanders, as the crews had to be mustered in the home port in order to qualify for the bounty. That year the restrictions were relaxed for the duration of the war; 22 years later when Waterloo brought peace, the practice was part of the whaling routine.[3] Shetlanders and Orcadians made a massive and not yet fully documented contribution to the Arctic whaling industry

Because the early whaling and sealing ships hunted around the Arctic islands of Jan Mayen Land and Spitsbergen, which was originally known as Greenland, the ships and their crewmen came to be known as Greenlandmen. Until steam, the whaling season lasted around three to four months, although bad weather could prolong it to twice that length. For that reason, by the 1850s the vessel would be provisioned for a longer period in case they were iced in. In the one to two months it took sail-powered vessels to reach the hunting grounds and return to Dundee, steam ships could get there and back, refit and sail on to the Davis Straits. After the 1870s many Dundee vessels sailed directly to St John's in Newfoundland, picked up a local crew of 'sweilers' and worked the Newfoundland and Labrador banks. Although Dundee vessels made the Newfoundland fishery an annual event, they were not the first to try it: as well as the early Basques, two Glasgow whaling ships headed for the Newfoundland banks in 1764,[4] but the attempt could not have been profitable enough to be repeated.

The whaling ship transported the hunters to the whaling grounds but was not directly involved in the hunt. When the ship reached the edge of the ice, one whaleboat would be on 'bran', which meant it was ready for a quick launch. The master or some trusted veteran would mount watch in the crow's nest, high in the mainmast. Armed with a telescope to look for whales and icebergs, and a speaking trumpet to give directions, he would command the ship from aloft. He may also have had a rifle for an unwary narwhal or seal. It was not unknown for the ship's master to be in the crow's nest for hours, in temperatures that could sink to thirty degrees below freezing. The ships hunted along the edge of the Arctic ice, or among broken ice, where the whales could be seen and trapped. Decade by decade, they had moved further away from the open waters, and decade by decade life was tougher and harder for the hunters. If the lookout in the crow's nest spotted a whale, the whale boats – small, open vessels with six men in each – would race toward the prey. There was a hierarchy in the boats, with three officers: a boatsteerer who steered the boat to the best angle for killing the whale, a harpooner who actually threw the harpoon or fired the harpoon gun, and a line manager who ensured the line from the harpooned whale to the boat did not become entangled around a stray leg or neck. The other men in the boat were purely oarsmen. The first boat to harpoon a whale was known as the 'fast boat' as it was 'fast' to the whale, and the crew gained extra money – 'fast money'.

Once harpooned, the whale would thrash its tail, which could break or capsize the boat, and would dive or tow the boat, sometimes for miles. The whale could swim at perhaps ten miles an hour, and if other boats were present they would strain to keep in sight of the fast boat. This was one of the most dangerous periods of the entire voyage for the whaling men. They could be towed into fog or broken ice, out of sight of the mother ship. Being lost in fog could lead to disaster, as happened to the Dundee whaling ship *Chieftain* in 1884 when most of the crew of a whale boat died of exhaustion and exposure. The whaleboats spread out across the water and when the whale surfaced, normally after about half an hour, the nearest boats would close in, the harpooner would plunge in a harpoon and the process would begin again. When the whale was exhausted it would lie on the surface and the hunters would close in and kill it with lances.

After the killing came the tow back to the mother ship where the head was cut off, and the whale was stripped of its blubber, a process known as 'flensing'. It was essential to flense as quickly as possible as the dead whale decomposed very quickly. The blubber was cut into squares, a process known as 'making off', and stored on board in casks and barrels or in special tanks built into the fabric of the ship. It was unwise to store great slabs of blubber loose in the hold as oil eased out and could create noxious and even potentially lethal gasses in the hold.

Such an event happened on board the Montrose vessel *Eliza Swan* in 1802, an event that was recorded in the customs records:

> On the 16th instant Alexander Young, jr. Master of the Eliza Swan of Montrose, just returned from a voyage to the whale fishing in the Greenland seas, reported the cargo of his said vessel, as containing among other things, 231 casks of blubber or thereby.
>
> By the log book there appears to have been no more than 231 casks filled with blubber, but the master states, that he apprehends there may have been more, but that owing to the confusion the crew were thrown into, at the time the casks were filling with blubber, by eleven of the people having nearly lost their lives in the hold by Mephitic Air which issued from a number of water casks which were stashed for the purpose of being filled with blubber, the exact number of casks filled, could not be ascertained.
>
> We have judged it proper to state this case to your honours, and to pray for your honours directions, whether under the circumstance before stated, if more casks shall be found on board, than the number specified in the report, they may not be added thereto, and admitted to entry[5]

The whale's jaw was cut out so the baleen, the great curtain of material that filtered the plankton that was the whale's sole means of sustenance, could be removed. This baleen was normally known as whalebone and was a valuable commodity. Flensing and making off were cheerful times as the crew knew the proceeds of the kill would supplement their basic wages. Once the whale had been flensed the ship would resume hunting. There were recognised techniques for ensuring a capture, such as keeping behind the whale until the harpoon was driven in, and killing a pup first to ensure the larger and therefore more valuable mother remained close by and vulnerable. The ship would remain 'in the ice' – in the whale hunting grounds – until she was 'full', meaning she could not hold any more whales, or until material damage or the onset of winter weather forced her to return to port.

Seal hunting was equally specialised, with a specific hunting season. Females gave birth on the ice some time after the middle of March and remained until the pups were weaned. Utterly cold blooded, the sealers waited nearby until the pups were worth killing, landed on the ice and either shot them or battered them to death with sealing clubs. If there was no pack ice, the sealers took boats around the edges of the floes and harpooned the seals. Although seal hunting was not as dangerous as whaling, the bladder-nose or hood seals could resist, dragging men over the ice or tossing them into the frozen sea. The males of this seal species were so named because they had a bag of loose skin on top of their head which was inflated when the seal was provoked. The hunters had to pierce this bag with a seal pick before they could club the animal. The bladdernoses tended to fight to defend their mates from the hunters, which made the more docile saddleback seals the first choice for the hunter; their name came from the broad black bands down either flank, although the pups were virginal white.

In the early years the sealers found packs of seals that stretched to the horizon in either direction. Two or more vessels could fish the same pack without sighting each other so there was no thought of conservation or of an end to the seemingly limitless supply of seals. By the early 1870s hunting had reduced the numbers to such an extent that the Dundee ship masters introduced a voluntary close season. They did not start the slaughter until 27 April and even then complained of the immaturity of the catch.[6] While the old seals naturally gave the largest amount of oil and so were prime targets, the young were easier to kill. Once weaned, these pups were left to fend for themselves; they remained on the ice as easy prey for hunters with the ferocious seal clubs. As Surgeon Trotter of the Fraserburgh whaling ship *Enterprise* noted: 'This day we got our first seal . . . one of the men shooting her from the boat and then another running onto the piece of ice and striking her on the head with a seal club. I was astonished at the immense quantity of blood which they contained.'[7] Trotter seemed equally surprised that the seals did not always die tamely: 'the male, a great big ugly black brute prepared to defend her against the coming assailants.'[8] The pups were killed without compassion: 'The young one was . . . clubbed. It was so small that it could be carried on one's hand.'[9] The dead seals were piled together in clumps known as 'pans' with the crew of each ship marking their own pan with a flag.

With the initial hunting complete, the sealing ships sailed further north in pursuit of their prey. The sealers did not hunt for pleasure but for profit; it was a cold-blooded business venture. If captured early in the season, the hunters reckoned forty mature seals made one ton of oil, but if the catch was of the smaller young seals, anything from 70 to a hundred seals would have to be killed to make a ton of oil. However, in a good hunting season a ship could capture perhaps 2,000 young seals and 600 older animals, making over 30 tons of seal oil once the blubber was boiled down. The hunt became frighteningly efficient as the sealers perfected their trade. If the seals were killed on the ice away from the ship, the animals were stripped of their skin and blubber immediately. The skins were dragged to the ship in bundles by means of a 'lowery tow' which was a rope ten feet in length (about three metres) and an inch in diameter. Sometimes the men had to drag the bundles for miles across the ice. Once they reached the ship the skins were flensed with a blubber knife and the blubber stored in casks or, as with whale blubber, in special tanks.

When the ships returned to port the blubber was boiled into oil which sold for anything between £25 and £35 per tun (a tun was 252 gallons) and, like whale oil, would be used for lighting or lubrication. In a sale of whale and seal oil at Peterhead in October 1853, merchants from Newcastle, Leith, Aberdeen and Dundee paid £36 a tun for whale oil and £33 10s for seal oil, with the entire cargoes of the Greenland ships being bought within the hour. Given the much more dangerous and longer voyage required to hunt whales than seals, the scant difference in price would not discourage seal fishing; investors would be more likely to put their money into the safer trade. After coming home in the late summer or autumn, the hunting vessels were usually laid up for the winter, and repaired from the damage done to them by the ice and storms of the north. Occasionally the vessels might be sent out on a conventional trading voyage in the winter. If the season had been profitable, the men could settle down for the winter, but if whales or seals had proved elusive, they would have to seek a berth on another ship. The managing owner, who had the ultimate responsibility for the company would sell the oil and calculate the profit for the other owners. In wartime, the whaling companies, masters and crew had further troubles, but the hunting and the prey would remain the same.

3

Prizes, Privateers and the Press

The *St Anne* Greenland ship belonging to Aberdeen, now an armed vessel in
the navy service took a French privateer about two in the afternoon
Read's Weekly Journal, 14 May 1757

While war on land is about manoeuvre, tactics and destroying the enemy,
war at sea is as much about economics and starvation. The purpose of a
national navy is threefold: to defend the trade of a nation, to prevent the
enemy from trading and to carry the army for invasion and raid. The epic
and bloody sea battles were merely a means to those ends. When the smoke
had cleared, casualties counted and honours handed out, the ships of the
victorious powers returned to the relentless, cold-blooded task of preventing
the enemy from trading.

In the eighteenth and early nineteenth centuries the Royal Navy was an
utterly professional tool of war. It specialised in warfare by blockade. The
term sounds innocuous and the method was fairly simple. Small vessels of
war cruised close to the enemy shore, with flotillas watching each trading
port and a powerful fleet of battleships waiting further out at sea. If any
enemy ship was seen, it was attacked and anything in port was liable to be
'cut out', which meant the Royal Navy sent in boatloads of men to capture the
enemy vessel and bring it to Britain to be sold. If enemy warships left port, the
small vessels would alert the waiting battle fleet, which would challenge the
emerging ships and a battle could ensue. The longer a blockade continued,
the more experienced the Royal Navy, constantly at sea, became, while the
entrapped enemy became correspondingly more demoralised, giving the
Royal Navy an overwhelming advantage in expertise and morale even before
battle was joined. If the enemy navy did not emerge, then the Royal Navy
severely curtailed or completely prevented trade, causing economic distress,
a lack of basic commodities and perhaps even starvation to the blockaded
country. The Royal Navy could be a very cruel opponent.

However, there were drawbacks. The longer the coastline to be blockaded,
the more ships and men the Royal Navy required, and there was a finite

number of experienced seamen in the United Kingdom. As the number of warships required for convoy and other duties increased, the crews became more stretched, the numbers manning each ship could lessen and their training and efficiency suffered. A constant succession of victories over superior forces may also have created an overconfidence, which may have been partly responsible for the apparent dip in the Royal Navy's efficiency from around 1810, when they suffered a succession of minor defeats. The most important was arguably the Battle of Grand Port in Mauritius in August 1810 when a French frigate squadron defeated a British force of similar strength. The War of 1812 against the USA began just as the Royal Navy was at its least efficient and it saw the capture of some small British warships by more powerful American opponents. However, there was a revival of British naval strength by 1815. The whaling industry, of course, was heavily involved in all the wars of this period. There is a simple question to ask: why were there so many wars involving European powers in the eighteenth century? There is an equally simple, if not simplistic, answer: dynasties and trade. Dynastic squabbles to decide which prince should sit on what throne were important, but trade dominated European political thought. Every nation wanted a greater share of the market and used armies and navies as a tool of aggressive mercantilism.

The wars revealed both the strengths and the weaknesses of the blockade system, and exposed British whaling ships to attack from enemy privateers and national naval vessels. Privateers played a huge part in the wars of this period. They were privately owned vessels that were licensed to carry arms and attack enemies of the state. The ship owner had to obtain a letter of marque from the Admiralty or the equivalent, and the legality of any subsequent capture was decided at an Admiralty court. Normally the bulk of profit from the sale of the prize was awarded to the ship owners, with the government of the licensing state taking around 10 per cent. Every maritime state used privateers, which were seen as a private arm of national navies. They could be of any size from simple rowing boats to sizeable ships capable of facing small naval vessels yardarm to yardarm. Nevertheless their primary function was as profit-making commerce raiders, and as such they were after the most lucrative merchant ships they could realistically capture, with the least damage to themselves. This system of private enterprise was a constant factor throughout the wars of the eighteenth and early nineteenth centuries, and only ended with the Declaration of Paris in 1856.

Whaling ships were valuable property and therefore a prime target for both privateers and government warships. Even an empty and elderly whaling ship was worth a few hundred pounds, while a new ship with a full cargo of blubber and bone could be worth at least £5,000. As a few examples of the cost of empty ships, in 1765 the London ship *Britannia* was sold at Lloyds Coffee House for £1,150[1] and in 1802 the *Lancaster Gazette* claimed that among the 36 Hull vessels fitted out for the whale fishing were two valued at £10,000 each.[2] With anything from fifty to a hundred and fifty British ships on the whaling grounds, and a huge area for the stretched Royal Navy to guard, it is not surprising enemy privateers and warships targeted the Greenland Sea.

Warfare added three threats to the Greenlandman's normal dangers of storm and ice; privateers, national navies and the Royal Navy impress service. These will be considered one after another. During the wars of the eighteenth century, the northern fishery became one more contested area. Britain and France were the main protagonists, with the Dutch not far behind, and at times Prussia, Denmark and the United States were also involved. In the eighteenth century, Frederick the Great had made Prussia a major power on land, but her navy was not significant. Denmark, however, was a fairly substantial sea power, with sway over Norway and the parts of north Germany immediately adjacent to Jutland. In 1751 the King of Denmark was also known as Lord of Greenland and there was a strong rumour that he intended to build a fort and a gun battery on Cape Farewell to control the entrance to the Davis Straits,[3] which would be a threat to British whaling ships. In the event there was no battery built, but the seas remained dangerous with enemy privateers.

There were two methods of defence for the whaling vessels; they could carry cannon, or they could rely on the Royal Navy, which provided convoys to and from the whale fishing grounds and patrolled the Greenland Sea. Often they did both. Whaling ships needed a licence to carry arms, with the owner applying to the local customs office. The owner also had to give security the weapons would be returned and had to account for any ammunition expended.[4] A change of use of the ship necessitated a different licence; for example, in 1809 the owners of the Dundee vessel *Horn* altered her use from the foreign and coasting trade to the whale fishery trade, and her original licence to carry arms had to be cancelled and a new one issued.[5]

In 1793, at the beginning of the French Revolutionary Wars, all Greenlandmen that used the British Channel – now known as the English Channel – were ordered to be armed for fear of privateers.[6] By the early nineteenth century most Dundee whaling vessels carried arms, with *Estridge* mentioned in 1804,[7] *Jane, Horn* and *Rodney* in 1805,[8,9] and *Advice* in March 1809.[10] The allowance of arms was fairly generous, with 'one carriage or swivel gun for every ten tons burthen of the said ship, one musket or blunderbuss, one pair of pistols and one sword or cutlass for every person borne on the books of the said ship with twenty rounds of powder and ball for every carriage or swivel gun and for each musket, blunderbuss or pistol.'[11]

Sometimes the Greenland ships were armed aggressively as well as defensively. For example in 1756 the government hired whaling vessels and fitted them out as 'cruising armed vessels',[12] a role for which their size, seaworthiness and sturdy construction made them ideal, as was proven in May 1757 when one of these ships, *St Anne* of Aberdeen, captured a French privateer.[13] There were also occasions when whaling ships could turn on their hunters, such as the whaling ship that turned to fight the Dunkirk 18-gun privateer *Neckar* in 1781. Suspecting the whaling ship might be a frigate, *Neckar* took fright and tried to run, but crowded on too much canvas and sprung her topmast. Encouraged, the Greenlandman closed, boarded and captured the privateer. *Marianne*, a London whaling ship, was even more successful when she captured a French privateer in 1781 and a 10-gun Dutch cutter privateer in 1782, while also retaking a Newcastle collier from the Dutch privateers who had captured her.[14] It is possible that the 1781 capture was that related by the Reverend John Mill of Dunrossness in Shetland who said: 'A Greenlander took a stout French privateer and brought her into Bressay Sound.'[15] By 1782 the entire Greenland fleet seemed ready to defend itself against anybody: all six Whitby vessels carried letters of marque[16] and the well armed Dunbar ships *North Star* and *Endeavour* sailed north under the escort of *Princess of Wales*, an ex-whaling ship converted into a 16-gun privateer.[17]

Privateering followed the same pattern in every war with enemy vessels prowling the main shipping routes and cruising for prey while avoiding confrontation with vessels that could fight back. Privateers were after profit, not glory. For example, in 1797 a privateer avoided the armed Dunbar ships *Blessed Endeavour* and *East Lothian* off Fair Isle[18] but the following year a French privateer chased *Rodney* of Dundee just off the knuckle of Buchan. When a high sea prevented the privateer bearing her guns on him, Captain Froggett escaped to Fraserburgh.[19] In 1804 Captain William Scoresby of Whitby also carried letters of marque. While he was in the ice he met four Dutch whaling vessels but did not attack as the Dutch also carried neutral Danish documents.[20]

In all the wars of the period, the whaling ships would cluster in prearranged spots, such as Largo Bay for the Dundee and Firth of Forth vessels,[21] and a warship or armed vessel would escort them north and often back to safety again. For instance, in June 1756 a 60-gun warship, *Roebuck*, sailed to Greenland to escort the whaling fleet and some returning Indiamen back to Britain.[22] Despite this escort, a privateer sailed close enough to *Tryal* of Leith to create some concern.[23] Privateers would cruise the shipping routes, waiting for the laden whaling ships, but sometimes they themselves were captured, as happened in 1762 when the Dunkirk 14-gun privateer *Duke de Broglio* chased the Leith whaling ship *Edinburgh* into the Firth of Forth. The Royal Navy sloop *Dispatch,* under Captain Bertie, captured her after a 30-hour chase and a brief fight.[24]

The American War of Independence (1775–83) was costly for British shipping as American, Dutch and French privateers caused havoc on sea lanes and along the British coast. In 1777 American privateers ran riot on the whaling fleet. One of the first British Greenlandmen to be captured was *Nautilus* of Liverpool, taken by the American privateer *Tartar* off the Lizard, while another American captured Aberdeen's only whaling ship,[25] and a third laid in wait off Orkney.[26] Another Liverpool Greenland ship, *Venus,* was taken off Barra in August that year.[27] Although the privateers sailed under the flags of enemy powers, the crews and officers could come from anywhere; for example, an 18-gun French privateer that took two whaling ships in 1779 was officered entirely by Irishmen.[28] Other British whaling ships that year benefited from the protection of HMS *Camelon*, and avoided the privateers.[29]

The losses may have encouraged the Admiralty to increase protection, for in August 1780 a seven ship fleet assembled off Aberdeen to protect the homecoming Greenlandmen.[30] That year the whaling ships proved they could fight back even without naval protection, for when a 16-gun American privateer attacked two English whaling ships in the North Sea, they beat her off after a two hour running fight.[31] Although the Royal Navy continued to convoy the Greenlandmen throughout the war, in 1782 the seven Whitby ships sailed together but unescorted, depending on their own armament for protection.[32] The government also erected shore batteries and in July 1782 *Princess of Wales* sheltered under the guns of Dunbar as two large vessels hove into view: there was relief when they were identified as English whaling ships. However, that incident highlighted Britain's poor performance in that war, where Dutch privateers raided Suffolk, British seamen served on board Dunkirk privateers and Americans bombarded Arbroath. Of all the wars of the eighteenth century, perhaps the American War of Independence best revealed the vulnerability of British trade and the British whaling industry to enemy attack.

The French Revolutionary Wars started in January 1793, and already by March there were orders in council that unarmed whaling vessels should 'proceed on her voyage north about and not through the British Channel.'[33]

It would be highly unlikely that vessels from Dundee or any other Scottish port would sail southward to reach the whaling grounds, but the order does highlight the danger of the seas around the British Isles, where French privateers could lunge from any of their ports to snap up a British merchantman and return home for lunch. At the start of this war, the Hull merchants immediately asked for Royal Naval cutters to protect their Greenland ships[34] and three years later, with five known privateers cruising off north and east Scotland, they had increased their demand to a battleship and some privateers.[35] Nevertheless, despite Royal Naval protection, enemy privateers continued to infest the North Sea. In February 1796 the Greenlandman *Gibraltar* of Hull was attacked just north of the Humber by a 16-gun cutter. *Gibraltar* fought back, but with only six four pounders she was heavily outgunned and was captured, looted and burned. Perhaps it was the column of smoke from her funeral pyre that attracted *Star*, sloop of war. A three hour battle saw both vessels damaged, and the privateer withdrew to Dunkirk. The privateer was French flagged but manned by Dutch, French and renegade English seamen.[36]

The following year a group of English ships repulsed a 16-gun Dutch privateer off the Firth of Forth.[37] In 1798 it was the Buchan coast that was most dangerous as a black painted privateer chased the whaling ship *Robert* to the protection of the battery at Peterhead. The danger continued in 1799 when the 16-gun French privateer *Le Resolve* captured the Dundee whaling vessel *Tay*, but on this occasion the crew was landed at Aberdeen. Although *Tay* had a larger crew than the privateer, she only mounted two guns.[38] It is possible an arrangement was made to pay a ransom to the French privateer master for their release, which was an indication both of the commercial aspects of warfare at this period and the good sense of both sides. In 1801, with the French Revolutionary Wars grinding to stalemate, the Admiralty still provided escorts as far as Shetland, but after that the Greenland ships were on their own.[39] The convoy system was reinstated for the Napoleonic Wars, leaving from the Nore and picking up the whaling ships at the Humber, the Tyne and the Forth.

However, British vessels were equally keen to capture enemy whaling ships and the first American prize taken in the American War of Independence was a 150-ton brig with a cargo of whale oil.[40] The Royal Navy also enjoyed the harvest with, for example, HMS *Cirte* bringing a Dutch whaling ship into Leith in August 1796[41] and in May 1798, Captain Bertie of *Ardent* captured a further nine Dutch vessels, which were taken into Yarmouth.[42] Forming an impenetrable chain of vessels across the ice, the Royal Navy captured more Dutch vessels in August.[43] Although some of the Dutch Greenlandmen sailed under the neutral Prussian or Oldenburg flag, they were still condemned as legal prizes at the Admiralty Court.[44] In June 1803, HMS *Leda* headed a four ship flotilla from Sheerness to hunt the homecoming Dutch Greenlandmen.[45] Again, some Dutch sailed under German flags[46] and once-friendly vessels became legitimate targets the day their governments sided with Bonaparte.[47] In 1807 Bonaparte and Tsar Alexander of Russia signed the Treaty of Tilsit, which made peace between the two Empires. However a secret clause allowed Bonaparte to seize the powerful Danish fleet, posses-sion of which would increase French naval power so it would again be a threat to Great Britain. Accordingly, a British naval expedition sailed to Copenhagen and forestalled the French plans by annexing the Danish fleet. This undeclared and undoubtedly illegal war also meant the Danish whaling fleet was vulnerable and the frigate *Quebec* quickly snapped up six Danish whaling ships,[48] with *Constant* adding another six.[49]

Sometimes the privateers themselves could be the victims, as happened in 1806 with the Leith 14-gun privateer *Simms*. She sailed to the Greenland Sea to hunt both whales and Prussian whaling ships but her timing was poor. A small French squadron escaped from the Royal Naval blockade off L'Orient and the frigate *Le Guerriere* captured and plundered *Simms*. The Frenchman released the crew, who made their way back to Peterhead. When they reported a further six French warships in the north – two in the Green-land Sea and four in the Davis Straits – the Admiralty sent *Texel*, a 64-gun ship partially crewed by Newhaven Sea Fencibles, plus three frigates and a sloop to capture the Frenchmen.[50] On her way north, one of the frigates pressed 18 hands from the London whaling ship *Dundee*, while *Blanche* captured *Le Guerriere* after an hour-long battle.[51]

National ships were also a threat to the whaling ships. In July 1758 two French warships captured three whaling ships and chased an Aberdeen privateer, *Hussar*, for five hours,[52] and in July 1780 there were a reported three enemy frigates and three sloops cruising off Shetland to ambush the returning whaling ships, Baltic traders and vessels from Archangel and Norway.[53] In 1794 the warship *Brest*, one of a seven-strong French fleet headed by the 50-gun *Le Brutus*, captured *Dundee* of Dundee off Duncansby Head, and although the Royal Navy recaptured her, most the crew were taken prisoner. That same French fleet captured the whaling ship *Raith* of Leith, removed most of the crew, placed 16 men on board and sent her to Bergen in Norway. Three of the original crew were left on board, but one was washed overboard. When the French got drunk, Burrish Lyons, the mate and the remaining Greenlandman, attacked them with flensing knives, drove half below and half into a small boat and took *Raith* into Shetland.[54] According to the Rev John Mill, Lyons was a Shetlander; he was later promoted to master of *Raith*.

News of a foreign warship could cause consternation among the whaling ships. When the whaling fleet in the Greenland Sea saw a couple of supposed enemy frigates to the north of them, they abandoned the fishing and set sail for home. However the panic was groundless as the ships were either Royal Naval vessels sent to protect the British whaling ships[55] or Russian vessels, for the Hull whaling ship *Ipswich* was boarded by the crew of a Russian ship a few days later.[56] Naturally the war in the northern seas involved others apart from Britain and her immediate enemies. For instance, in the whaling season of 1794, the French captured a large number of Dutch whaling ships.[57]

The final threat to the whaling men came from the impress service. This was a branch of the Royal Navy dedicated to recruitment, and in England at least, dated back centuries. There were attempts to press Scottish seamen in the seventeenth century, but after the Union of 1707 the miniscule Scottish Navy merged with the Royal Navy and the press became an ogre north as well as south of the Border. The name originated in the 'prest' money which was paid to a seaman to enable him to travel to a rendezvous. However, the general conception was altered to press or press gang. The impress service was an unpleasant reality in seafaring life throughout the eighteenth and well into the nineteenth century.

There was no conscription into either the British Army or the Royal Navy but there was a quota system, where each port in the United Kingdom had to produce a number of seamen. However this system was neither reliable nor sufficient as the ports tended to pass on the unwanted or undesirable men of the port. The always overstretched navy made up the inevitable shortfall by resorting to the impress service. The popular image of the press gang roaming maritime Britain randomly 'pressing' stray seamen or unwary labourers into naval service belies a reasonably well organised and efficient organisation (see Appendix 6). There was a permanent naval rendezvous at various ports, including Dundee, ready to grab any unwary seaman or welcome any volunteer. The Dundee customs records contain many references to wages paid to the wives of Dundee men in the Royal Navy. Given the hardships, indeterminate periods of service and poor pay in the Royal Navy, it was not surprising most seamen hoped to avoid being pressed and in 1798 some of the crew of *Rodney* slipped ashore at Aberdeen to avoid being press ganged. Although the whaling industry had been partly created to build up a reservoir of seamen, those who sailed on whaling vessels could obtain a protection certificate, which rendered them immune from naval service. These protections are frequently listed in the Customs and Excise records, usually showing the rank of the men and sometimes their port of origin.

The protection system gave some security from Royal Naval interference, but seamen had to abide strictly by the letter of the law. The certificate only applied to the vessel for which they had signed articles – a contract – and only for that particular voyage. Once the vessel was back in its home port, or even in home waters, the seamen seemed to have been regarded as legitimate targets for impressment. The seaman also had to ensure he kept the protection certificate with him at all times; if he failed to produce it on demand he was liable to impressment. Protections were always in demand during wartime, but the Admiralty did not always see eye to eye with the merchant mariners and could try to ignore protections. Although the Seven Years War did not officially start until 1757, hostilities began in 1755 in North America, and conditions at sea were also uneasy. That year the Lords of the Admiralty announced they would not press 'any of the persons who have served in this year's Greenland Fishery.'[58] Early the following year the Admiralty announced they would not recognise protection certificates, but countermanded that order in March.[59]

However, although the Navy were bound to obey the law, they also knew the limitations of protection. At the end of July 1756 a body of forty whaling men marched to the Custom House in London to apply for new certificates. Two separate press gangs attacked them, but the Greenlandmen fought back, with one whaling man stabbed in the hand, and Lieutenant McKenzie of the Royal Navy slashed across the head, while others of the press gangs were variously injured. Three men were pressed.[60] That same summer there was a proposal to recruit the whaling men into the navy during their off season, and allow them back to their own trade in the spring,[61] however the idea was dropped. It was more common for Greenlandmen to sign on another ship, often in the coal trade where they were also protected.

Sometimes the whalers' resistance had fatal consequences, such as the occasion in August 1759 when a press gang boarded a whaling ship as soon as she docked at Deptford. In the ensuing scuffle a Greenlandman chopped off the press gang lieutenant's wooden leg as well as his arm. The lieutenant died later.[62] There was a similar situation in Liverpool when HMS *Vengeance* pressed the master and crew of *Golden Lyon*, but the master was later released.[63] The impress used the same technique of ambushing newly arrived whaling ships during the American war, with press gangs waiting in Newcastle in August 1779. The crew of *Kitty* left the ship before they were pressed, while *Noble Ann* put back out to sea, chased by an impress cutter and two tenders.[64] A more successful press in London in 1781 removed nearly 400 whaling men newly returned from the Arctic and shipped them off to the Royal Navy,[65] and the same procedure the following year again stripped the London Greenland ships of their crews.[66] Even in 1787, during peacetime, the press gang hit Whitby as the whaling ships came home from what had been a difficult season.[67]

As well as outright violence, whaling seamen resorted to legal means to resist the press. In 1776 Lord Mansfield presided over a case where a whaling man requested a.habeas corpus after he was pressed on board *Mars*. He claimed that there was a clause in the Act of Parliament that stated no harpooner, boatsteerer or line manager should be pressed. He won his case.[68] However, when the odds against Britain stacked up during the American Revolutionary War and ships and men became scarce, some MPs wanted to legalise impressment of all the protected seamen including whaling men[69] and the Admiralty commandeered a number of whaling ships for government transports.[70] This exacerbated the wartime shortage of whaling vessels so Hull only sent out four in 1781.[71] As the war continued to go badly, Fort Charlotte at Lerwick, originally built during the Dutch Wars of the seventeenth century, was modernised. A 12-gun battery was erected to defend Bressay Sound where the whaling ships anchored.

Despite the Navy's efforts in port, they probably pressed most men at sea. Their technique was to wait off shore for homebound merchantmen, press most of the crew and allow the master, mate and perhaps the ship's boy to navigate back to port as best they could. The customs records have a notice of such a case in July 1810 when a Royal Navy vessel reported as HM Gunboat *Pickle* ambushed the Dundee whaling ship *Advice* off the north coast of Scotland. The Royal Navy seemed quite indignant that the whaling men gave 'considerable opposition', and there was talk of withholding the bounty from *Advice*. To avoid such incidents, some crews landed at remote locations and made their own way home. Sometimes the situation escalated into true tragedy. In July 1794 HMS *Aurora* fired a signal cannon to order the homeward-bound Hull whaler *Sarah and Elizabeth* to close. As the ships came together, *Sarah and Elizabeth*'s crew ran below deck and secured the hatches, but the Navy boarded. A deluge of Royal Navy seamen and marines hacked open the hatches and ordered the Greenlandmen up. When they refused, the marines fired a volley of musketry down the hatchway; one man was killed and three wounded. Captain Effington ordered that most of the whaler's crew were taken on *Aurora* and put in irons. Although a coroner's court found Effington guilty of murder,[72] the Hull Assizes later exonerated him.[73] In 1798 there was a similar situation when two men of war approached the Hull whaler *Blenheim* the instant she berthed. When the warships sent boats to press *Blenheim*'s crew, the Greenlandmen fought back with blubber spades and lances. As more navy boats approached, the Greenlandmen locked their own captain and the pilot in his cabin, fired a swivel gun at a boatload of navy men and fled into the streets of Hull.[74] Captain Mitchinson of *Blenheim* was later charged with the murder of two Royal Navy seamen. When he was acquitted, a body of sailors removed the horses from his coach and dragged it through Hull in triumph. Unfortunately the captain was not inside, but the incident reveals something of the feelings of Greenland seamen for the Royal Navy.

Seamen could be pressed at sea during peacetime as well as wartime, such as the case in August 1790 when HMS *Champion* sent boats to board a Whitby whaling ship and was met with armed resistance. Captain Edwards of *Champion* had to run out his cannon before the whaling men backed down; the entire crew were pressed and men from *Champion*'s crew sailed the ship to Whitby.[75]

Whaling men were obviously valued for their nautical skills for augmenting the constant threat of impressment there were occasional calls from the navy for Greenland volunteers. For example, when the British captured the Danish fleet in 1807, the Admiralty asked for Greenlandmen and other protected seamen to bring the captured vessels to Britain.[76] There was a bounty of £2 10s offered as well as normal rates of pay,[77] which might have been welcome to any hard pressed family in Hull or Dundee. Finally, the government could also hire whaling ships for national service, which limited the number of vessels available for fishing, but not the owner's profit.[78] Samuel Standidge of Hull made £17,000 for hiring *British Queen* to the government during the Revolutionary War, and that was just one example, albeit a profitable one.[79] This requisitioning of civilian vessels continued throughout the life of the industry, with the shore based whale catchers also snapped up in the twentieth century.

The final nautical war of the period erupted in 1812 as Great Britain and the United States faced each other across the Atlantic highway. For once the Royal Navy did not get things all their own way and were jolted out of their complacency before they took things in hand. As always, the whaling trade was affected. The war was ostensibly about nautical issues, such as US ships harbouring British deserters and Americans complaining about contraband and the press gang, but as the U.S. maritime states voted against war, the real reasons were more complex. Bonaparte's political manipulation of embargo with an arguably naive US government that had a desire to twist the British lion's tail, coupled with a number of US politicians hoping for a Canadian land grab were more likely the real causes. As in the previous American war, privateers swarmed across the Atlantic and up to the whaling grounds, this time backed by a small number of powerful frigates who were used as very effective commerce raiders.

One of these frigates, *President*, who carried 56 guns and 475 men, captured *Lion* of Liverpool and *Eliza Swan* of Montrose. She ransomed *Eliza Swan* for £5,000.[80] At the time it was reported Commander Rodgers of *President* had captured eight whaling ships and although his crew apparently boasted they wanted to fight a British battleship, Rodgers quickly retreated to the Greenland Seas when the Royal Navy came to hunt him. *President* flaunted two banners, one of which stated 'No Impressment' and the other 'This is the Haughty President – how do you like her?'[81] In the event it was the smaller British frigate *Endymion* which defeated her. Sometimes the results were even more embarrassing for the Americans. In December 1814 an American privateer tried to capture a Whitby whaling ship but found the tables turned when the Greenlandman boarded her and took her into Whitby as a prize.[82] Overall the War of 1812 was a minor affair compared to the long struggle with France, and to the Greenland trade, except for the cruise of *President* and the temporary increase in privateering, it had no more than irritation value.

With the end of the Napoleonic and American Wars, one major phase of whaling history was complete. After 1815, the ogres of the press and the spectres of privateers and men of war faded from the whalers' minds. The British whaling industry had come through well, but there were greater challenges ahead than French, Dutch or US cannon could provide.

4

The Dundee Whaling Industry

Dundee of Dundee had one dead fish and had been damaged in her hull
Owen's Weekly Chronicle, 8 July 1758

On 5 April 1753 William Cheyne eased *Bonny Dundee* out of Dundee and out of the Tay on the first stage of her voyage to the Greenland Sea.[1] Later reports named her as *Dundee* without the prefix but, whatever her correct name, documentary evidence suggests she was Dundee's first whaling ship. Unlike London and Hull, Dundee was not a major player in the British whaling industry during the eighteenth century. She usually sent out just one or two ships each year. They sailed regularly but without making a huge impression on the town. However, she would continue to send whaling ships to the Arctic until 1914.

If Dundee's participation in the eighteenth century was unspectacular, it was also steady, and had enough success to persuade the ship owners to continue through the difficult early years. There were some good catches; for example, in 1755 'one of the whale-ships belonging to Dundee is returned from the Greenland Sea with five whales'.[2] The following year Captain Cheyne of *Dundee* caught four whales and was going after a fifth, but diverted to save the crew of a wrecked Dutch ship.[3] By 1757 there were two whaling ships sailing from Dundee as *Grandtully* joined *Dundee*.[4] Many ships were lost the following year and *Dundee* sustained some damage, but both Dundee ships returned safely.[5] In 1759 the Dundee ships caught only one whale[6] but in 1769 *Dundee* caught six[7] and in 1787 she brought home 3,250 seals,[8] with *Tay* catching 10 whales in 1791 while *Dundee* returned clean.[9] Dundee was one of the most innovative of British whaling ports and, after the close of the traditional whaling season in 1784, sent two ships north of Shetland to search for whales.[10] As the experiment was not repeated, it could not have been successful, and not until the early years of the twentieth century was a shore station established in the Shetland Islands. Nevertheless, the trial proves Dundee's questing nature.

The wars of the eighteenth century were particularly testing for the whaling industry and Dundee vessels suffered as much as any, with whaling vessels particularly prized as their cargoes could fetch thousands of pounds. While the American War of Independence was undoubtedly the most unfortunate for the country as a whole, Dundee suffered more during the French Revolutionary Wars, when a French warship captured *Dundee* and a privateer snapped up *Tay*. When *Tay* was captured she had a full cargo so was valued at around £6,000, a major loss to her owners.[11] The Napoleonic Wars also saw the impress service causing trouble for Dundee whaling vessels. Even so, it was business as usual, with *Mary Ann* returning from the Davis Straits in 1804 with all her casks full, oil choking her pumps and two whales ready for flensing.[12] In 1807, *Horn*, under Captain Valentine, caught nine whales, as did *Mary Ann*,[13] and the following year *Rodney* captured 12,[14] so despite the vagaries of war, whaling remained profitable.

By 1813 Dundee had 8 whaling ships compared to Aberdeen's 15, Leith's 10 and Hull's 55,[15] so Dundee remained a middle ranking whaling port. When the French and American Wars ended in 1815, the Dundee whaling fleet settled down to peacetime conditions. She was also successful in her cargoes in this period, and enjoyed the benefits of a sea bereft of privateers and coast safe from the press. Technically the impress service continued until the Crimean War but there were no more press gangs to haunt the nightmares of homeward bound seamen. There remained the normal seafaring hazards of poor weather and the perils of hunting for whales in high latitude ice fields.

Dundee gradually increased her number of ships to 10 with *Friendship*, a Royal Navy prize made free, and *Dorothy*, a former exploring ship added to the fleet. However, *Rodney* had been lost in 1810, and *Tay* and *Mary Ann* in 1819.[16] That was one of the bad years, with 10 British ships sunk including *Raith, Royal Bounty*, and *Thomas and Ann* of Leith. Dundee bought new vessels to replace the casualties. *Three Brothers* made a good catch of 18 whales in 1820 but in 1822 she was beset in Davis Straits alongside *Success* of Leith. Both ships broke free and sailed 20 miles before an area of thicker ice stopped them. It was a further four days until they could inch into a lane of open water.[17] *Calypso* of Dundee was one of the six ships sunk that year in Baffin Bay. By that time the whaling fleet faced other challenges apart from ice. In 1817 Dundee boasted 24 whale-oil lamps for street illumination, but that year saw the founding of the Dundee Gas Light Company and the whaling companies lost an important customer. Within a decade, Dundee was a gas lit town and the whaling companies had to search for consumers.

In 1821 *Dorothy* had a scare when she struck a rock just outside Dundee harbour and the steam ferry *Union* had to tow her off. That year, 13 British whaling ships were lost out of a fleet of 159, but Dundee was unscathed. In 1823 Hull was still the leading British whaling port with 41 ships, followed by Peterhead with 15, Aberdeen with 14, Dundee and Whitby with 10 each, Leith with 6, and Kirkcaldy with 4.[18] The catches in the 1820s could be impressive; for example, in 1823, after a long whaling season, the Dundee ships *Achilles* and *Thomas* both brought home 37 whales, *Dorothy* caught 27, and *Estridge*, 28.[19] The following year, when Dundee vessels imported a fifth of the entire British catch of whale fins,[20] the whaling bounty ended and the whaling companies were on their own. 1825 was a poor season that saw the loss of *Estridge* and low catches for most of the British fleet, including the Dundee vessels, with only 43 whales caught in total, compared to around 260 in 1823. Oil prices rose correspondingly and in 1826 shareholders of the Friendship Whale Fishing Company were looking for a buyer.[21] That was another bad year with only sixty whales captured, and even a Hull vessel was advertised for sale in Dundee.[22] In 1827 the nine Dundee vessels brought back 130 whales,[23] but there were still shares in *Friendship* and the whaling ship *Dorothy* on the market.[24] That year 92 British ships sailed north, so Dundee owned nearly 10 per cent of the entire British fleet. The next two years were both good; *Dorothy*, *Princess Charlotte*, *Achilles* and *Advice* all brought home bumper catches in 1828 and the 1829 catches were reasonable.

As the 1820s show, whaling was a roller coaster of an industry, often poised on a knife edge where success or failure depended on the luck of a single voyage. Good catches meant years of great profits, but there was always the possibility of calamitous losses if the ships were unsuccessful. Shipwrecks were a regular occurrence with, for example, *Achilles*, which sank in the disastrous year of 1830,[25] *Advice* lost in the Davis Straits in July 1859,[26] *Dundee* crushed in the ice in June 1782[27] or *Jane* which ran aground at the entrance to the Tay in 1809. A bumper catch such as the 37 whales caught by *Achilles* in 1823[28] would mean a healthy profit for the owner, but when a vessel returned clean such as *Dundee* in 1798, the company would frequently make a loss. Most Dundee whaling companies were small, with only one or two vessels, so a poor catch by one ship was not counterbalanced by the profits from others, and it was often the case that the entire whaling fleet experienced a bad season as in 1825 and 1826.

There were terrible years when a number of ships went down; 1822 was one such, when six British ships were lost in the ice, including *Calypso* of Dundee; the ice stove in and badly damaged another ship and thirteen more were beset for weeks. After the roller coaster of losses and stupendous successes of the 1820s, the 1830s proved even more dramatic. Out of the Dundee fleet of nine ships, two, *Achilles* and *Three Brothers*, were sunk in the disastrous season of 1830, but the worst year for Dundee was 1836 when two of her ships, *Advice* and *Thomas*, were stuck in the ice. Although *Advice* eventually freed herself, around 80 men from the two crews died. When *Advice* came into Dundee harbour crowds gathered to see the stricken ship. She survived another 20 years in the whaling trade, despite losing six men in the 1847 season.[29] Perhaps surprisingly, whaling masters were rarely blamed for the loss of their ship. When *Achilles* and *Three Brothers* were sunk in 1830, the masters of both were back at sea the following year with their replacements, *Alexander* and *Ebor*. Appendix 4 records details of ships lost from the Dundee whaling fleet.

By 1838 there were seven ships sailing from Dundee, which was nearly thirty per cent less than the peak in the early years of the century. Such losses damaged Dundee's confidence in the industry and in 1839 there were rumours the town might withdraw from the whaling trade as her ships only captured 13 fish between them.[30] However, Dundee continued unlike most English ports, which discarded their whaling fleets, and for the next two decades Peterhead was the most important British whaling port. The 1830s had been a bad decade overall, but the losses of 1836 were unique only in the scale of disaster. There was a constant slow bleeding of men who fell victim to accident on board ship, in the small whale boats or out on the ice. Usually the local press only reported the deaths with a laconic few words such as: 'a young man belonging to Broughty Ferry who went out with the *Advice* fell a sacrifice to the perils of the fishing'.[31] The deaths could be particular to the whaling industry: for example, in 1821 *Calypso* lost two men when a whale smashed their whaleboat by a flick of his flukes,[32] and in 1825 Mr Davidson, the mate of *Estridge*, survived the sinking of his own ship, was taken on board *Advice*, only to drown later while harpooning.[33] In 1838 one of *Alexander*'s whaleboats harpooned a whale which became stuck on an ice floe. The whale splintered the whaleboat with a flick of its tail; one man was drowned and two others had their legs broken. Two more of *Alexander*'s men died in 1853 when a captured narwhal pulled them overboard. Accounts of accidents like these crop up throughout the history of Dundee whaling, for instance, when James Lamb, a harpooner on *Erik*, died in 1881 after a whale slashed him with its tail.[34]

As well as fatalities particular to whaling, there were the usual maritime accidents and occurrences, such as the events of 1831: one man died when he fell from the mainyard of *Princess Charlotte*; the mate of *Friendship* drowned in the Davis Straits; and a seaman on *Horn* died of a severe cold.[35] That same year James Ravie, a seaman on *Dorothy*, died of tuberculosis[36] which the cramped accommodation on board ships ensured was relatively common. In 1847 bad weather lengthened the season and scurvy erupted in the Dundee fleet. *Horn* and *Princess Charlotte* were affected, and six men died on *Advice*. There were also rogue waves, such as the one which swept Captain James Sturrock overboard in 1854 and injured the mate. In 1874 there were two deaths on *Camperdown;* one man dying of a cold and another being drowned.[37]

Life on shore could be equally dangerous for the seamen: 'On Saturday night a sailor who had lately arrived from the Northern Seas was knocked down in the Overgate on his way home and robbed of all the money in his possession.'[38] A Greenlandman back home from a successful voyage would be a tempting target for a footpad. There were also occasions when the Greenland seamen were the vehicles of their own misfortune, as when a harpooner 'who had been enjoying himself with some comrades . . . tumbled headlong into the water'. This inebriated Greenlandman was rescued and revived in the bath house at the harbour.[39]

The whaling industry affected Dundee in other ways. The Greenland ships unloaded their cargo either at the harbour or at the beach to the east,[40] alongside each whaling company's boiling yard, where the blubber was boiled to extract whale oil. The yards were at the Seagate in the heart of the city and when the blubber was being boiled, the stench forced the good people of Dundee to keep their doors and windows firmly shut. A contemporary description of a whaling vessel arriving at Dundee describes the scene:

> Besides the blubber in the casks, there is always an immense accumulation of filth in the hold, consisting of large masses of the carcass and tails of the whale, stuffed in between the casks; and often a full ship has even her boats on deck filled with the blubber. The whole of these materials being in a rancid and putrid state, generally swarming with maggots, the stench they occasion may be better imagined than described.

The passage speaks of the blubber becoming fermented, bursting out of the casks, while the process of landing is 'accompanied with much bawling and noise and may be accomplished in the course of a few weeks, if a proper allowance of whisky has been administered . . . to overcome the squeamishness . . . the sickening fumes all the while are widely diffused'.[41] The quoted passage was found in a small pamphlet produced with the intention of preventing a whale industry at Burntisland, so it could well be biased. Nevertheless, there is no doubt that blubber boiling was unpleasant. Once landed, the blubber was boiled either in the open or in simple sheds, for ventilation was essential for those men who operated the boilers. The resulting oil was stored in huge tanks, with the Dorothy Whale Fishing Yard selling two that held 1,110 tons of oil in 1840. These tanks were 30 feet by 15 by 10.[42] The area around the boiling yards was described as having 'no genteel houses' and 'a filthy neighbourhood . . . surrounded by . . . noisome manufactories . . . foundries and the like.'[43] The fumes were said to carry far across Dundee. There were other methods of reminding Dundonians of the downside of the whaling industry. The *Advertiser* of 26 October 1821 carried a letter complaining about a 'country cart' driven by an 'unconscious clodhopper' that spilled boiled blubber waste through Dundee. The stench was apparently appalling. Although the 1824 Police Act tried to regulate the stink of boiling blubber, nothing was done and the Dundonians continued to hold their noses when the whaling ships arrived. Few people realised that the terrible stench was the result of decomposition of the blubber and any animal matter attached to it. If the blubber is boiled as soon as the whale is killed and flensed, the smell is no more offensive than that any other fat.

The 1840s started badly with a catch of only three whales in 1840, the subsequent sale of *Friendship* and the temporary withdrawal of *Fairy* from whaling to the emigrant trade. Under a new shipmaster, *Fairy* returned to the Arctic in 1843 to face mayhem and mutiny but was eventually put up for sale. Dundee's whaling fortunes improved with good catches in 1845 and again in 1849. By the 1850s, Dundee's fleet was reduced to four vessels and then to only three when the elderly *Horn* came ashore in Fife in 1852. The season of 1856 contained ominous shadows of 1830 as the ice closed on a small group of ships. When *Princess Charlotte* was trapped between two floes and crushed, Captain Alexander Deuchars blew her hull open to rescue the men's clothing, but the rum was liberated too, and after a bout of heavy

Table 4.1 **Dundee's position in 1847–57**

Port	Whales	Seals	Oil (tons)	Baleen (cwt)
Peterhead	238	726,312	12,161	3,209
Fraserburgh	11	79,709	1,101	
Banff		9,045	39	
Aberdeen	197	10,735	1,921	2,228
Dundee	270	1,690	2,910	3,733
Kirkcaldy	160	9,650	1,911	1,878
Bo'ness	33		490	568
Hull	198	131,518	3,765	2,988

Source: Ingram files

drinking, men from the Hull whaler *Truelove* challenged the Dundee men to combat. In 1857 Hull sent out the first steam vessel and when Dundee followed suit, the town began the steep climb to become Britain's premier whaling port.

Steam power altered the balance of whaling to Dundee's favour. The town already had an established shipbuilding industry with nearly half a century of experience of steam ships, so the step to steam whaling was almost inevitable. The writing was on the wall for sail-powered whaling ships when Alexander Deuchars took command of *Tay*, a sailing ship converted into a steam whaler, and the sail-powered *Alexander* was sold as a coal tender. Dundee was set to become the most important British whaling and sealing port. The introduction of steam power also helped her forge a close connection with St John's in Newfoundland from where around 400 vessels sailed for the sealing. St John's provided a base for Dundee's Arctic whalers and a market for her ships.

In 1858, on the cusp of the change, Peterhead was still Britain's premier whaling port as Table 4.2 shows.

By 1859 Dundee had six whaling vessels, half of them steam. Following the example of Hull, Dundee converted the sail-powered whaling ship *Tay* to auxiliary steam power, and followed with the steam ship, *Narwhal* and *Dundee*. After a century of being one port out of many whaling ports, with a small to average whaling fleet, the advent of steam gave Dundee a major boost that sent her to the top of the Arctic league. The smutty funnels of *Tay*, *Dundee* and *Narwhal* pointed a grimy finger to the future and for the next 50 years Dundee enjoyed ascendancy as Britain's premier whaling port.

Table 4.2 Whaling statistics, 1858

Port	No of ships	Whales caught	Seals caught	Whale oil (tons)	Seal oil (tons)	Baleen (cwt)
Peterhead	27	31	79,838	351	947	426
Aberdeen	6	27	3,290	242.5	25	354
Hull	7	28	959	356	8.5	426
Fraserburgh	5	11,649	Nil		145	
Dundee	4	14	Not known	262		212
Kirkcaldy	3	7	Nil	84.25		116.5
Bo'ness	1	1	Nil	13		14

Source: Ingram files

From 1862 Dundee vessels began to regularly operate from St John's in Newfoundland, with *Polynia* the pioneer. By the early 1870s Alexander Stephens had established a whale boiling yard in St John's to process the catch, and then built a similar boiling works in Dundee, known as the Arctic Yard, at the south west of Victoria Dock. The building was situated on a corner of the old Alexander Stephens shipbuilding yard and looked like a two storey shed covered in galvanised iron. To eliminate the stink of boiling whale blubber, Stephens led a pipe from the top of the boiling tank to the furnace, so the worst of the stench was hopefully burned away.

Steam power gave the whaling industry a tremendous boost, and Dundee ships began a regular programme of double voyages, one for seals and one for whales. There had been some earlier attempts at double voyages: London vessels tried after the bitter winters of 1763 and 1776,[44] and in 1785 and 1786 the Dundee ships, joined by one from Perth, had attempted a double season, but bad weather and contrary winds spoiled the trial.[45] Now steam power alleviated the need to wait for a favourable wind and two trips a year became the norm. The number of vessels sailing from Dundee increased: 7 in 1860; 8 in 1861; 11 in 1866; 15 in 1878. The combination of steam power and the demands of the jute industry had forged a unique force in Dundee.

But even with steam it was not an easy ride, with whales becoming harder to catch and even seals elusive. As Dundee ships ventured ever further afield, the losses in vessels and men continued. *Jumna* was lost in Melville Bay in 1863, the same year that Gourlay Brothers became the first jute company to directly enter into whaling. Their ship *Emma* went down the following year, with the survivors rowing for 24 bitter hours before a Norwegian vessel rescued them. Six years later, 18 of *Ravenscraig's* crew were stranded on a breakaway ice floe until *Alexander* and a Dutch vessel rescued them. The ice claimed *Alexander* later that year. So despite the improved vessels and all the effort, whaling was as costly in ships and men as ever and catches continued to diminish.

Table 4.3 shows the number of ships sailing from Dundee and catches of whales and seals for selected years over the period 1864 to 1911. Considering the increase in power of the whaling vessels and the lack of competition, the fall in whale catches compared to the earlier years of the century shows just how much the whale stock had been depleted. The seal figures are also revealing, showing the sheer extent of the slaughter with the inevitable result of a decline in seals.

Whaling was always a roller coaster of an industry, with bad years nearly inevitably following good, so there was rarely an opportunity to see a continual upward climb of profits. Except for the constant search for fresh

Table 4.3 Dundee ships, whales and seal catches for selected years

Year	Ships	Whales	Seals
1864	8	31	23,911
1870	10	61	87,768
1874	11	190	44,087
1880	14	114	75,260
1884	16	79	57,409
1890	10	18	43,811
1894	8	19	18,170
1900	6	16	18,093
1905	10	23	408
1910	10	18	4,549
1911	8	7	3,505

Source: Dundee Agricultural and Fishery Records, Dundee Archives

hunting grounds, there was no discernible pattern in the industry. Figure 4.1 shows the number of whales caught over a 20-year period when Dundee was the leading whaling port in Britain.

The graph reveals the unstable nature of the whaling industry in the later decades of the nineteenth century. Even with steam powered vessels and a century of experience, the Dundee whaling masters could not guarantee success. A number of variables combined to create a successful hunt, from favourable weather to a knowledgeable shipmaster and possibly luck. Experience mattered: the fate of *Fairy* in 1843 showed exactly what happened when a shipmaster did not know his business and the catches of veterans such as Captain Adamson of *Princess Charlotte* or Adams of *Arctic* speak for themselves. But even the most expert whaling master could not catch whales when they were not there, and diminishing catches in the latter part of the nineteenth century reflect the cumulative results of nearly three centuries of slaughter.

Figure 4.2 shows the number of whales caught by the Dundee fleet, showing the totals in five-yearly groups. It reveals the peaks and troughs of the industry over a 90-year period starting in 1820.

The totals reveal the unstable nature of the industry. The peak in the 1870s must have raised hopes for the future of the industry, but proved to be an anomaly as catches fell again and never recovered.

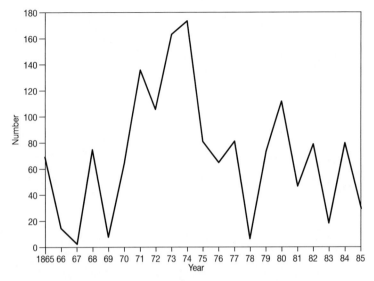

Figure 4.1 Dundee whale catches

Source: Compiled from the Ingram Records and Dundee Archives: AF 32.45

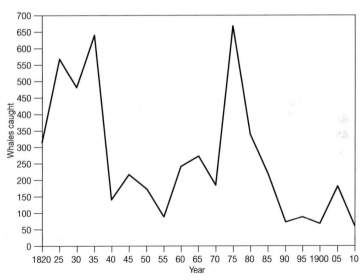

Figure 4.2 Five-yearly Dundee whale catches

Source: Data taken from Ingram files and Dundee Archives AF 32.45

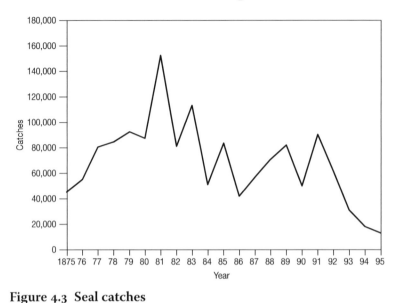

Figure 4.3 Seal catches

Source: Compiled from Ingram records and Dundee Archives AF 32.45

Seal catches were equally erratic but the eventual decline was, if anything, even more depressing to the hunters. From hunting shoals of seals whose numbers were incalculable in the early period, the ships scrabbled with single figure catches as the industry dragged to its close.

Figure 4.3 shows the number of seals caught by Dundee vessels in the 20 years from 1875 and 1895. The peak years of the early 1880s contrast vividly with the decline after 1891 when catches slumped year after year.

From the 1870s Dundee masters and vessels became involved in Arctic exploration. There had been a connection between Dundee and exploring ever since 1821 when the ex-discovery ship *Dorothy* had joined the Dundee fleet, but the latter decades of the century saw Dundee whaling ships and masters become ever more heavily involved. In 1872 the explorer Leigh Smith chartered the Dundee vessel *Diana*, under Captain Fairweather, to search for Baron Nordenskjold in Spitsbergen. The following year Captains Walker and Adams of *Ravenscraig* and *Arctic* helped relieve the stranded men of the US exploration ship *Polaris* and in 1882 *Aurora* was chartered to rescue the American Greely expedition. However, perhaps Captain Milne was best known for his efforts in helping Arctic exploration, as he advised and aided Roald Amundsen on his successful voyage through the North West Passage. The King of Norway knighted Milne for his services.

The Dundee fleet peaked at seventeen vessels in the 1880s and then declined. Only the textile industries, and especially the need for whale oil to soften raw jute before processing, allowed Dundee's whaling industry to survive decades after other ports had given up. In 1881 the Dundee shipmasters imposed rules that restricted the use of steam power near whales and required vessels to use only wind power north of Cape Horsburgh unless the ship was steaming to Lancaster Sound. Even the enthusiasm for Newfoundland sealing dissipated with only *Terra Nova* sailing there in 1895. In 1912, with whale stocks a shadow of what they had been, Dundee whaling masters considered adopting a close season of 15 years, but nothing came of this. By that time the Dundee ships worked deep in Lancaster Sound and into Hudson's Bay, for which Robert Kinnes, managing owner, had to pay a licence fee to the Canadian Government.[46] Catches continued to fall, but there were occasional successes. For instance, in August 1906 James Vannet on SS *Morning* recorded 'Saw a lot of whales . . . got fast to one about 7 pm and had her killed in about an hour.'[47] Despite the more advanced vessels, there were still ship losses: 'sighted three boats coming from the northward which turned out to be the *Windward*; they lost their ship on Carey Islands.'[48] Right until the final year of its existence, Arctic whaling was a dangerous industry that demanded sacrifices from the men and ships that sailed north.

The final years were a sad story of helpless decline. By 1911, while Dundee still tried to hunt whales in the old traditional ways in the old traditional whaling grounds, there were Norwegian factory ships in the Antarctic and shore-based whaling stations evolving in Shetland and Harris. That year *Diana* made a profit of only just over £175 but was fitted out for the next year. In 1913 there were 17 Norwegian ships operating from South Georgia, and only two Dundee vessels in the Arctic, with three more laid up in the harbour. In 1914 *Active* and *Morning* sailed on Dundee's final season in Arctic whaling. *Active* arrived home on 28 October: the Great War had begun. The Dundee Arctic whaling industry ended in a whimper, rather than a roar just as the First World War brought Armageddon to so many Scottish industries and destroyed so many Scottish families.

After the First World War Dundee lost interest in Arctic whaling. Robert Kinnes sold his northern Canadian trading posts to the Hudson Bay Company, moved to Crieff and operated the Crieff Tannery instead. The old Dundee whaling masters died off one by one and the Greenlandmen would no doubt regale their grandchildren with tales of life in the old days, of famous whale hunts and adventures with polar bears. In Dundee the memories, fading with each generation, remain in the names of the Arctic Bar, of Baffin Street and Mary Ann Lane.

5

Why They Hunted

The Dundee Union Whale Fishing Company and the Dundee Whale Fishing Company will expose to sale by public roup at their warehouses here on Thursday the 7th February next at twelve o' clock noon about twenty five fine Davis Straits whale fins to be put up in lots to suit intending purchasers

Dundee Advertiser, 17 January 1828

There are many different types of whale in the sea and, at one time or other, the whaling men would hunt most of them. Whales are divided into two main groups: *Odontoceti* and *Mysticeti*. The former are toothed whales and the latter toothless. The sperm whales, prey of the United States whaling ships, are among the toothed whales and there are many tales of battles between whaling crews and these splendid mammals. However they are rare in the northern seas, although there are occasional sightings. All the whales are warm-blooded mammals but to the whaling men, they were known as fish or whale fish and the hunting process was whale fishing. The Dundee whaling men hunted the baleen whale, of which there are ten known species, further divided into three family groups. These families are the right whale, the rorqual, and the grey whale. Instead of teeth, these animals have plates of baleen in their mouths, through which they filter their plankton food. Baleen was known as whalebone to the whaling men and, because of its strength and suppleness, it was a useful commodity in an age before plastic. Of all the Arctic whales, the British whaling men preferred the bowhead whale, *Balaena Mysticetus*, which they termed the Greenland right whale. The name bowhead relates to the animal's head, which curves upward from its body. It is a relatively slow swimmer so the whaling ships could catch it and, even more importantly, when it was killed, it would float on the surface for easier towing back to the whaling ship. Most vital of all, the jaw of a large Greenland right whale contained as many as 700 pieces of baleen.

The Greenland right whale was longer than the whaleboats from which it was hunted. Even without teeth it could be dangerous, with many instances of a hunted whale overturning a whaleboat by a lash of its tail. As an example, two crew members of *Thetis* – Stewart Chaplain, the boatsteerer, and Mr Henderson, the carpenter – were killed in this manner when one of the much smaller bottle-nosed whales capsized their whaleboat. Hunting the whale was not a sinecure.

When the whaling ships returned to Dundee, the blubber was unloaded and taken to the company boiling yards near the docks. In the early days each whaling company had their own boiling yards in a section beside the Seagate, with each one named after the company. These yards occupied a decent amount of ground, with the Friendship Whale Yard being 80 feet broad and stretching from Seagate down to the then line of the River Tay.[1] All that remains is the street name Mary Ann Lane after the Mary Ann whaling company of the early nineteenth century.

Whale blubber consisted of between 50 and 80 per cent oil, which consists of glycerides of saturated and unsaturated fatty acids. The blubber was boiled in great copper vats, although iron vats may also have been used. The recipe for whale oil was simple: add water to the blubber and boil for at least an hour; separate the oil; cool it for a few hours; run it off and keep for a day. After this it was ready to be sold. The whale oil came in four grades, with the palest, a very light yellow, being the highest grade.

The oil had many uses. In the early years it was used mainly for lighting and heating. Oil-fired street lights kept the city safe in the hours of darkness. However, there were never enough street lights and a high wind could blow them out, leaving the traveller at the mercy of footpads or liable to flounder into the gutters that carried all the human and animal waste. Two types of oil lantern were used in homes, one small for individual use and the other, a larger triangular lantern for lighting bigger areas, Factory lights kept the cog wheels of industry turning. Whale oil lit the lamps of lighthouses around the coasts of the British Isles and was used down the mines in Davy's safety lamps. If the lamp was filled with oil, it could burn for a full six hours, the length of a miner's shift underground.

Whale oil could also be used to tan leather and in sail making, two industries which were extensive in Dundee. Later, it was used to lubricate machinery; to grease wagons, pulleys and the Balbeuchly engine of the Newtyle Railway.[2] Whale oil was also used in soap making and in some varnishes and paints. Farmers also found it useful: it put gloss on horses in agricultural shows, and a mixture of whale oil and whisky in equal proportions was said to be a cure for wind in the stomach for black cattle. Apparently, the surplus matter left after boiling the blubber was used as a fertiliser.[3]

The high noon of whale oil ended with the introduction of coal gas for public, factory and eventually domestic lighting. The discovery of petroleum in 1859 signalled the beginning of the end of Arctic whaling, although the industry had a long and painful decline. It is ironic that whaling became most efficient only when the trade was already doomed. Steam powered whaling vessels arrived almost simultaneously with petroleum. However, Dundee threw Arctic whaling a brittle lifeline with the jute industry. Whale oil was found to be the perfect agent for softening jute fibres before they were processed into a useable textile; not only did it make jute easier to work, but it also gave the fibres a silk-like sheen. In the latter decades of the nineteenth century it was used to a massive extent to soften jute in the factories and mills that gave Dundee her unique character (see Appendix 7).

The volume of oil brought in to Britain naturally depended on the number of whales caught. In 1815 the British whaling fleet brought home around 11,000 tuns of oil; the next year the figure rose to 13,590 and in 1817 it fell to 10,500 tons. There was a shockingly poor year in 1822 with an estimated 7,000 tuns. Sometimes there was major speculation in the whale oil market. In 1818 a Hull oil broker named Cleasby bought huge quantities of oil to create a monopoly that forced up the price of oil from its usual 25s a tun to more than 60s. Cleasby was taken to court but, as he had done nothing illegal, he was allowed to continue trading.[4] Sometimes speculation about the size of the catch drove the price up even before the whaling ships returned, as happened in October 1824 when oil prices rose from £22 to £30 per tun when the fleet returned late.. As ever, there were profiteers in times of crisis and one man packed an extra £1,000 into his bank account, which was a massive figure for the time.[5] The following year, the whaling failed and the price of oil rose to a then-appalling £35 a tun. However, some retailers kept the price down by adding cheaper linseed oil to the whale oil. The compound thus produced was said to burn just as well as pure whale oil.[6]

Each whaling vessel strove to catch as many whales as possible and in a good hunting year, a single ship could bring back as many as 37 whales ensuring a plentiful supply of oil. The 1832 season was very good for the Dundee fleet with, for example, *Friendship* under Captain Davidson bringing home 29 whales yielding 209 tuns of oil and 12 tons of baleen, and *Dorothy* catching 35 whales, with 290 tuns of oil and 10 tons of baleen. That year oil was £20 a ton and the combined oil cargo had a value of £38,809 with the baleen fetching a further £17,250 making a total of £56,059.[7] The following year was even better, with the whaling fleet making more than £65,000.[8] The whaling industry obviously gave a major boost to the Dundee economy.

However, 1832 and 1833 were exceptional years cramped by a frame of disaster. In a bad season the ships brought home only two or three whales and the oil prices rose accordingly. After the terrible season of 1830 when 19

British whaling ships sank and a further 21 returned clean, there were fears of a steep rise in oil prices. Dundee whale oil faced serious competition in the form of lighting gas from the gasworks that opened in Peep O' Day Lane in 1826 and also as a lubricant. In the mid 1830s, a Mr Joseph Jamieson of Perth created a blend of vegetable oil that was said to be better and cheaper than whale oil and without the offensive smell.[9] Despite the competition, Dundee whale oil was still essential for many households and the streets of Dundee were reportedly busy with people rushing to the oil dealers.[10] The fortunate, greedy or astute could still rake in their money, as when *Fairy* returned with her catch of three whales and the oil sold for a great profit. The price continued to rise[11] to as much as £32 a tun by 1839.[12]

Baleen was the second commodity to be torn from the whale. Being flexible, durable and tough, it had a hundred uses in the Victorian world, from chair backs to carriage springs, hair brushes to whips, umbrellas, hat frames and nets to its best remembered use, stays in the female fashion trade. In common with whale oil, prices fluctuated throughout the life of the industry with many factors affecting the price. For example, when women's fashion demanded corsets made from whalebone, baleen was in demand and the price rose, but when tastes changed and clothes became loose fitting at the turn of the nineteenth century, prices fell from around £186 a hundredweight to as low as £30 in 1802. The weather was also an important consideration as it affected the yearly catch. The terrible whaling seasons of 1837 and 1838 reduced the catches and thereby increased the price of baleen. Throughout the remainder of the nineteenth century, the price rose and fell like the waves of a choppy sea but reached new heights – £2,900 per hundredweight in 1903 – as catches diminished at the beginning of the twentieth century.

Although the Dundee industry focussed primarily on whales, reduced catches and fluctuations in price led to diversification. After the whale, the next in importance was the seal. Young seals had blubber two or three inches thick; old seals had twice that. Both provided oil which was slightly cheaper than whale oil. Seals were also killed for their skins which were used for leather. Prices for skins were relatively stable; 5s in the late 1870s and early 1880s but falling to 3s 6d in 1885 before rising to around 4s 6d at the turn of the century. Sealskin would usually be tanned and used for shoe making, or dressed and used as an exotic covering for trunks or similar items. The Arctic Tannery in Dundee was a fairly substantial business where sealskins were converted to various leather items such as schoolbags and even in relatively modern times, there was a market for little cuddly baby seal ornaments made from real sealskin.

By the 1870s, the once immense colonies of seals had been decimated and in 1871 the ship masters created a voluntary close season for the slaughter so there was no hunting until the 27 April.[13] Even at that date, the hunters found many of the seals to be small and immature. In 1877 an international agreement continued the close time, with the killing season allowed from the 3 April. By 1912 there was a proposal for a fifteen year close season but by then the Scottish Arctic sealing industry was all but dead.[14]

Seal oil prices also fluctuated from year to year. In 1878 it sold at a decent £32 a ton but it moved from £25 in 1880 to £31 in 1883 before dropping to £20 in 1885. Polar bears were also hunted and the occasional cub was brought home alive. For instance, in 1812 a young bear was taken to Edinburgh University and fed on bullock's liver. Walrus, known sometimes as 'seahorses', provided blubber and a skin that was apparently perfect for polishing bicycles while the tusks were excellent for false teeth. Narwhals, known as unicorns or 'unis', were prized for their long, twisting horns which were used for walking sticks among other things. Dundee Museum has a couple of excellent examples of these sticks. In 1818 a Newcastle whaling ship brought back a live narwhal around 20 feet in length which created some interest at the time. However, most of the narwhal ivory sold at £1 or £1 10s a pound, was exported to the Far East for religious decorations. The leather was used for shoes. Along with the bottlenose whale and the beluga or white whale, the narwhal skull contained spermaceti, semi-transparent material that was used for candles and, in an era of quack medicine, for dubiously effective ointments. In 1882 oil from the bottlenose was selling at £60 a ton.

By the closing decades of the Arctic whaling industry, the hunters were harvesting anything and everything that might make money. For example, the small ketch *Albert* killed 22 bears and 59 foxes in 1905, and was even involved in an expedition to hunt for gold. The whalers also brought home musk ox[15] and fished for salmon. At the very end of the Arctic period, the whaling companies diversified to find anything that could make a profit. Robert Kinnes, founder of Robert Kinnes and Sons Limited, the trading company for the Tay Whale Fishing Company of which he was managing director, and a major force in the industry, mined for mica in Baffin Island. Despite some success, it could not stop the inevitable closure of the whaling industry.[16]

Overall, the whaling industry contributed a great deal to the Dundee economy. Whale and seal oil, whalebone, sealskins and the various supporting commodities from other animals all brought wealth to the town and created hundreds of jobs, but to some extent, the whalers were victims of their own success. Their efficient hunting created a dearth of the very creatures that brought profit and, even as the industry modernised with steam vessels and better weapons, the invention of petroleum removed a major market. Dundee was fortunate that the jute industry gave a long extension to Arctic whaling, but the industry faced an inevitable demise no matter to which devices the ship owners and shipmasters of Dundee resorted.

6

The Greenland Whaling Ships

> Hawke, Greenland ship of Anstruther is arrived at that place from the Fishery but without success. She was obliged to leave the Ice, having received considerable Damage in her Hull. The Captain reports that the weather has been extremely stormy; that many ships have suffered and some are entirely lost and that the Fishing in general has been very unsuccessful.
>
> *Public Advertiser*, 13 July 1758

Dundee whaling ships operated in some of the worst sea conditions in the world. They sailed from the Tay early in the spring and headed north, first to Orkney or Shetland to complete their crew, and then across the Atlantic to St John's in Newfoundland or north to the Greenland Sea. At any time from departing the Tay, the ships were in danger and the deeper into the ice they sailed, the worse the danger became. The best fishing lay right beside the ice, where the danger was also greatest. In his definitive history of British whaling, Gordon Jackson states that 'few vessels have ever been subjected to the immense physical and psychological strains that were frequently the lot of whalers . . . no whaler could withstand unrelenting ice pressure for long'.[1] It was not surprising that many never returned to Dundee. This chapter describes how the whaling ships developed to cope with these extreme conditions. Appendix 1 provides detailed descriptions of each of the vessels that sailed as part of the Dundee Arctic whaling fleet from 1753 until its demise in 1914.

To cope with the conditions, the whaling men needed sturdy vessels. Growing experience throughout the eighteenth and early nineteenth centuries taught them what was required to withstand the pressure of ice in the north. A typical whaling vessel of that period would be around 100 foot long and between 250 and 340 tons. Captain Scoresby of Whitby believed 350 tons was the best weight. A typical whaling vessel would be three-masted and either ship-rigged, with square sails on all masts, or barque-rigged, with square sails on the fore and main masts and fore-and-aft rigged on the mizzen. The crew would have between 45 and 50 seamen.

At that period it was unlikely that a ship would have been built specifically for whaling – it would be just a sturdy ship converted and strengthened to operate in Arctic waters. She would have been 'doubled', that is, she would have an extra layer of planking added to her hull with a third layer at her bows which would make the first and most frequent contact with the ice. Strengthening the ships was not a cheap process: the Tay Whale Fishing Company paid the carpenter James Smart £854 8s to have *Princess Charlotte* doubled in around 1819.[2] The ships would probably have 'ice plates' at their bows too, which were shields of wood or metal to help her break through the ice sheet, and internal bracing beams of some twelve inches (30 cm) thick to further strengthen her.

Even with all this added protection, it was so common for whaling ships to be lost that in 1784 there was some surprise in the tone of the *London Chronicle* when it reported: 'the Greenland fishery has ended this year without the loss of a single ship to any of the powers involved'.[3] Ships could be lost even before they reached the ice. In 1776 the London vessel *Syren* was 'cast away on the North part of the island of Unst on a very barbarous part of the coast and all the crew perished'.[4] In 1812 *Fountain* of Lynn was wrecked on the Bell Rock off Arbroath and in 1813 disaster struck the Aberdeen fleet as they left their home port. Possibly lulled by a period of good weather, five Aberdeen whaling ships were in the bay when an easterly gale sprang up. Three vessels escaped but *Oscar* and *St Andrew* tried to sail out to clear Girdle Ness. The storm drove *St Andrew* onto the shore beside Aberdeen North Pier, while *Oscar* was tossed onto the rocks at Greyhope Bay, beside Girdle Ness. The men crowded the boats, but huge breakers swamped them and forty-three drowned.

It was quite common for whaling ships, particularly sail-powered vessels, to get stuck in the Arctic. Surgeon Trotter of the Fraserburgh ship *Enterprise* wrote in 1856: 'a great many ships have got beset in the ice, unable to get out again at present'.[5] Many journals and accounts of the high latitudes contain at least one mention of vessels trapped in the ice. John Nicol, one of the few eighteenth-century 'before the mast' mariners who left a written account of his life, remarked on his whaling ship being ice-bound: 'we were for ten days completely fast in the ice . . . and the ship was so pressed by it everyone thought we must either be crushed to pieces or forced out upon the top of the ice, there ever to remain'.[6] It was when the vessels were stuck in the ice that the worst disasters occurred. For example, in 1776 *Providence* of Whitby was stuck in the ice, with the loss of 26 men. There was one particularly bad season in 1787 when at least 11 ships were sunk by 'getting inclosed by the vast islands of ice which are always floating in the Greenland Seas . . .

but were this year more numerous and stupendous than any man employed in the fishery had ever seen before.'[7] The Reverend John Mill of Shetland showed scant sympathy when he said: 'Tis a wonder of mercy that so many of these curs'd ruffians are preserved.'[8]

In the disaster of 1830, most of the whaling fleet were threading a narrow clear passage across Melville Bay when the ice closed on them. Negotiating such a passage was an arduous task. The ship would have to be towed by muscle power alone, with the men wearing a canvas 'row raddie' or tracking belt to which a line was attached. Tied together and to the ship, they would literally haul her bodily through the clear water; a stout-lunged bagpiper or their own singing often encouraged them in this process. George Laing, the Scottish surgeon of the Hull whaling ship *Zephyr*, mentioned the song 'Oh Logie of Buchan' as being sung in 1830:

Oh Logie o' Buchan, O Logie the Laird
They hae taen aw' Jamie, that delved in the yaird
Wha played on the pipe, and the viol sae sma'
They have taen awa Jamie, the flow'r o' them a'

On 24 June 1830 a south westerly screamed on to the long line of ships and slammed shut the gate to the west. Alexander Kidd, on board *Achilles* of Dundee, reported it as 'a sudden and violent irruption took place about one . . . and the *Achilles*, the *Baffin* and *Rattler* of Leith and a French ship, the *Ville de Dieppe* . . . were rendered complete wrecks.'[9] The wind altered to the SSW, with sleet and snow hitting others of the fleet. The men had hacked out ice docks with their great nine-foot saws, but the storm was too strong and pushed them shut. Alarmed, the men bundled their belongings on to the ice, then carried up as much food as they could before the relentless thrust of ice lifted the vessels clear or hammered them down. *Laetitia* of Aberdeen was tossed on her side, dismasted and wrecked; *Princess of Wales*, also of Aberdeen, soon followed. As the days wore on, casualties mounted; *William and Ann* of Whitby, *Eagle* of Hull . . . the list is sad, sickening and relentless, as the ice made mockery of man's attempted domination.

Yet despite the catastrophe, 1830 was not only remembered for the loss of proud ships, but for the almost unbelievable aftermath. In most businesses, such tremendous losses and near-death experiences would create melancholy and despair, but the Greenlandmen were not easily given to such emotions. Where others might have mourned, they turned disaster into a party, looting wine and spirits from some of the vessels; they burned the ships and drank themselves sober for days in what became known as the Baffin Fair. Legend tells of up to a thousand men living on the ice, drinking steadily, sheltering in canvas tents or in the shadow of upturned whaleboats as the fleet slid down in flames, the reflection of which flickered from the underside of the low white clouds. Others trekked for days across the ice to find a serviceable ship. Surprisingly, there were only ten deaths as a result of these misadventures, but the whalers were not so lucky in other years.

Although fewer ships were sunk in the 1836 season, the loss of life was far greater, following on from the wreck the previous year of *William Torr* of Hull with all hands. In 1836 six ships were trapped in the ice. These vessels were *Dee* of Aberdeen, *Swan* of Hull, *Grenville Bay* of Newcastle, *Norfolk* of Berwick and two Dundee vessels, *Thomas* and *Advice*. In December, the Lords of the Treasury refused a petition from the merchants, shipowners and magistrates of Dundee to send a relief ship. However, in January 1837, their Lordships agreed they would pay a bounty to 'any vessel which may render assistance to the detained whalers'.[10] In response, the Dundee whaling ships *Horn* and *Princess Charlotte* fitted out and left early, while a Stromness surgeon named Hamilton offered his services free of charge. The government bounty was fixed at £300 for the first five vessels to sail before 5 February with extra provisions for the beleaguered whaling ships, and a sliding scale of bounties for actually relieving the ships depending on how deep in the ice they were lodged, and compensation for vessels that escorted the rescued ships to a secure port.[11] *Traveller* of Peterhead and *Dunscombe* of Hull also sailed early,[12] but none of the whaling vessels were able to help the crews of *Thomas* or *Advice*, most of whom died. *Thomas* sank under the ice and *Advice* staggered to Ireland with her crew raddled with scurvy.

Captain Adamson of *Princess Charlotte*, however, was able to effect the relief of *Swan* of Hull, a vessel which had been trapped 15 miles to the westward of Hare Island. Captain Dring was preparing to abandon the ship in mid May when she saw the searching *Princess Charlotte*. The Dundee ship sent a relief party on board and organised a rescue which included physically sawing through 3,000 foot (about 1,000 metres) of ice and involved *Dorothy*, *Horn* and *Heroine* of Dundee and *William and Anne* of Hull. On 21 May, thanks to Captain Adamson and *Princess Charlotte*, *Swan* was free. As most of *Swan's* crew were too weak to work, Captain Adamson sent some of his men on board and *Swan*, accompanied by *Dunscombe*, sailed back to Hull.

Although 1830 and 1836 were unusual for the number of deaths, the ice was a constant hazard. In 1834 the Dundee vessel *Dorothy* was stuck and the master, Thomas Davidson, 'called all hands and warped the ship through'.[13] Even as late as 1884, when most whaling vessels were steam powered, the ice could be formidable, as this short passage by Matthew Campbell, who sailed in the Dundee vessel *Nova Zembla* shows: 'At 12 pm stuck fast in the ice and backed astern but of no avail . . . called all hands to roll the ship, which they did with a will, so much in fact that her boats almost touched the ice.'[14]

The design of the ships was very important in the ice. In 1791, when *Neptune* was sunk by two ice floes meeting, *Royal Bounty* of Leith escaped 'by being a sharp built vessel'.[15] The later Dundee shipbuilders took note and when they designed whaling ships, used every ounce of experience a century of ice navigation gave them.

Next to ice, stormy seas were possibly the worst danger whaling ships would face. Journals, logbooks and newspaper reports constantly highlighted the importance of storms to the success or otherwise of the fishery. For example, the 1754 season was so bad that when *City of Aberdeen* returned the 'harpooners on board, some of whom had 30 voyagers in the ice, say they had never seen such bad weather.'[16] Four years later, when *Hawke* of Anstruther returned damaged and clean from the Greenland Sea, she reported 'extremely stormy' weather that made the 'fishing in general . . . very unsuccessful'.[17] *Oswald* of Bo'ness also reported 'very stormy weather'[18] which helped claim eleven ships that year. In 1762 Captain Cheyne of the Dundee ship *Grandtully* reported: 'the Fishery in general is bad owing entirely to stormy Weather for never was there greater Plenty of Fish seen in Greenland'.[19] In 1790 'tempestuous' weather was 'unfavourable to the fishing'[20] and in 1788, 'hard gales of wind . . . and a storm of wind' forced *Six Brothers* of Leith to abandon a captured whale with 12 whaling lines as 'the sea [was] running mountains high.'[21]

That same year of 1788, a number of vessels used the strong winds to their advantage when they were stuck side by side in the ice. They fastened a cable one to the other along the whole line of ships and when a northwest wind came, the combined force of seven ships cracked open the ice and they escaped.[22] However the storms of 1789 took some beating. When *Ranger* of Hull was sailing to the whaling grounds, a single wave swept 14 men overboard but the very next wave crashed 10 back on deck.[23]

In the season of 1825 the Dundee *Advertiser* reported: 'the reason given of the bad fishing is the condition of the strong north-east winds, which had occasioned the strong ice to come down which could not be penetrated.'[24] Seven years later the same newspaper mentioned that the Dundee ship *Horn* 'sustained very serious damage from the ice during a gale of wind in Lancaster Sound . . . and had to abandon five fish after having them alongside.'[25] In 1856 Surgeon Trotter of *Enterprise* spoke of heavy weather: 'clear today but with a tremendous sea: forced to take two of our boats on deck [from hanging over the side] and also to block up one of the stern . . . windows'.[26] Captain Robertson of the Bo'ness ship *Ocean* also reported on stormy weather he met in the spring of 1787:

> The Ocean had, by the 28th Ult, the sixth day from sailing, got so far as 67 degrees 35 min north latitude, 3.15 west longitude when a severe gale came on . . . in handling the top sails Peter Steen, one of the sailors was killed by a fall from the maintop sail yard. The gale increasing, the ship was laid to. Next morning it blew still harder, several heavy seas were shipped; one in particular tore up the larboard gunwell, carried away timber heads, capstone, stations and quarter sherds also stove four boats on the main deck.[27]

The wind did not have to be storm force to cause problems. In the days of sail even a moderate wind from the wrong direction could cause delays. For example, in 1758 the entire Leith Greenland fleet was forced back into harbour only one day after setting out.[28] An easterly wind also caused difficulty in 1764, as the whaling fleet could not get into the ice for the whales.[29] Sometimes there was no wind at all, but rather than having a holiday, seamen engaged in whale hunting had to work harder than ever. For example, on *Dorothy* in 1834, when there was a period with hardly any wind, the master 'called all hands to tow the ship'.[30] Fog was also a hazard, with the 'poor fishing' of 1761 blamed on 'incessant foggy weather'.[31]

While the weather was obviously vital to the whaling fleet, the whaling masters adapted their work to suit the conditions. By the 1780s they had decided that a hard winter encouraged the whales further south, so the ships did not need to enter the more hazardous northern seas. The seasons of 1765 and 1778 had been successful after such cold spells.[32]

Dundee was an early adopter of steam power in whaling ships and by the 1860s, Alexander Stephen of Dundee was building steam ships specifically for the whaling trade. There were advantages and disadvantages in steam. The advantages were speed and the ability to steam against the wind. On her trial, *Tay*, a sailing ship converted to steam in 1858, steamed at 7 knots. That may not seem impressive, but it was in the ability to maintain that speed day after day that steamships scored, for sail powered ships were only faster if the wind was right for them. Steamships could also ram their way through ice that defied sailing vessels. One major disadvantage of steam power was the expense, for engines had to be built and fitted, and required coal which was not free. *Tay* carried 300 tons of coal. A second disadvantage was the amount of stowage space the engine room removed. *Tay*'s engine was built by J. P. Almond of Newcastle and when it was fitted, she lost 160 tons of cargo space. There was also the possibility the engines might fail as happened on *Tay's* maiden voyage in 1858 when she had to return to Dundee from the sealing rather than calling into Lerwick to replenish her coal bunkers. Despite these setbacks, however, her initial whaling voyage was a success as Captain Deuchars caught six whales as well as lending coal to *Diana* of Hull and a spare rudder to *Chase*, also of Hull.

The new steam whalers used every technical innovation they could to overcome the hazards of high latitude navigation. Even the early *Tay* had a retractable propeller. The screw propellers were possibly the most vulnerable parts of the steam ship and were frequently damaged. For instance, in 1862 *Polynia* damaged her propeller and had to sail to St John's to be repaired and in 1891 *Thetis* broke her propeller while sealing in the Greenland Sea. As well as their vulnerability, screw propellers had other disadvantages. In 1881 the Dundee whaling masters decided that screws scared off the whales and had a mutual understanding that whaling ships should use sail alone when whaling north of Cape Horsburgh, but that they could use the engines if they were travelling to Lancaster Sound. They decided to restrict their use of steam power after 20 July, when the season was at its height, although steam was permitted when the ships were towing whales.

Esquimaux was typical of the Dundee built steam vessels of the later nineteenth century. She was launched in 1865, and in common with other steam vessels, coal occupied a great deal of her carrying capacity. She had 110 tons of coal in her bunkers, and burned 7.5 tons a day when under steam alone, which was fairly typical of her class. *Terra Nova*, launched two decades later and 100 tons heavier, burned about 14 tons a day at full speed, but had about 2 knots more. Arguably the finest of them all, *Terra Nova* had bow planking of between four-and-a-quarter and five-and-a-quarter inches of thick hard wood, with three inches of bark or greenheart outside that. That protection ran for about nine feet aft of the stem, with the addition of three-and-a-half inch thick steel plates on the stem itself.

Both vessels were built at Alexander Stephens' yard in Dundee. Stephens' ships were not only owned in Dundee, for Newfoundland owners also bought them for the sealing trade. Many explorers also sought Dundee-built vessels for the more arduous voyages. *Esquimaux* was sold to the United States and renamed as *America*, but one of the most successful converted discovery ships was *Aurora*, Stephens-built and used by Sir Douglas Mawson in his Australian Antarctic Expedition of 1911. In his book *The Home of the Blizzard*, Mawson describes the type of vessel he sought: 'a vessel built to navigate amid the ice'.[33] Mawson wrote about the 'elasticity' of the wooden construction easing the 'shock of impacts with floating ice'. As well as the wooden hull, *Aurora* had a cutaway bow, with the upper part of the bow overhanging, to rise above the ice pack and gradually lessen the vessel's progress. The bow brought the vessel above the ice, and then eased it down so the weight broke through the pack. Mawson gave fulsome tribute to *Aurora*, writing of the oak, fir and greenheart hull, the solid wooden bow sheathe with steel plate, the frames supported by oak beams and the internal bulkheads. She had a 98 horsepower engine that drove a four bladed propeller that gave a speed of up to 10 knots.

The later Dundee whaling ships were superb vessels for their time and place with 150 years of ice experience in their design so when the British Government decided on an Antarctic expedition in 1900, they came to Dundee for the local expertise. The resulting vessel, *Discovery*, now resides on Dundee's waterfront and is probably the closest thing existent to a Dundee whaling ship. To look at her on a foul day, when an easterly wind cuts white water on the Tay, and think of the savage seas of the Arctic, is to get closer to the experience of the whaling men than any book can conjure up.

7

The Business of Whaling

To be sold by private bargain
One share of the capital stock of the Dundee Union Whale-Fishing Company
with or without the undivided profits of the last voyage
Dundee Advertiser, 10 February 1825

Although the popular image of nineteenth century whaling centres on a small boat against an Arctic background, with a harpooner balanced in the bow ready to hurl his harpoon at a spouting black whale, the harpoon was only the sharpest point in a long sword. Whaling was always first and foremost a cold-blooded business venture, despite the romantic image of adventure and survival against the odds. Profit was the driving force behind the whaling industry; when whale hunting made money, the number of whaling vessels increased; when the inward flow of money decreased, the industry faded. Investing in the ships was always a huge gamble as every trip was fraught with danger, from the complete disaster of the loss of a ship to the possibility of a poor season, but a good season could see large profits.

It was not until the government offered financial incentives in the form of cash bounties that the Scottish whaling industry really started. In 1733 the government put forward a scheme with a bounty of £1 for every ton weight of a ship of 200 tons and upward that ventured on the whaling trade. That was a good first step, but not until the bounty doubled in 1750 was there a surge of interest. During lean years the bounty was an invaluable lifeline for the industry, but by the 1780s the Board of Customs thought the industry 'so flourishing as not to stand in need of the aid of bounties'.[1] In 1789 the bounty was fixed at 30s a ton; it was reduced to 25s in 1792 and 20s in 1795.[2] At that low level, whaling became an even more precarious financial adventure. Even so, in 1815, when the Tay Whale Fishing Company paid the master of *Advice* £82 11s 6d for wages and £496 4s for the remainder of the crew, the government bounty of £300 would go a long way to meeting the costs.[3] The bounty stopped altogether in 1824 but by then the whaling industry was well established. However, the price of whale oil fell concurrently with the demise of the bounty, dropping to £23 a ton as mineral oil production grew[4] from a high of £55 in 1813.

With the bounty, the British whaling fleet multiplied from a miniscule figure in 1749 to 83 in 1756, with by far the greater part in England, with London the main centre. Nevertheless, the government was not handing out money for nothing; there were stipulations and strings attached. To obtain the bounty, each ship had to sign on five supernumeraries, or greenmen. Initially, these greenmen were expected to be first voyagers – men with no previous seagoing experience – but by the second decade of the nineteenth century, seamen with no Arctic experience were also considered as greenmen. Customs officials checked the whaling ship before she sailed to ensure she had whaling equipment on board, and was not trying to defraud the government by claiming the bounty but not sailing anywhere near the whaling grounds. The master and mates had to swear an oath that they were going whaling, and keep an accurate log that recorded every change of course, every sighting of land and every time they saw a whale, together with soundings and bearings. The ships were also to remain in the fishing grounds until a specific date unless they had already succeeded in capturing 30 tuns of oil and 30 cwt of bone.

Despite the strict regulations, there were numerous applicants for the bounty, and the whaling fleet grew year on year. In 1788 it cost around £1000 to send a whaling ship of between 300 and 400 tons to the Arctic, but the bounty would pay for the cost of the voyage. The catch was not pure profit, however, for the whaling company still had to pay for the ship and hand out a dividend to the partners.[5]

The Bounty had been intended to encourage the growth of British whaling by providing a financial incentive and safety net. Fluctuations in bounty payments and in the size of the whaling fleets, often ran roughly in parallel, as in the 1790s. When the value of the bounty diminished, fewer entrepreneurs risked their ships and capital in the precarious trade of whaling. The number of ports that had dabbled in whaling diminished and the trade became polarised in the hands of a small number of ports, with increasingly specialised whaling men and ships. These ports were located on the East coast of England and Scotland: Dundee was one such.

The expense grew as ships became larger and voyages longer: in 1824 a trip to the Greenland Sea cost around £2,000, while the longer journey round Cape Farewell to the Davis Straits cost around £3,000. However, by the 1830s the whales were already becoming harder to find in the old hunting grounds of the Greenland Sea and southern Davis Straits. There had been a couplet:

With Riff Koll Hill and Disco dipping
There you will see the whale fish skipping[6]

But that did not apply in the later stages of whaling. Disco is a large island off the west coast of Greenland where the whaling ships often rendezvoused. Even in the middle of the nineteenth century whales were expected there, but as the years passed they moved northward and westward deeper into the ice fields. It would appear that each extra mile cost around £1, so making it harder for the industry to be profitable as the whale fish no longer skipped as Disco dipped beneath the horizon. More specialised vessels plunged deeper into the ice, but the rewards were not always there.

Buying a ship was the major investment for those who adventured into the whaling industry, but prices varied tremendously. A newly built steam vessel would cost a fortune; for example *Terra Nova* cost £16,000 to build in 1884. When *Tay* was refashioned from sail to steam in 1858, she cost a reputed £17,000, but she was one of the earliest steam powered whaling ships and the first of an entirely new breed. *Ravenscraig* was also a steam whaling vessel that operated out of Dundee. In 1879 she ran onto a reef in a snowstorm and, with her screw lost, no power and making water fast, she listed heavily. The crew had to abandon her with some speed. *Ravenscraig* was valued at £11,000, with her cargo at £3,000, which was a massive loss to any company.

Even second hand ships were not cheap, with *Intrepid* of Peterhead costing £5,000 in 1863 and *Erik* sold to Peterhead for £10,200 in 1883. However *Esquimaux* fetched only £4,455 in 1895, a year when whaling was in a slump. Older and less complex vessels were far more affordable. For example *Columbia* cost £750 in 1867 when she was purchased as a store ship. The sail powered vessels, once converted for use in whaling, could be relatively expensive, though. In 1841 *Friendship*, although around 40 years old, was offered for sale at £800, while in the same year, *Fairy* was priced at £1,500.[7]

Given the capital outlay, it was hardly surprising there were few ships with a single owner. In common with other British ships, whaling ship ownership was divided into 64 shares. They were usually owned by a company with a managing owner and a number of shareholders, who could own only a single share, or many more. Occasionally one man, or a partnership, would own all shares. Share transactions were commonplace, with the Dundee Shipping Register recording the name of the shareholder and how many shares they had. Over the century and a half of the whaling industry in Dundee, a number of companies were formed; some lasted a considerable number of years while others folding fairly quickly. Details of the Dundee whaling companies are provided in Appendix 5.

The first known Dundee company, the Dundee Whale Fishing Company, caught the whales but had no facilities for selling the catch, which were sold by 'public roup' or auction in the company's warehouse. In September 1826 this company considered merging with other companies including the Dundee Union Whale Fishing Company. The names of the proposers included all the major shareholders and whaling ship owners in Dundee, including David Brown, James Soot, John G. Russell and Robert Jobson junior. The Dundee whaling companies were dynamic, always willing to try new techniques or search for new whaling grounds. It was this elasticity that pushed Dundee to the forefront of the industry in the 1860s and kept her there for the next half century.

Whaling was a fairly complex business, with profit depending on a number of variables from the weather to the skill of the master, and the state of the market when the ships returned. If every vessel returned with a full cargo, the oil market could be glutted with a consequent fall in prices, but if the whales or seals were hard to find, the ships could return clean. Whatever the catch, the vessels had to be maintained and the wages paid, so the ship owners or shareholders would have to bear the costs. The companies often appointed a 'ship's husband' to act as an agent of the owners of the cargo and sometimes the owner himself would take on this role. He travelled with the vessel or remained with her when she was in port and took care of all the business arrangements for the cargo. He was also sometimes known as supercargo. A good, or lucky, ship master could be with the same ship or company for many years, but if the master was unsuccessful, his career could be short. A bad season could be very expensive; for instance, in 1867 the Tay Whale Fishing Company lost £6,000 when the fishing failed.[8]

By the middle of the 1860s, the majority of the Dundee fleet was steam-powered, but although there were greater chances of a good catch, there were also greater costs. In 1870 a company would have to pay £2,000 to send a steamer on a single voyage, or £5,000 for the double voyage of sealing and whaling. In the mid 1880s a whaling ship cost around £12,000 with insurance of £4,000, and each ship had to catch four whales before they broke even.[9] Insurance was a major cost throughout the whaling industry, but it provided a vital safety net for what was a high risk investment. In 1816 the Dundee ship *Tay* was insured at a total cost of £367 17s through three different companies, one of which was J. G Russell of Dundee, whaling ship owners and managers in their own right; the world of whaling was small and often intertwined. The other two insurance companies were John Thain and C.A. Miller, both of London.[10] But insurance did not always guarantee shipowners' financial security. That same year *Earl of Fife* of Banff was driven onto the bar off Banff and wrecked. The crew were saved but the ship and stores were lost. There were three insurers: Lloyds of London, a Leith company and an Aberdeen company. Lloyds paid up promptly but both Scottish underwriters refused to pay, saying the owners should not have abandoned the ship. They later changed their excuse, refusing to believe the ship had been properly equipped for a whaling voyage. The owners only got their money when they took the insurers to court in March 1818.[11]

The managers of whaling companies were undoubtedly good business men and managed their assets to the best advantage, selling them before their value depreciated too far. For example *Terra Nova* cost £16,000 to build but her cargo of 34,500 seals in 1891 was valued at £18,500 and she was sold for £11,060 in 1893. Whaling ships frequently changed hands, being sold by auction or private bargain. A typical advertisement would be as follows:

By Private Bargain

The Fine whale fishing ship DOROTHY 356 tons per register, with all her FISHING STORES; as she presently lies in this harbour

The vessel was completely fortified and fitted out by government for the Northern Expedition a few years ago; and is at present in excellent condition; and her fishing stores are nearly new

The Dorothy can be sent to the fishing without any expense except provisions.

For particulars apply to Mr Peter Thomson, manager

Dundee, November 8 1826.[12]

The following month the company advertised the sale of their second ship, *Friendship,* together with the 'yard, boiler, cast iron tanks and commodious warehouses adjoining.'[13] The prices asked for the ships can give an indication of their depreciation. For example, *Dorothy* was for sale once again in 1827, with an asking price of £2,000[14] but sold for £4,200, having been bought for £7,300[15] in 1821.

One ship's good catch could make a company financially viable for a year. For example, when *Campbeltown* of Leith caught four whales in 1774, it was estimated the cargo would bring in 'near three thousand pounds,'[16] a large sum at the time. But conversely, the loss of a ship could signal the death of a whaling company. In 1874 *Tay* was lost in the ice and the Dundee Arctic Fishing Company folded. A new company, the Dundee Polar Fishing Company, took its place and bought two ships, *Jan Mayen* and *Nova Zembla* from Hamburg in recently united Germany. The new company had mixed fortunes, with no dividend at all in 1881 but a 15 per cent dividend two years later.

By the late nineteenth century Robert Kinnes and George Welch were the major players in the Dundee whaling industry. In January 1881 both were appointed joint managers of the Tay Whale Fishing Company, which ran *Victor, Active, Jan Mayen* and *Intrepid*. In July that year, a single share in the company cost £70, with a thirtieth share of *Active* costing £225, which was £25 above the asking price, so even at that late stage, with whales scarce, investors still believed there was a viable future in the whaling industry.

After the cost of the ship, wages were probably the next major expense. With a large crew of around 50, and a high number of specialists, it can be imagined that the shipowners needed good catches to pay their costs. Naturally the ship's master was the highest paid man. In the year 1829, Captain Thomas Davidson of the Dorothy Whale Company earned £291 10s 9d in total, although his standard wage was only £60 (see Table 7.1). It is obvious that there was a huge financial incentive to have a successful catch on each voyage.

Table 7.1 Shipmaster's income, 1829

Reason	Amount earned
One year's wages	£60 0s 0d
Oil money: 207 tuns at 20s per tun	£207 0s 0d
Fish money on 16 sizeable at 63s	£50 8s 0d
Bone money on 11 tons 5 hundredweight at 63s	£35 8s 9d
Striking money on one fish	1s 1d
Half proceeds of rump and tails	£12 8s 6d
Cash paid out agreeing hands etc	£5 0s 0d
Cash paid pilotage, 24 dozen eggs etc	£1 16s 0d
To interest on £256, 4 months at 4%	£3 8s 6d
Total	£375 10s 10d

Source: Dorothy Whaling Company Wage Book, Dundee Museum

As with the shipmaster, the men were paid a flat rate per month, with a number of bonuses depending on how successful the season had been. The bonuses were for oil money, fast boat money for the men in the whale boats that harpooned the whale, and skin money, depending on the number of sealskins brought home. The bonuses acted as an incentive for the men to work harder and on a successful voyage could easily double the take home pay. An unsuccessful voyage, however, would leave the men virtually penniless, so they might have to search for another berth over the winter. The shareholders would have no dividend if the ship failed to catch a decent quota of seals or whales. Table 7.2 shows typical wages for whaling seamen in 1874.

In 1869, falling profits caused the owners of Dundee whaling companies to propose a reduction in wages, with mates and engineers losing £2 a month and seal oil money reduced by 2s 6d a ton. Fast boat money was to be abolished completely. These changes would have affected most

Table 7.2 Whaling seamen's wages, 1874[17]

Rank	Wages per month	Whale oil per ton	Seal oil per ton	Bone per ton	Half pay
Mate	100s	7s 3d	5s	10s 6	50s
2nd Mate	70s	6s 9d	5s	10s 6d	40s
Specktioneer	60s	7s 3d	5s	10s 6d	40s
1st harpooner	55s	6s 9d	4s	10s 6d	40s
Loose harpooner	65s	3s 6d	3s 6d	10s 6d	32s 6d
Boatswain	50s	2s 6d	2s 6d	5s	25s
Line manager	45s	2s	2s	4s	22s 6d
Able-bodied (AB) seaman	40s	1s 9d	1s 9d	2s	20s
Engineer	100s	7s 3d	5s	10s	50s
1st Fireman	60s	3s	3s	5s	30s
2nd Fireman	55s	3s	3s	5s	27s 6d
3rd Fireman	50s	2s 6d	2s 6d	5s	25s
2nd carpenter	55s	2s 6d	2s 6d	4s	27s 6d
1st cooper	70s	3s	3s	5s	35s
2nd cooper	45s	2s	2s	4s	22s 6d
Cook	45s	2s	2s	4s	22s 6d
Surgeon	40s	2s	2s	4s	Nil
Sail maker [AB]	50s	2s 6d	2s 6d	4s	25s
Sail maker [OS]	45s	2s	2s	2s	22s 6d
Steward	50s	2s	2s	4s	25s

whaling seamen, and the mates and specialists in particular. One hundred and fifty whaling seamen met in the Masonic Hall in the Murraygate and sent a deputation to the owners stating they would not accept the cut in wages. They stated they would not sail if their wages were reduced, and they were supported by seamen in other whaling ports who refused to take their places. Wages were so vital for the men and such a large expense for the company that they were bound to lead to friction.

After wages came provisions for the men and all the expenses of fitting out a vessel for the rigours of the Arctic. The whaling companies frequently advertised for supplies, for instance:

> To Graziers: wanted for Dundee Whale fishing: carcasses of 25 fine fat bullocks from 32–40 stones each, to be delivered company's warehouses Dundee 4–23 February. Apply Walter Newall.[18]

Some of the accounts of the Dorothy Whale Fishing Company still survive in a number of bundles of payment slips held in the archives of Dundee University and in documents in Dundee Museum. Unfortunately there is no way of knowing if the bundles represent a full account of all the expenses faced by the company, but reading through them gives a good idea of the expenditure of a typical early nineteenth century whaling company. The expenditure for 1830 is set out in Appendix 8. That year, the Dorothy Whaling Company paid out at least £2,093, excluding the wages bill, before they could start to make a profit. The expenditure included £726 for carpentry work for ships and the boiler yard and a further £63 for work on the new boilers at the yard, plus £21 12s for a new mast for *Friendship* and over £76 for new wood for the decks. These figures may not be typical but they provide a reminder of the constant drain of overheads on a whaling company, where the ships operated in harsh conditions, so the profit from the capture of a whale might be tempered by damage to the ship or loss of equipment. In 1830 the company paid £24 for a new whaleboat, which suggests there was one lost or damaged in the 1829 voyage, while the amount paid for carpentry work suggests damage sustained in the ice.

There are other points of interest in the accounts including a bill for £6 for 'two tides of barge for lightening *Dorothy*'.[19] In 1829 *Dorothy* returned from the Arctic with 37 whales. Such a large cargo would weigh her down, increasing her draft so she was possibly too deep to enter the harbour, so necessitating the use of a lighter to take off a portion of her cargo. The accounts also mention pilotage paid for taking the ships in to harbour and out of the Tay. The Tay is not easy to enter, with a strong current, shifting sand bars at the entrance and tidal sand banks far up river. One whaling ship,

Jane, was lost at the entrance to the Tay in 1809, so investing a few pounds in a professional pilot was common sense.

There were also the everyday, often forgotten hidden costs that ate into the profits, such as shore dues on the oil the company exported to London and Glasgow and the dock dues and the freight charges on oil and bone. With ships operating in such a hostile environment there were constant maintenance costs, such as the £77 for ropes and sails that year, and sundry payments such as the five shillings for sawdust, which was sprinkled on deck during flensing to soak up the blood and blubber. Other charges were more expected, such as the payment for repairing and sharpening harpoons and for carrying them to and from Pittenweem in Fife, or the 11 dozen bungs for the blubber casks.

Overall, the accounts of the Dorothy Whale Fishing Company show just how important the whaling industry was to the economy of Dundee. As well as providing employment for the seamen, this one small two-ship company supported shipbuilders and carters, other shipping companies, grocers and farmers, joiners and smiths. Dundee Central Library has an account book for the Tay Whale Fishing Company which also gives details of customers and prices. These accounts show that in 1816, £57 8s 6d was paid for beer and £24 10s 5d for rum for *Estridge* alone. The harpoons were purchased from William Clark of South Shields, the ropes from the Tay Rope Works Company and Thomas Webster and Co, Rope Makers, and a whole raft of local merchants from bakers to plumbers benefited from the whaling industry.[20]

Whaling companies brought back a number of saleable commodities from the Arctic, but the two most important were oil from whales and seals, and baleen. The whale oil market was both national and international, with domestic, commercial and industrial users. Oil prices were published in many newspapers; for instance, in August 1814, the *Lancaster Gazette* published the following list: 'Greenland oil per tun: £35; South Sea Whale Oil per tun: £34; whale fins per tun, South Sea £40–£50; Greenland whale fins: £75 per tun of 252 gallons'.

In the early nineteenth century whale oil was used almost exclusively for lighting so that one historian thought it 'made a bigger contribution to safety in the streets of London than the policeman.'[21] It was used in many towns, including Aberdeen,[22] Dundee and Edinburgh. In 1816 the whaling ship *Estridge* certainly sent oil to a company called Smith and Swan in Edinburgh, and to William Waddle in Leith. Smith and Swan was founded by Thomas Smith (1752–1814) who had been responsible for lighting both the Old and New Towns in Edinburgh, so Dundee whale oil was burned in the capital. In 1814, the entire British whaling fleet produced an estimated

9,000 tons of oil, which reduced oil prices and the cost of soap and candles.[23] In 1816 they brought home around 12,500 tons of oil, but the following year only around 11,000 tons. Prices rose accordingly as the oil speculators had a field day, with oil being quoted at up to £45 a tun compared to the average price of £27 the previous year.[24]

The price obtained for oil mainly depended on the amount brought onto the market, which in turn was dependant on the catches of whaling vessels. For instance, 1765 was a successful year, so there were more whales brought back and oil prices fell.[25] The greater the volume of whale blubber brought back, the lower the prices for oil. In the early years of Scottish whaling, the oil came from many different whaling companies who could sell their goods by public roup.[26] This system could lead to major oil firms grabbing a monopoly of the market. At the beginning of the nineteenth century, the firm of Peter and Christopher Wood, with warehouses at the Sands of Leith, was the largest purchaser from the Leith ships; for instance, in 1814 the vessels *Dexterity*, *Thomas and Ann*, *William and Ann*, *Raith* and *Royal Bounty* all sold their catch to that one company..

Dundee whaling companies had many customers. As well as exporting whale oil to France by the barrel load[27] they sold oil in various quantities all around Scotland as well as to Sunderland, London and Memel in East Prussia (now known as Klaipeda in Lithuania). Oil from the vessel *Dorothy* alone was sold to some 41 different customers.[28] In 1833 customers included the Commissioner of Police for Dundee and consumers in Rotterdam, Liverpool and Newcastle.[29] However, it was not all profit, for the company had to pay £3 13s freight for 24 casks to Newcastle[30] and £12 8s freight for 30 casks of oil to Glasgow. There was also freight of bone for Bremen, with the Dorothy Company paying the Hull Shipping Company 5s.

With such a wide number of consumers, the income base of the whaling industry was virtually assured. But all the fluctuations of supply and the security of demand were thrown into turmoil after the advent of gas lighting in the 1820s. In January 1822, 53 gas lanterns replaced 79 oil lamps in Edinburgh, just in time for the visit of King George IV; by October that year, 947 gas lamps replaced the 1,370 oil lamps that had previously illuminated the streets of the capital. The new lighting was said to be both cheaper and more effective,[31] and Edinburgh pushed forward, with Sir Walter Scott laying the foundation of an oil-gas works at Tanfield in 1824.

In 1826 one Dundee whaling company was selling its assets, which shows how a drop in profits could adversely affect the company,[32] while a proposed merger of the remaining Dundee whale fishing companies that same year[33] may indicate how difficult trading conditions altered competition. The years 1828 and 1829 reveal the roller coaster reality of the whaling trade, with the nine Dundee vessels bringing in 1,800 tuns of oil in 1828 which made £70,000, but only half that amount the following year.[34] After the poor season in 1830, Dundee witnessed 'an absolute run' upon the oil dealers[35] which raised the prices so the cargo of one vessel sold for a startling £60 per tun.[36] The vital importance of good catches to oil prices is obvious when two years later, after a successful season, prices dropped to £20 per tun.[37]

With the gradual replacement of oil by gas for domestic lighting and the disasters of the 1830s, whaling companies the length of Britain began to desert the trade. The Dundee companies were luckier than most. The Dundee staple trades of linen and especially jute were to prove the industry's most reliable customer, and by 1858 they demanded 2,200 tons of whale and seal oil a year.[38] As the jute industry expanded, Dundee whaling companies responded by expanding their fleets, just as steam whaling ships came into production. Yet even as Dundee faced a whaling boom, the progress of petroleum from 1859 struck another major blow for whale oil as a fuel. From that date the industry faced a double challenge: the search for customers and shrinking supplies as the whale and seal stocks diminished. Nevertheless, in Dundee the whaling industry remained alive and kicking. In 1863 Gilroy, Sons and Company bought the whaling ship *Emma* from Hull, becoming the first jute company to directly enter the whaling trade. The Dundee Whaling industry sailed through its final half century of existence on a wave of jute. While the other British ports relinquished any interest in whaling, Dundee continued to send ships north. But although whale oil remained important, there were other commodities that brought in money.

Baleen or whalebone was probably the second most important item brought back from the Arctic. Baleen depended on market forces just as much as oil did, and in the early years was as much influenced by catches by non-British ports. For example 1766 was a poor year for the British ships, but vessels from North American ports seem to have had a better season and their catches were expected to depress prices.[39] The prices fluctuated year by year, but undoubtedly rose toward the end of the Arctic whaling period presumably as the product became scarcer. The variations in price throughout the nineteenth and into the twentieth century are illustrated in Table 7.3.

Although conditions for the whaling industry grew ever tougher, there was still the possibility of profit until late in the day. In 1893 a large whale with around 30 tons of oil and a ton and a half of baleen could make as much as £5,000, so Dundee continued to send her ships north, hoping always that next year things would improve.

Table 7.3 Whale bone prices

Year	Price per ton
1823	£187 10s
1824	£125
1833	£150
1856	£290–£315
1865	£525
1874	£540
1879	£700
1882	£1,150
1884	£1,200–£1,450
1891	£2,650
1893	£1,000–£1,600
1900	£1,400
1901	£2,000
1902	£2,500
1903	£2,700–£2,900
1904	£2,800 dropping to £2,000
1905	£2,750 to £2500
1908	£2,000

Source: Dundee Advertiser

The whaling ships also brought back seal skins. In 1800 sealskins sold in London for 70s to 80s per dozen for small seals and up to twice that for large. The skins were for sale on the London market throughout the eighteenth and into the nineteenth centuries. Sealing became very important for Dundee. In 1879 the Dundee sealing made £40,500. The following year, 1880, Dundee vessels brought home 1,215 tons of seal oil, with a value of £30,375, and 88,040 seal skins valued at £22,010. The whaling that year brought in £115,091. Even the produce of a single ship could realise an impressive sum. In 1861 the new steamer *Narwhal* brought home a cargo valued at £13,000, which raised a profit of £7,000 for the owners. As the stocks of right whales and even seals diminished, the whaling vessels diversified their attentions to other Arctic animals, from narwhal to bottlenose whales and even bears, reindeer, ptarmigan and Arctic foxes; anything that could turn a profit. By 1882 bottlenose whales were a common catch, with *Intrepid* bringing home 23, *Thetis* catching 8 and *Polar Star,* 67. The oil from bottlenose whales sold for £60 a ton, as opposed to £33 a ton for the right whale, so it was a valuable commodity.

The whaling industry also benefited Dundee indirectly. Dundee gained a reputation as a builder of vessels ideal for Arctic conditions, and Alexander Stephens built many vessels for other sealing ports. Some of these ships had fascinating histories but, save for their origins, little connection with Dundee. They include *Adventure*, built in 1906 by Dundee Shipbuilders Ltd and owned by Hervey of St John's Newfoundland. She was Dundee's first purpose built steel sealing ship, with 400 men employed in building her. As always, Dundee showed innovation, equipping her with search lights to spot seals in the dark. *Adventure* also carried the Royal Canadian Mounted Police to Hudson's Bay and rescued the crew of the Dundee vessel *Paradox* in 1909. She ended her career in Russia.

The Alexander Stephen-built vessel *Bear* became almost legendary in the USA. She was originally built for Grieve of Greenock but in 1884, the US Government purchased her to help search for their missing Greely expedition. When *Bear* sailed into New York harbour after the rescue, her officers were lauded as heroes. The US government kept hold of *Bear,* refitted her at Brooklyn Navy Shipyard and used her to keep order on the North Pacific sealing grounds, where she earned the nickname 'White Angel of the Arctic'. She acted as a police ship during the Klondike gold rush and then continued her adventurous career by enduring fogs and gales of 150 miles per hour, rescued crews from shipwrecks, survived her own near shipwreck in 1924, helped chase smugglers in 1931, starred in a film and became the first US ship to capture a German vessel in the Second World War. She finally sank off Nova Scotia in 1961 after a career to make any shipbuilder proud.

There were other vessels that made money for Dundee: *Bloodhound*, later named *Discovery*, again built by Alexander Stephen and used in the 1876 search for the North West passage; there was the hard working, Newfoundland-owned *Commodore,* once laden so deep with sealskins the crew could reach over the bulwarks and dip their hands in the sea. Arguably most famous of all was *Discovery* built by Dundee Shipbuilders at Panmure Yard, Marine Parade, and used by Captain Scott of the Antarctic. She now sits in her splendour beside the Tay. There are many others: *Eagle*; *Fogota*; *Hector*, reported lost in a storm in 1872 but arriving safe and sound without losing a man; *Iceland*, which broke her propeller shaft on the Grand Banks but

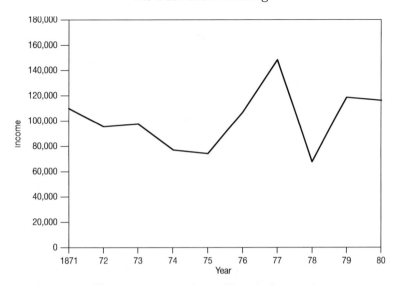

Figure 7.1 Annual income from whaling 1871–1880

Source: Ingram and Dundee Courier

was towed to safety; *Lorna Doone* that sailed to Siberia in 1927; *Mastiff* and *Neptune*. All these vessels were built in Dundee because of the whaling and Arctic expertise.

Overall, the whaling industry was very important for the economy of Dundee. Figure 7.1 shows a decade of whaling income at a time when Dundee was the most important whaling port in Britain.

Once again, the nature of the industry is obvious with no pattern; income rose and fell year by year. That was the pattern throughout the history of whaling, yet all the while, seal and whale catches were gradually but inexorably diminishing. The remembered image of whaling may be of the harpooner and the beautiful ships, but it was always about money. It was a business, and when the whaling ships stopped making money, Dundee Arctic whaling ended.

8

The Whaling Masters

There is an old superstition that the captain of whalers, when they die, takes the form of a raven.

A. Barclay Walker

The master of a whaling ship occupied a unique position. Often he was part owner of the vessel, very occasionally he brought his wife to sea, but always he was responsible for the success or otherwise of the voyage, and the safety and well-being of the crew. Harpooners, line managers, mates and speck-tioneers, all had their place in the vessel, but ultimately the master made the decisions: the buck stopped with him. Many qualities were necessary for a successful whaling master.

He needed to be a skilled mariner, but he also needed the particular dexterity of ice navigation, recognising the various types of ice, where it was safest to navigate and where the whales were most likely to be. The master had to have a thorough knowledge of terms such as 'growlers' for small icebergs that growled though the sea, the 'bergy-bits' that fell from the large icebergs, 'bay ice' that was a mixture of ice and snow on top of the sea, pancake ice, field ice, pack ice, brash ice, streams of ice and hummocky ice. He would know how and when to carve out ice docks with the great nine foot long ice saws, and how to tell an ice sky from a water sky; when to anchor to an ice berg and when to have the hands tow the ship through a narrow passage. The master needed weather lore too, with a northerly swell foretelling a storm, a Cape Searle mist warning of fog, and if a shout to an iceberg brought an echo, the wind would come from the north.[1] A good whaling master needed to be an excellent man manager for the whale ship crews had a reputation for truculence, he needed charisma and, above all, he had to have luck.

Some whaling masters achieved national recognition such as Captain Scoresby of Whitby who wrote what may be the definitive account of Arctic whaling, *An Account of the Arctic Regions, with a History and Description of the Northern Whale Fishery*. Others were of local importance such as

Captain Thomas Dawson who made forty-two trips to the Greenland Seas, many of them as master of *North Star* and *Blessed Endeavour* of Dunbar. Latterly he was considered as the Commodore of the Greenland whaling, and his labours kept Dunbar in the whaling trade. He died in 1815 aged 88.[2]

Very few men had all the necessary attributes to be a success. A list of the Dundee whaling masters reveals many men who commanded for one voyage or two before conditions or an experienced crew found out their weaknesses and they withdrew from Arctic seamanship to a lesser or easier trade. The master of the lost *Columbia* in 1869 is a testimony to that, as the crew sued the whaling company because of his inexperience and incompetence. Presence was important, but size was not. Captain William Milne was one of the most successful of the later whaling masters, yet he stood little over five foot tall. Sobriety may have been an asset, for Captain Thomas 'Coffee Tam' Robertson was a total abstainer, but on the other hand, Captain Fairweather is said to have died from delirium tremors. Some were pillars of society, but Thomas Robertson was not the only whaling master who got himself in trouble for suspected smuggling and William Adamson had to answer for his crew resisting the press.

There were some who criticised the whaling masters. By law, every whaling ship carried a surgeon, frequently a newly qualified doctor or even a student just learning his trade, and these young men often kept a journal of, what was to them, a novel adventure. The surgeons were reputed to have the easiest job aboard, but were often given the added responsibility of keeping the ship's log and acting as clerk. In 1834 one such surgeon was John Wanless, who sailed on the Dundee whaler *Thomas* and gave the world the benefit of his teenage wisdom when he stated:

> The abilities of masters of whaling fishing vessels are highly praised and valued when they prove successful but what can be more erroneous than to say a man is possessed of powerful intellectual faculties . . . let it suffice that the qualification of a whaling captain are very limited.[3]

Wanless later emigrated to Canada and made a name for himself in the field of medicine.

Other, more experienced men were not so critical. Chief engineer Alexander Smith sailed on *Camperdown* in 1861 and spoke highly of her master: 'Captain William Bruce who to some extent was part owner . . . quite free from the avarice and meanness so prevalent among our captains and ship owners'.[4] Captain Markham of the Royal Navy sailed with Captain William Adam on a whaling voyage and praised him as 'the jovial and kind hearted captain'.[5] The dedication of the whaling masters may be proved by the number who actually died on board their ships. For instance, Captain Ireland and Captain Deuchars both died at sea in 1824 and Captain Sturrock in 1854, with Captain Adams in 1890 and Captain Alexander Fairweather in 1896.

The whaling masters were frequently family men with wives and children waiting for them at home. For example, Captain Milne had ten children in his fifty-five year marriage; he balanced them equally, with five boys and five girls. A captain's wife shared the same heartache and joy as the wives of the crewmen. For instance, when *Thomas* was lost in 1836, her master, Captain Davidson, was taken aboard *Advice*. Unfortunately, *Advice* was icebound all that winter and finally reached port in Ireland until the summer of 1837, with a crew of corpses and scurvy-riddled dying. One of the few survivors was Captain Davidson. Waiting anxiously in Dundee for news, the captain's wife learned of his survival and was told he was sending a letter by the mail coach. Hurrying to the coach, Mrs Davidson waited for the letter, but when her husband stepped out in person, she fainted on the spot. There were a few occasions when Dundee whaling masters took their wives with them to the Arctic. James Murray was one, and William Penny another. Penny was one of the big names in mid-century whaling but he seemed to have been matched by his wife Margaret Irvine, who on one occasion took charge of the ship when Penny was out whaling and reputedly saved it from running into danger.

It is very noticeable that whaling masters often shared the same surname. Ireland; Adams; Sturrock and especially Deuchars were prominent among the Dundee fleet throughout the nineteenth century. Sons often followed their fathers to sea, frequently serving on the same ship; for instance, Captain Ireland took his son James to sea in *Rodney* in 1812 and *Friendship* in 1814. The Adams family are possibly better remembered because they flourished in the latter part of the century when the fame of Dundee whaling reached its apogee. Captain William Adams was born in 1837 and married twice, with five children. His son Thomas died at sea aged 18 while his son William followed him into the whaling trade. The elder William had a half-brother named Hector who was also a whaling man. Whaling seems to have been in the blood of families such as that.

The name Sturrock was also scattered through the crew lists of nineteenth century whaling ships. Of the ship masters, Captain David Sturrock may have been the most unfortunate, losing his son to a shooting accident while on a whaling voyage in 1846 and losing his ship, *Horn*, off St Andrews in 1852 He survived that only to be swept overboard and drowned while commanding *Heroine* two years later. The wave that claimed him also fatally injured his nephew James, leaving David's son, also James, to continue the tradition as master of *Alexander.*

Of all the whaling dynasties of Dundee, the Deuchars were perhaps the most prolific, but arguably the least remembered. As masters, mates and crewmen, they occur wherever a Dundee vessel hunted for whales. There were at least five whaling masters of the surname Deuchars in the nineteenth century, from Alexander born in 1808 to William born in 1849. The vessels they commanded read like a Dundee whaling fleet: *Mary Ann; Achilles; Dorothy; Advice; Princess Charlotte; Alexander* and *Intrepid.* It would be impossible to read about nineteenth century Dundee whaling without tripping over the name Deuchars. However, despite the proliferation of the name, the Deuchars clan did not enter legend as the Adams family did. They were always the hard working professionals and never the stars. To give one example of the Deuchars influence in Dundee whaling, in 1836 when *Advice* was trapped in the Arctic ice, her master was George Deuchars, her mate was Alexander Deuchars and her second mate was James Deuchars. They were a prolific breed. Dundee mariners were also a close caste as proved by the marriage of William Deuchars to Isabella Cuthbert Ireland in Dudhope Crescent in the early 1890s; two seafaring families with strong whaling connections uniting in marriage.[6]

Overall, the Dundee whaling masters were a varied body of men, with the best of them probably equal to any ship master anywhere in the world. The whaling dynasties prove their commitment to the sea and their long attachment proves their success. Appendix 2 provides thumbnail sketches of some of the more prominent whaling masters.

9

The Greenlandman's Experience

On each of the steamers there was a football team, and when any two
steamers met, either on the ice or in a harbour, they had a friendly game.
                                                           Captain James Fairweather

Without the whaling men, there would have been no whaling industry. They
sailed the ships and rowed the boats; they hauled the sails and thrust the
harpoons, they flensed the whales and skinned the seals; they manhan-
dled the barrels and towed the ships. The whaling men or Greenlandmen
survived some of the worst conditions of any seamen in the world and
returned home to wives or sweethearts and family life, interspersed by the
occasional roaring visit to a public house in Dock Street or the Overgate.
Unique among seamen, their work included rowing open boats for hours or
days, regular encounters with dangerous animals, the possibility of catching
scurvy or being poisoned by gas and the constant threat of frostbite. Yet
they are normally invisible, unless specifically sought for. Their names
are recorded in crew lists, in certificates of discharge and in a hundred
newspaper columns, but merely as names or cold faceless statistics. They
are merely allowed the odd peep from behind the shaded glass of history,
distant blurred images manning hard worked whaling vessels or giving
perspective to a photographer's shot of ship or shore. Unless they died on
duty or were guilty of some spectacular crime, they were barely recognised
as people; they were just the cogs that drove the wheels of an industry that
made money for the shareholders. In a British context they were useful for
sailing the ships but were seldom given credit or treated with anything much
above contempt.

Whaling men could be recruited from the fishermen of coastal villages,
from the sons and nephews of veteran Greenlandmen, from merchant
seamen or from the unwanted, as happened in London when Sir John
Fielding formulated a plan for sending orphan boys to sea and in 1772 sent
the first two onto *Rising Sun* of London.[1] They were as exploited as any
seagoing labourers in history, overcrowded in foc'sles that were a breeding

ground for tuberculosis, subject to impressments in time of war, always in danger and often underpaid. The Greenland men were often depicted as wild and wayward, yet they were people. They were warm-blooded, affectionate men with a past and aspirations for a future. They laughed and cried and loved and were loved in turn. They had wives and children; lovers and siblings; they suffered in the bad times and rejoiced in the good. They were the dreaded Greenlandmen whose reputation for drunken violence inspired Sir Walter Scott; they were amongst the toughest of Scottish seamen, themselves a breed not renowned for delicacy and temperamental frailty. To the Shetlanders, they were the Southern Boys; to the Inuit of Eastern Canada they were friends and companions and often lovers. They were the Dundee whaling men, a unique breed of sailors from a unique port town.

And Dundee is a strange city. At one time it existed and expanded because of its strong maritime connections, yet even today, many native Dundonians choose to think of themselves as scions of the jute industry which barely lasted a hundred years, rather than descendants of a magnificent nautical tradition. A great sweep of road disconnects Dundee from its seafront, and although there are attempts to physically reconnect the city to the shore, the mental and emotional attachment appears limited. In a city of self-proclaimed discovery, the only statue with a maritime connection is to Admiral Duncan who stands in splendid isolation at the head of Castle Street, pointing his telescope inland, with his back, like Dundee's, turned to the sea. It is a sad reflection of a near rejection of the past. Dundee's docks and shipping were an integral part of the town, with whaling ships built locally, owned locally, with local masters and a large percentage of local men among the crews.

Dundee Museum has a spreadsheet with information, often taken from the logbooks of ships, on some 4,000 seamen who served in Dundee whaling vessels. A survey of the first 200 men whose place of origin is given reflects the importance of whaling in Dundee's economy and the involvement of seamen from other leading whaling ports in Scotland and beyond. Almost half of these seamen came from Dundee and Broughty Ferry with about 11 per cent from Shetland and a further 11 per cent from Peterhead, Dundee's closest rival as a whaling port. Just under a tenth came from the Fife fishing ports of St Monance and Pittenweem and the remaining quarter included men from Perth, Aberdeen and a score of ports from England and the east coast of Scotland. The Greenlandmen had a hard, if interesting, life. In common with other seamen, as soon as they signed articles at the company office, they were legally bound to sail on a specific vessel on a particular voyage. If they failed to appear, they would be in breach of contract and could be fined or jailed. If they turned up, as the vast majority did, they would embark on a voyage that could bring relative prosperity or the possibility of death.

In the early decades of Dundee whaling, all the voyages were to the Greenland Sea rather than the Davis Straits. The general pattern of the voyage would be similar for most whaling ships, from whatever port they sailed. In 1780 Dr Sigismund Bacstrom, later to be famous as an alchemist, wrote an account of his voyage to Spitsbergen as a surgeon aboard a London whaling ship, and his experiences were probably typical of most other mariners of the period. Bacstrom stopped at Lerwick for inexpensive provisions and spoke of the 'hospitable reception' despite their being wind-bound for fourteen days. John Nicol from Currie also called at Lerwick when he sailed as a cooper in the London whaling ship *Leviathan* in the 1780s; his ship called to complete the crew.

After Shetland, at 71 degrees north, where there was perpetual daylight at that time of year, Bacstrom wrote:

> We were overtaken . . . by a most tremendous gale of wind from the north east which lasted three days and nights. Our ship lay more than once on her beam ends, and everyone on board thought she could never right again . . . a storm in those high latitudes is so intensely cold, when it blows from the north or northeast that it is impossible to look in the wind's eye as the cold is such as literally to tear the skin off the flesh.[2]

Nicol also encountered 'very stormy weather . . . it blew a dreadful gale.'[3] And Robert Kinnes on *Active* in 1900 recorded: 'Vessel made 15 knots to 12 noon . . . very stormy, sea washing on deck . . . ship a sea which came into skylight and drenched the captain and I sitting below . . . seas coming in every direction bed soaked with wet.'[4]

From around 76 degrees north, Bacstrom sailed for a number of days through flat water and pancake ice – small circular flat floes – followed by an area of icebergs 'five or six times' larger than the ship. This was dangerous water for the ship, particularly when the bergs were close together, so the captain climbed to the foretop to direct the passage of the ship. On this voyage: 'We saw the land of Spitsbergen east from us. It is seen at an almost incredible distance sometimes at thirty leagues; a proof of its immense height. It generally appears amazingly bright, of the colour of the full moon; while the sky above it looks white and cold.'[5]

Bacstrom's vessel probed further north, but 'a solid continent of ice' stopped her at 79 degrees. Securing the vessel with an ice anchor, they kept two boats in the water and killed seven whales. They berthed at Magdalena

Bay in northwest Spitsbergen to make off the blubber. Whereas Bacstrom was lucky in his weather after his early storm, Nicol recorded his feelings when *Leviathan* was stuck in the ice: 'You must behold . . . your approaching fate, without the power of exertion, while the crashing of the ice and the less loud but more alarming cracking of the vessel serve all to increase the horrors of this dreadful sea-mare.'[6] One trip to the Greenland Sea was enough for Nicol: 'I did not like the whale fishing. There is no sight for the eye of the inquisitive after the first glance and no variety to charm the mind. Desolation reigns around.'[7]

Bacstrom was one of many surgeons who left journal accounts of their adventures on whaling voyages and these accounts give a perspective on whaling which make fascinating reading. For example, the journal of Stewart Peters, the surgeon of the Dundee whaling ship *Resolute* in 1882, reveals a number of ailments among the men: 'James Milne, harpooner suffering from dysentery'; 'Thomas Leask has got something in his hand, which is greatly swollen'; and 'David Scott . . . suffering from toothache.'[8] The journal of Surgeon James Allan of the Dundee ship *Aurora* in 1893 adds to the atmosphere of danger with mention of the 'men at wheel tied with ropes.'[9]

Although it was very seldom mentioned, seasickness must have been common among the greenmen. Alexander Smith, the engineer on *Camper-down*, mentions such a case in 1861: 'John Dacre, our second engineer who was voluntarily resigned as unfit for duty in consequence of his constant liability to seasickness.'[10] However there was little sympathy; here is the log of David McAdam, surgeon, *Horn*, 1839:

> Sea sickness at sea is similar to toothache ashore, for from an acquaintance with both, both are bad enough . . . but they alike have little sympathy from their fellow creatures. Copious draughts of salt water, pea soup over boiled, a walk up the rigging during a breeze, these and others of a similar nature were the remedies the compassionating tars recommend to their afflicted brethren.[11]

Disease was also a concern, particularly if bad weather prolonged the voyage in the days before the 1854 Merchant Shipping Act made antiscorbutics obligatory on British merchant ships. For instance, in 1847 heavy weather delayed the fleet, with the result that 15 men on *Horn* and five on *Princess Charlotte* were seriously sick with scurvy. *Advice* suffered worst with two men dying on board and four others after their arrival at Orkney where the master hoped to purchase fresh food. One of the casualties, David Ogilvy, was on his 39th Arctic voyage. The surgeon might also have to deal with tuberculosis or dysentery, as in the case of James Milne the harpooner on

Resolute in 1882. There were also accidents, as happened to the line manager Robert Peterson on *Esquimaux* in 1890. He was found dead in a pool of water, presumably after sliding on some sloping ice. When he signed articles, he claimed to be 59 years old, but the census gives his age as 74. His effects, mostly clothing, were contained in one sea chest and a bag.[12] It seems a small reward for a hard life at sea. Sometimes shipboard accidents led to complications such as swollen hands.[13] But generally, the crew remained healthy in the far north.

By the 1860s, when Dundee was the leading whaling port in Britain, the seaman would sign either one or two sets of articles. The first would be for a short sealing voyage to the Greenland Sea and the second for the longer whaling trip to the Davis Straits. Each seaman was issued with a certificate of discharge on the termination of his voyage; this certificate acted as proof of good character and of the man's experience. It is sometimes possible to trace large parts of a seaman's career from his certificates of discharge where they have been retained. One set discloses the bare bones of the voyages of William Stenhouse of Kirkcaldy in Fife, who sailed on Dundee whaling ships from the 1870s to the 1890s. His record is detailed in Table 9.1.

William Stenhouse married Susan Watson in the parish church of

Table 9.1 Whaling career of William Stenhouse[14]

Dates	Rank and stated age	Ship and voyage	Master	Given character
04 May 1872 – 11 November 1872	Able-bodied seaman aged 22	Polynia: Davis Straits	William Walker	Very good
27 February 1873 – 24 April 1873	Line Manager aged 23	Polynia: seal fishing	David Kilgour	Very good
01 May 1873 – 24 October 1873	Line manager aged 24	Polynia	David Kilgour	Very good
01 March 1875 – 26 April 1875	Boatsteerer aged 25	Polynia	David Kilgour	Very good
03 May 1875 – 11 November 1875	Boatsteerer aged 25	Polynia	David Kilgour	Very good
01 March 1876 – 21 April 1876	Boatsteerer aged 26	Polynia	David Kilgour	Very good
03 May 1876 – 31 October 1876	Boatsteerer aged 26	Polynia: whaling	David Kilgour	Very good

Dates	Rank and stated age	Ship and voyage	Master	Given character
01 March 1877 – 24 April 1877	Boatsteerer and skeaman aged 27	Polynia: sealing	David Kilgour	Very good
03 May 1877 – 07 November 1877	Boatsteerer and skeaman aged 27	Polynia: whaling	David Kilgour	Very good
04 March 1878 – 18 April 1878	Boatsteerer and skeaman aged 28	Polynia: Greenland seal fishing	David Kilgour	Very good
25 April 1878 – 01 November 1878	Boatsteerer and skeaman aged 28	Polynia	David Kilgour	Very good
1879–1882	Various	Voyages to Archangel and Baltic		
01 February 1883 – 27 October 1883	Harpooner aged 33	Narwhal: sealing and whaling	Jeffrey Phillips	Very good
28 January 1884 – 02 September 1884	Mate aged 34	Narwhal – sealing and whaling. Vessel lost Davis Strait	Jeffrey Phillips	
29 January 1885 – 22 October 1885	2nd mate aged 35	Jan Mayen – Newfoundland and Davis Strait	William Deuchars	Very good
03 March 1886 – 30 October 1886	Mate aged 36	Nova Zembla – Davis Strait	William Allan	Very good
08 March 1887 – 20 January 1887	Mate aged 37	Nova Zembla: Davis Strait fishing	William Allan	Very good
20 March 1889 – 1 November 1889	Only mate aged 39	Nova Zembla: Davis Straits	Jeffrey Phillips	Very good
12 March 1890 – 20 November 1890	Only mate aged 40	Nova Zembla: Davis Straits	Jeffrey Phillips	Very good
05 February 1891 – 24 October 1891	Only mate aged 41	Esquimaux: sealing and whaling	Jeffrey Phillips	Very good
06 February 1892 – 18 November 1892	Only mate aged 42	Esquimaux: sealing and whaling	Jeffrey Phillips	Very good
08 February 1893 – 10 November 1893	Only mate aged 43	Esquimaux: sealing and fishing	Jeffrey Phillips	Very good
07 February 1894 – 16 October 1894	Only mate aged 44	Esquimaux: sealing and fishing	Jeffrey Phillips	Very good

Abbotshall in Fife in 1875 and by 1910, he had become the harbourmaster at Kirkcaldy. His career shows the natural progression of a successful Greenlandman with a reputation of a good character. Normally, the whaling seaman would begin as a first voyager or greenman, and progress from there to ordinary seaman (OS). He could be any age, but most ordinary seamen were in their teens when they undertook their early voyages. Some men progressed no further, either through a lack of ambition, or lack of skill, bad luck or a character failure such as an over fondness for drink.

The beginning of any voyage was much the same. There were often wild celebrations before the ships departed, and crowds gathered to wave their husbands, brothers, fathers, sweethearts and sons goodbye. In the early days the ships were purely sail powered so would have to wait for a favourable wind to leave harbour. An easterly wind blowing into the mouth of the firth would inevitably prevent the ships from leaving. With the advent of steam, the Tay ferries could tow the ships into the Firth of Tay, as happened in 1825 when the wind failed to blow at all, and when it did appear as the ships lay in the roads, it came unyieldingly from the east. The same thing happened in 1826 when *Dorothy* was wind bound off Dundee. Even when the wind was kind, the ships could remain in the Tay for a day or two as the crews sobered up.[15] Some voyages began with many of the hands drunk, as happened in *Eclipse* in 1894. Logbooks and journals were often laconic about this emotional stage: 'mustered on the 8th April and hauled out of dock on the 10th April and left the Tay on the 14th April and proceeded with light and variable winds';[16] '11 June Monday: left Camperdown Dock at 1 pm – waited in River half an hour – one man short got him on board and proceeded. 4–10 Pm landed pilot – heavy swell . . . proceeded under steam – no wind'.[17]

The new hands would get used to conditions on board and the close proximity with the other men: in 1894 there were 34 men crammed into *Eclipse's* forecastle doubling up on bunks that were 2.45 feet by 6 feet by 3 feet – as one man rose from his bunk to work, another, at the end of his stint, would take his place.[18] They would learn that many people on board also doubled up their positions at work as well as in their bunks. For example, the mate, second mate, specktioneer and the cooper also acted as assistant harpooners on the whaling boats, while the boatswain and skeaman could be assistant boatsteerers. On the whaling ship the mates and specktioneers each stood a watch, the harpooners could stand a trick at the wheel, the boatsteerers could be employed in the foc'sle, and the boatswain was always in charge of the masts and rigging. When the blubber was flensed, the skeaman was in charge of everything underneath the main deck.[19]

It was common practice for whaling ships to call at Stromness or Lerwick

Sandon Perkins, explorer and lecturer, on board the whaling ship *Morning* in 1906.
(Courtesy of University of Dundee Archive Services)

Dundee whaling ships supplied Arctic objects for museums and zoos. This may be the polar bear brought to Dundee in 1881 by Captain Adams of *Arctic*. (Courtesy of University of Dundee Archive Services)

This seaman is splicing a foreganger line onto a gun harpoon. The foreganger attached the harpoon to the actual whale line, samples of which are coiled beside him. (Dundee Art Galleries and Museum (Dundee City Council))

ABOVE. Barque rigged whaling ship in home waters. This vessel has her whaleboats upside down on deck and a crowd of men standing forward. She may be *Terra Nova* in the Tay. (Courtesy of University of Dundee Archive Services)

LEFT. Whaling vessels hunted for other mammals as well as whales and seals. This photograph shows a narwhal being lowered onto deck. whaling men often referred to these animals as 'unicorns' or 'unis'. (Courtesy of University of Dundee Archive Services)

The deck of a whaling ship was a busy place when a whale was being processed. This large slab of blubber has just been cut from a whale; the process was known as 'flensing'. (Courtesy of University of Dundee Archive Services)

Dundee whaling men made frequent contact with the Inuit of eastern Canada and Greenland. This image shows an Inuit couple on the deck of a Dundee ship.(Courtesy of University of Dundee Archive Services)

Active leaving Dundee. Departure was a very emotional time as families waved farewell to men they would not see again for months. (Courtesy The McManus and University of Dundee Archive Services)

ABOVE. Figurehead of *Active*. Many seamen were superstitious about figureheads and ensured they were kept in good condition. (Courtesy The McManus and University of Dundee Archive Services)

RIGHT. *Eclipse* under sail through broken ice. Her whaleboats can be clearly seen hanging from their davits ready to be launched if a whale is sighted from the crow's nest. (Courtesy The McManus and University of Dundee Archive Services)

ABOVE. By the latter decades of the 19th century Dundee whaling men played football on the ice. This photograph shows a football team composed of men from *Active*. (Dundee Art Galleries and Museum (Dundee City Council))

LEFT. This is a hand-held harpoon. The harpooner stood in the bows of the boat and threw the weapon two handed into the animal. This harpoon is held in the McManus Museum, Dundee. (Dundee Art Galleries and Museum (Dundee City Council))

By the 1860s, Dundee had a reputation for building some of the strongest Arctic vessels in the world. This photograph shows what sort of conditions the Dundee whaling ships worked in. (Dundee Art Galleries and Museum (Dundee City Council))

Two barque-rigged Dundee whaling vessels side by side in the Arctic. When vessels met it was common practice for masters and men to visit each other. The ladder descending from the bowsprit of the nearest vessel suggests this may be the case here. (Dundee Art Galleries and Museum (Dundee City Council))

to enhance their crews and pick up stores. By the 1860s, steam power ended much of the uncertainty of the voyage and it was a simple 30-hour steam to Shetland. Thomas Macklin recorded in 1874: 'We in the first place are going to call at Lerwick . . . for the purpose of adding to our crew a number of Shetlanders, these men being said to be good and experienced sailors';[20] and Matthew Campbell in 1884: 'The captain went ashore today and engaged the Shetland men'.[21] After completing the crew, the ships sailed northward to the Greenland Sea or round Cape Farewell to enter the Davis Straits. Even before they reached the whale hunting grounds, the dangers of the sea were never far away: 'two men missing from the mate's watch, must have been washed overboard';[22] 'port bulwarks smashed . . . two men washed away from wheel and wheel spokes broken'.[23]

The ship headed north, or west into the Davis Straits, and the ice: 'Came in contact with the pack ice it made the vessel heel a bit ultimately she forced it aside and then . . . did not expect to get much sleep with the bumping . . . through the night'.[24]

However, things were much worse when the ships were deep in the Arctic. At the northern end of the Davis Straits lies Melville Bay where: 'so much danger there is, of losing ships in this bay, may be judged from the following . . . all the ships before entering get up all their provisions on deck so as to be ready to leave at a moment's notice . . . also every man picks up his chest'.[25] At this time the Greenlandmen would prepare the hunting equipment: 'at noon called all hands to clean the harpoons. Harpooners employed splicing on the foregoers'.[26] The foregoers or foregangers were the ropes that connected the harpoons to the long whaling lines. The next stage would be to get the boats ready as the ship reached the whaling grounds on the margin of the ice: 'hoisted the boats up from below – coiled the lines and set up the crow's nest. Ship plying to the northward and along the edge of the ice'.[27]

From ordinary seaman (OS), the next step up was to able-bodied seaman (AB), which was a man with nautical skills, more responsibilities and higher wages. Able-bodied seamen were the backbone of any ship and would be welcome additions to any crew. If the seaman decided to specialise in whaling, there were three officer ranks: linemanager; boatsteerer and harpooner. William Stenhouse filled them all, one after the other. When the ship sighted a whale, small boats were sent out on the open water or among the broken ice. Each whaleboat held a crew of six; three oarsmen and three specialists. The boatsteerer had the responsibility to steer the boat up to the whale, ideally coming up behind the animal and close enough for the harpooner to strike. Next to the master, the harpooner was arguably the most important man on board; the success or failure of the voyage, and the amount of wages earned by the crew or profit gained by the company, depended on his skill with the harpoon.

Once again, journal entries can reduce this dramatic picture to pure routine: 'Thos Davidson struck fish'[28] or 'with boats on the bran, John Duncan struck a fish, Thos Dowie steering . . . Robert Watson in the boat with the first harpoon.'[29]

Although many pictures depict the harpooner standing in the bow of the whaleboat and hurling a hand harpoon, guns were easing out muscle before the start of the nineteenth century. In 1793, *Eliza Swan* and *George Dempster* of Montrose carried a harpoon gun apiece, although there was a minor dispute with the customs as to whether this gun was a weapon or an implement of fishing.[30] The harpoon guns were not cheap: in 1817 the Tay Whale Fishing Company paid £39 6s for a harpoon gun for *Advice*[31] which was about six month's wages for a skilled man. By the 1860s the majority of harpoons were fired from a gun situated in the bows of a whaleboat.

Most whaling journals, as opposed to logbooks, give at least one description of the harpooning of a whale. In 1861 Alexander Smith of *Camperdown* reported: 'and then followed the report of a gun followed by the well known, wild delirious joyfull shout of a fall, fall, a Faa-a-a-all assuring us we were fast to a fish.'[32] Other entries are more laconic, such as: 'an old Greenlander named Jack Knight fired his gun and got fast, hoisted his flag.'[33] Once the harpoon struck, the whaleboat would raise a flag to announce it was their whale – a procedure that could give rise to the occasional dispute between rival vessels claiming the same whale. It was now a fast boat – a boat that had got fast to a whale – and the crew had earned a bonus.

The next period was possibly the most dangerous time for the Greenlandman as the whale reacted to the harpoon entering its body. It could lash with its tail, upsetting the whaleboat and tipping the men into the water, or, more usually, dive deep and swim fast to escape. It was now that the linemanager came into his own as he managed the whale line. He had to ensure the line came out taut and straight, without any kinks that could loop around the leg or neck of one of the boat's crew, sending him into the sea.

The whale could tow the boat for miles, only surfacing when it had to breathe. Other boats from the same ship would come to help, adding their harpoon to the original, adding to the weight the whale had to drag and therefore speeding the process of exhausting the animal. When the whale was spent and lay on the surface, the Greenlandmen would kill it by thrusting great lances into the vital spots. Until the early twentieth century, there was no thought of compassion or conservation among the Greenlandmen.[34] It was their job to kill whales and they did so with as much efficiency as they could.

The Greenlandmen's wages depended on the number of whales and seals they slaughtered. As the years passed, the whale stock diminished so the wages depended more on other animals. For example, for William Stenhouse's eight month and ten day voyage as mate on *Esquimaux* in 1894, he was paid a flat rate of £5 per month, which made him £41 13s 4d as basic pay, but he also earned £9 17s 4d for his share of the seal oil money for the 7,194 seals they captured, plus £1 17s 9d skin money as his share of the seal skins, calculated at 5s 3d per skin. As *Esquimaux* failed to capture a single black whale, there was no bonus for that, but they brought back 30 tuns of white whale oil, which netted Stenhouse £10 2s 6d, so his pay packet was £63 10s 11d.

Sometimes the men did the work, but the company was late in paying. Such a case happened to two of the men of *Dorothy* in 1828. They sent a letter to the ship's agent, Mr James Justice:

13th November 1828
Mr Justis Eaghent
For the Dorothy
Petter Street no 3
Dundee
St Andrews November 13 1828

Mr Justis

Sr as it was a overlook of you not to pay our fast Boat money we would take it verey kind if you would send it by the bearer Mrs Seller [?] as we here that all the ship's company is payed it we had three fast boats each of our paybel fish by so doing you will oblidg your humble servents

Mathew Lister
Peter Ritchie[35]

In this letter Matthew Lister and Peter Ritchie, crewmen on *Dorothy* in 1828, had not been paid their fast boat money, the money due to them for three times being part of the crew of a whaleboat that made 'fast' to a whale, the most dangerous part of the occupation. The lack of such money would make a large dent in their pay packet, but the fact that they entrusted the letter to the bearer, Mrs Seller, also says a lot about the community from which the whaling men came. The whaling men came from fishing families where the women habitually controlled the purse strings.

After the kill came the row back to the ship, possibly accompanied by one of the Greenlandmen's ubiquitous songs. If the weather was foul or the distance long, this could also be an exhausting time, and there was always the possibility of losing touch with the ship. In 1884, three of *Chieftain's* boats were lost in a fog. Two were picked up by passing ships but the third was missing for weeks and when she was finally picked up, all of the crew had died of exposure except James 'Toshie' McIntosh, who had been in command of the boat. Fog had other dangers too, even on board the ship, as on *Active* in 1900: 'fog freezing in the rigging and dropping icebergs on deck'.[36] There were no safe times in the whaling industry.

Given that the whaleboats survived the perils of storm and fog, the whale was lashed alongside the ship: 'got her alongside and began to flinch . . . bone measuring 10 feet 8 inches clear'.[37] The flensing – stripping the whale of its blubber – was cheerful if dirty, since the men knew at this point that they would have oil money to add to their pay packets and the voyage would be a financial success. It was here that the specktioneer and the skeaman came into prominence; Stenhouse rose from harpooner to skeaman. The specktioneer was the head harpooner, and the man responsible for supervising the removal of the blubber from the whale. The skeaman, from Dutch *schieman*, captain of the forecastle, was in charge of the hold. He had to ensure the blubber was stored properly, to ensure the maximum use of available space, and safely.

The more whales caught, the higher the wages, so the men worked quickly. But hunting was only part of the job. The Greenlandmen spent much longer working the ship, with the logbooks and journals full of comments such as: '8 AM the sea beginning to slack off all hands employed on towing the ship to the northward along the land ice';[38] when frustrated by light winds: 'called all hands to tow the ship';[39] or the more common 'called all hands made up Sail';[40] when the ship was stuck in ice the message would be: 'called all hands and Warped the Ship through'.[41] Even when the weather was quiet, the deck of the ship could be busy: 'When our blacksmith, Carpenter and Sail-maker are all at work and the other men being at something or other, it puts me in mind of a Seaboard Parish . . . it just wants a few gossiping, loitering women and a few fair (or ugly) maidens to complete the picture.'[42]

When they were catching whales or seals, the men worked long, backbreaking hours but in between they had time for hobbies or games. Their skill at scrimshaw – where sections of whalebone were carved, often with a needle scrounged from the sail maker, and the resulting image inked with soot and oil – is well attested although it is not always easy to ascertain whether a piece of scrimshaw was genuinely carved by a whaling man. The origins of this practice are said to be Inuit. Toward the end of the century, as professional football became popular in Scotland, the crews of rival ships formed teams and booted leather balls about on the ice. There were also card games, boat races and, as expected, singing and dancing, particularly when the Greenlandmen were with the Inuit. When *Diana* was in Disco Bay in 1903, Alexander Lamb wrote 'some of the natives came aboard at night ... they were all very much amused at a phonograph which they heard'.[43] The two communities seemed to share some common pleasures: 'a boat load of natives came aboard ... and we started a concert and dance'.[44]

During the interludes between hunting trips, many lasting friendships were forged with the Inuit. The Greenlandmen knew them as Yakkies, a term that carried no disrespect. Captain Clark said: 'some of the men took up with the Eskimo women and had them living on board with them'.[45] However, not everyone approved of this; in 1894 a seaman named Redgrave on *Eclipse* wrote: 'we were at once boarded by a cargo of Female Yaks called Koonies and every man had his squaw. It was positively sickening'.[46] Inevitably there were children born from these liaisons, and the Inuit brought them up without complaint or prejudice in an example of interracial tolerance seldom equalled elsewhere. There were, of course, some differences: it is unlikely that many of the Dundee men had previously met women who washed their hair in urine to bring out the shine, and the Inuit would find the Dundee idea of monogamy peculiarly at odds with the whaling men's behaviour alongside the Davis Straits.

However, contact between Scots and Inuit was not confined to the North American continent. Numerous whaling ships brought Inuit visitors to Scotland, many of whom entertained the locals with their kayaking skills. Other Inuit revealed different talents such as Shoodlue, a medicine man from Black Lead Island who visited Dundee and became famous for his love of marmalade and for playing his melodeon at the Hillbank Hall. Etwango also made many friends in Dundee, spoke to a large assembly at Kinnaird Hall and left with good wishes, a melodeon for his wife and presents for their child. Overall, the two peoples made a fair partnership until economic alterations and the First World War forced a parting.

The whaling men also made contact with European settlers in Greenland, but not always amicably. In 1818 a boat's crew of the Hull whaling ship *Eagle*, aided by men from *Swan*, vandalised the winter home of a Danish family at Four Island Point, and they also dug up the graves of some Inuit and Greenlandman buried there.[47]

Food was often a sore point to British mariners and was often in limited supply, but whaling ships seemed to prove the exception to the rule. Although there was little imagination in the supplies they carried, most vessels carried an adequate stock to feed the men for the duration of the voyage, with a small excess to cover periods when they were trapped in the ice. Some ships sailed with half carcasses of cattle hoisted aloft and in the 1780s, whaling ships carried fresh beef, which they preserved by dousing in salt water.[48] It was not uncommon for the whaling companies to advertise for provisions, usually stressing a desire for quality produce, such as:

> Ox Beef Wanted
> The Union Whale Company are ready to CONTRACT for three tons
> prime OX-BEEF
> Apply to J. G. Russell, Manager
> Dundee, November 29 1826[49]

or:

> Contracts Wanted
> For furnishing the Tay Whale Fishing Company's ships with the
> undermentioned provisions for the ensuing voyage to the Whale Fishery:
> Best of beef, pork, potatoes, barley, pease, salt butter, small beer and rum
> Offers will be received at the company's offices until Friday the 29th current
> Dundee February 13 1828[50]

The journals kept by young surgeons or others frequently mention the food on board ship, and despite the intentions of the owners to purchase quality produce, the results were not always viewed as such. For example, soon after their departure from Scotland in 1834, Surgeon Wanless on board *Thomas* wrote:

> The Stores of Tobacco, Sugar, Tea and Coffee were served out to all hands . . . the tobacco seems very good but the others are not so . . . it should be looked after by a judge, the material before it is put on board a Ship whatever and what does not answer the sample sent to the committee of managers should be returned with a verdict proving the vendor to be a thief.[51]

Nevertheless, on other occasions the teenage Wanless seemed happy with the food: 'The sail maker has been making bags with canvas for boiling the puddings . . . I am rather partial to it myself. It is composed of suet and flour meal and tastes exceedingly well with molasses or sugar.'[52] Other concoctions were not so favourably received: 'We had for supper what is called a compound of potatoes, beef and water hashed through each other . . . and boiled, answers well enough when the weather is cold yet is rather heavy.'[53]

After the 1854 Merchant Shipping Act, conditions on British ships improved, but individual masters and ship owners were often parsimonious about supplies. Before signing articles, each seaman had the opportunity of perusing the terms and conditions of the forthcoming voyage, which set out exactly what the food would be. For example, in the 1860s, *Intrepid* had beef, pork and fish days, with one and a half pounds of beef, one and a quarter pounds of pork or half a pound of fish per man per day. There was also half a pound of flour on pudding days, with six pounds of biscuit a week, and an allowance of sugar, coffee, tea, molasses, potatoes, butter, cheese, oatmeal, pease, rice, barley and vegetables 'at the master's discretion.'[54] It may be significant that some of the trouble that broke out on *Diana* in 1893 centred on an alleged theft of stores, suggesting that the master's discretion did not always satisfy the hunger of the hands. However, there is no record of any man starving to death on a Dundee whaling ship, although it is possible that a lack of food debilitated the men who died on board *Advice* in 1837. At any rate, in 1884 Surgeon Campbell on *Nova Zembla* claimed: 'We have three meals a day, breakfast at 8 AM, dinner 12 AM, tea at 5 PM as an example of dinner I will quote here, what we got today. As first course we had oxtail soup, second do salt beef and fresh potatoes, for dessert we had rice.'[55] Food such as that would have been welcomed in most homes in the country.

Returning from the Arctic was every bit as emotional as leaving. When the ships came home, there were crowds waiting to meet them. Usually there was joy at the reunion of husband and wife, son and mother, or father and children, but there could also be terrible sadness as women learned their men had been lost. In the days before radio, bad news would only have filtered back by word of mouth carried by homecoming vessels, so there would be terrible anxiety for the waiting women until they actually saw their men. In 1868 James McDonald, the surgeon of *Tay*, died on the homeward voyage; as *Tay* neared Broughty Ferry one of the crew rowed ashore and sought Mr Piper, the seaman's missionary, hoping he could break the news gently to McDonald's wife. Unfortunately, she had heard about *Tay*'s approach and was already waiting at the quay when she docked. Other wives had multiple losses to cope with. One woman in Newhaven, now part of Edinburgh, had a husband, a brother and a son all at sea. Her son fell from the shrouds of a merchant ship and died, in 1762 her brother died at sea on the Leith whaling ship *Edinburgh*, while a week later, another whaling ship, *Tryal*, brought home the dead body of her husband.[56] For some people, the return of the whaling ships signalled the beginning, rather than the end, of work. The Dorothy Whale Company records mention payment to Elizabeth Hunter for cleaning over a ton and a half of whalebone which has been described as 'a tedious and disgusting process.'[57]

The image of the whaling men is frequently at odds with the reality. In

1775 the reverend John Mill of Shetland called the whaling men 'the worst of people' and 'curs'd ruffians' while he worried they might get drunk and burn Lerwick down.[58] Nevertheless, evidence gleaned piecemeal from a score of diverse sources argues that they were no different from any other seamen, with wives, families, and personal lives and problems. Captain Markham wrote of a whaling man who said his wife 'would have cried a pint of tears' while W. Burn Murdoch said 'almost all the crew, old and young, are married'.[59] Dundee Museum holds a number of photographs of whaling men and their wives, including the Cork born Nicholas White who served as a harpooner and steward on *Balaena*. He married Margaret, settled in Dundee and raised a family.

There is also a photograph of the handsome John Callendar Wales and his attractive wife, Christina Boyd. Wales is wearing a well cut three piece suit and Boyd, a smart pleated gown. Unlike the wild Greenlandmen of legend, neither would look out of place in the smartest establishment in Dundee. Wales was a cook on *Diana* between 1901 and 1905, during which latter year he married Boyd and settled in Dundee as a baker. There are also numerous instances where the whaling men assigned their wages and oil money to their wives; the wages of Robert Peddie, specktioneer of *Friendship*, were collected by his wife Margaret Stiven according to the wages book held in Dundee Museum. Agnes Myers also collected the wages of her Heligo-land–born husband Charles, who sailed on various Dundee whaling ships in the 1860s. Dundee Museum also holds documents asking the Dorothy Whale Fishing Company to pay Janet Cunningham the oil money due to John Cunningham. The document is dated 1829 and is signed with a cross for John Cunningham's mark. These selected examples tend to show that at least some of the Greenlandmen were responsible family men.

But whaling men were not angels. They had an inclination to stand up for themselves when they thought they were badly used or they were being taken into unnecessary danger. There was a number of recorded mutinies on Dundee whaling ships, including *Fairy* in 1842 and *Diana* in 1893, and an incident involving *Intrepid* at Reykjavik in 1883. Yet although there were cases where Dundee Greenlandmen were less than perfect, for all the thousands of whaling men who frequented Dundee over the decades of the industry, there was only one recorded case of murder.

Richard Leggatt was an experienced Greenlandman, having sailed to the Arctic from at least 1888. He was known as a quiet man who did not drink, but instead, he spent the long months worrying about the fidelity of his wife, Elizabeth. In 1896 *Terra Nova* had a bad season and Leggatt returned with as slim pay packet, so Elizabeth had to continue working as a weaver in Mid Wynd Works, Hawkhill. In the meantime Leggat lived in their John Street flat with their 14-month-old daughter. Perhaps it was the frustration of a long voyage with little pay, or possibly Leggatt genuinely believed Elizabeth was having an affair, but he lifted a revolver, shot her and later handed himself to the police. Although Leggatt was the only Dundee whaler arrested for murder, there was at least one case where a Greenlandman was arrested on board ship. In 1819 a man named Hugh Mackay signed articles on board the Peterhead whaling ship *Alpheus*, but when the ship returned to Scotland, George Campbell, King's Messenger, boarded and arrested him for horse and cattle theft. Mackay's real name was John Gunn, alias Miniart, and he was sent to Inverness for trial.

The whaling men too, were often subjected to hazards when they returned. Recently home, many would crowd into the public houses to celebrate their safe homecoming, and drunk Greenlandmen with a season's wages in their pockets were easy targets for the prostitutes and footpads who infested the closes and unlit alleys of night time Dundee. For example, on 2 October the *Advertiser* carried this small, if sobering piece: 'On Saturday night a sailor who had lately arrived from the Northern Seas was knocked down in the Overgate on his way home and robbed of all the money in his possession.'

Overall, the Dundee whaling seamen were as diverse as any group of working men. They worked hard at sea, sometimes earning good wages, and at others barely scraping a subsistence living. Their monotonous diet enlivened only by the imagination of the cook, they drank the rum or beer with which they were issued and looked forward to going home. They sang and danced, and occasionally had romantic flings with Inuit women. They endured the bitter cold, the frost and screaming gales of the north, and returned to their wives. The Greenlandmen had a mixed reputation, but if they worked and played hard, they also contributed to the character and spirit of Dundee in a manner few have equalled before or since. Appendix 3 draws on a variety of sources including ships' logbooks, journal entries, newspaper accounts and Customs and Excise records to provide a brief picture of some 250 men who sailed aboard the Dundee whaling ships.

10

The Last Hurrah:
The Dundee Antarctic Expedition

As we warped through the dock gates the last of the crew bade good bye to
their wives and children . . . Leaving many a face wet with tears.
W. G. Burn Murdoch, *From Edinburgh to the Antarctic*

By the 1890s it was obvious the whaling industry was ailing. Catches were
down, profits were down and the whale hunters could only dream of the
old days when ships came back so full their whaleboats were stuffed with
blubber. Despite the most modern techniques of whaling, steam launches
and shore stations, despite a widening of the net to include a whole host
of varied prey, new whaling grounds were necessary. Indeed, there was a
growing realisation that the 'perfection of the means of capture' was the
cause of the scarcity of whales in the northern seas.[1] With the Arctic apparently fished out, it seemed obvious that the fleet should try the Antarctic.
The Scottish explorer Sir James Clark Ross had taken two ships to the far
south between 1839 and 1843 and discovered Victoria Land. He had also
reported seeing 'great numbers of the largest sized black whales' and thought
'numbers of ships might procure a cargo of oil in a short time'.[2] It was on this
slender premise that Robert Kinnes' Tay Whale Fishing Company based its
expedition to the Antarctic in 1892.

South Sea whaling had been undertaken for decades, with ships, mainly
from London, scouring the seas, although the industry was far smaller
than its northern counterpart and the Antarctic Oceans had never been
fully exploited. There had been sealing trips, such as that of James Weddell
who sailed from Leith in 1822, but no systematic hunt for whales. Perhaps
the distances involved were considered too vast or the rewards not worth
the effort – in 1892 whalebone from the south sold for only £1,000 a ton
compared to £3,000 for the same product from the Arctic.[3]

Nevertheless, as whales in the Arctic seemed a diminishing resource,
predatory eyes turned southward. The arrangements for the Dundee
expedition were laid in 1891. The expedition consisted of four vessels, all
managed by Robert Kinnes: *Balaena* with Alexander Fairweather as master;

Active commanded by Thomas Robertson; *Polar Star* commanded by James Davidson; and *Diana,* commanded by Robert Davidson. The following year, the four ships returned early from the Greenland Sea to be fitted out for the south. The expedition had a bad start with a dispute about wages, but eventually the seamen accepted a monthly wage of £3 5s.[4] There was a further setback when, during the trials following her refit, *Balaena's* engine broke down in the Tay on 26 August and she was ignominiously towed back to dock by a tug.[5] However once she was passed fit, everything was ready.

As well as the whaling men, the expedition included the scientists William Speirs Bruce, who sailed on *Balaena,* and Charles W. Donald who was on *Active.* Bruce was later to lead the highly successful and professional Scottish Antarctic Expedition of 1904. The artist W. G. Burn Murdoch travelled with the expedition aboard *Balaena* with the spurious title of 'assistant surgeon', drawing one shilling a month pay.[6] On his return, he produced a splendidly readable book about the voyage and a selection of paintings.

The ships left Dundee on 9 September 1892 to the usual emotional farewell. According to Burn Murdoch, the crew of *Balaena* was 'a jolly motley crowd . . . men and boys . . . of every sailor type . . . Arctic whalers, red cheeked and bearded, tanned South Spainers . . . quiet men and boys from the east coast fishing villages and gentle men from the Shetlands'.[7] It seemed as if Dundee had drawn on the best maritime traditions of Scotland for the expedition. Although they did not know it, the Antarctic whalers had embarked on the last hurrah of the Dundee whaling fleet, the longest and most desperate venture to salvage a dying industry. They were the last best hope and they carried with them the experience of nearly a century and a half of Arctic whaling.

Rather than sail south and through the English Channel, the ships sailed north through the Pentland Firth. They hit such stormy weather that it was three weeks before *Balaena* cleared the southern tip of the British Isles: heavy seas carried away the *Active's* galley and injured the cook. As so often on whaling voyages, there were stowaways – *Polar Star* had 15 on board and *Diana* landed five at Stornoway. As they sailed, Burn Murdoch picked up snippets of whaling and seafaring lore from the men, from superstitions including the molly [storm petrel] named John Jack that had been a Greenlandman who died in the ice, to scandals such as the practice of some owners of sending men to sea in overinsured, leaky coffin ships.[8]

The growling dispute about wages resurfaced when *Diana* called at Queenstown (now Cobh) in Ireland for coal and repairs and able-bodied seaman David Turnbull was deducted £4 10s for alleged theft of stores. Around half the crew refused to sail further on their present pay scale; they claimed *Diana* was unseaworthy, swarmed ashore and hit the local pubs. Captain Davidson called the Mercantile Marine supervisor who made an inspection and attested *Diana*'s seaworthiness, but the crew continued their protest until the owner came from Dundee to sort things out. He provided a pilot and ordered the master and engineer to put to sea. *Diana* sailed from Queenstown and headed south carrying the mutineers with her.[9]

The rough weather continued, costing *Active* two boats, some sails and a section of bulwark. She had to call at Funchal, Madeira, to recoal. The four ships did not remain in company but made their independent way south the entire length of the North and South Atlantic Ocean. When *Balaena* crossed the equator on 26 October, there were the usual undignified ceremonies for those who had never been so far south before.

Despite the disputes and rough seas, all four ships called in safely at the Falkland Islands without any casualties, although they had to wait until January 1893 for *Polar Star* to join them. At the Falklands, trouble again broke out on *Diana* as various items, including sugar, ham, butter and a whole sheep, were reported stolen from the ship's stores. This seems to have blown over, and from the Falkland Islands the ships headed for the Weddell Sea and the Erebus and Terror Gulf. The whaling men saw finner whales, and on 16 December 1892, scores surrounded *Balaena*, but these animals were not then the prey. For all their high hopes of finding virgin whaling grounds, the ships had no success at whale hunting, so the four captains decided to hunt the seals instead.

The change in strategy proved successful. On her first day of hunting, 4 January 1893, *Balaena* captured 450 seals. Most of the seals were among the pack ice and were so innocent of man that they made no movement to escape when the Greenlandmen set about them with rifle and club. The men of *Balaena* were so successful that at one time there were 200 seals waiting to be made off, and their weight burst the main hatch. *Balaena* alone captured around 5,200, with 180 tons of blubber.[10] It was when *Active*'s boats were sealing that a blue whale surfaced nearly under the bows of a whale-boat. George Matheson of Peterhead, second mate of *Active*, fired a harpoon into the whale, and four other boats moved in for the kill. However, the whale was so strong it towed them all, and *Active* joined in herself. Even with her engines going full astern, *Active* was not powerful enough to tow the giant whale. After a fourteen hour struggle the whale escaped. It was seen later, embellished with two harpoons in its side, but otherwise apparently unharmed.[11]

The seal hunting covered the costs of the expedition. The Dundee men based themselves in South Georgia and sailed to 68 degrees south, working a new ocean that provided a mixture of storms, calm and fog, and completely lacked shelter except when the ships anchored in the lee of an iceberg. The constant swell around the pack ice made life uncomfortable and the seamen thought the ice different from that in the Arctic, with the top layer reported to be so soft that men sank 'knee deep' as they captured seals, while the icebergs were flat topped compared to the towering peaks of the Arctic.[12] The Antarctic seals were also different; they were much larger than their Arctic counterparts, with some reaching 16 feet in length, and Captain Fairweather stated that they were the finest he had ever seen.[13] *Polar Star,* the smallest vessel with the least powerful engine, began her sealing later than the others, and when she was only half filled, a gale drove her north from the sealing grounds and Captain Davidson decided to call a halt to the hunting. Despite this foreshortened stay in Antarctica, the men of *Polar Star* made a couple of interesting, if unaccountable, observations. The mate and second mate thought they saw the paw prints of a bear: there are no bears in the Antarctic, but these were both experienced Arctic seamen who should have known bear tracks when they saw them. Captain Davidson also believed they had sighted land about ten miles south of the South Shetland Islands, in an area of only open sea.[14] Even the most experienced of shipmasters could make mistakes.

As well as catching seals, the expedition was involved in a little exploring work, with Captain Robertson in *Active* sailing to the north shore of Erebus and Terror Gulf, where Captain Ross had probed 60 years before. He sailed into a sound never previously explored and passed stark cliffs of ice that rose 50 feet in the air. Robertson termed this area Active Sound, and an adjoining firth became the Firth of Tay. He named various geographical points after *Active's* owners, so a bay was christened Gibson Bay, and a headland of basaltic cliffs became Cape Alexander. Robertson also sailed around an island at 63 degrees south, 55 west and named it Dundee Island. Yet for all *Active's* exploration, it was *Diana* that pushed further into the southern ocean, but found no sign of the right whales.

During this expedition the first known photographs of the Antarctic were also taken. However, the scientists and the whaling professionals did not see eye to eye, with the scientists more interested in the minutiae trawled from the sea bed, while the whalers hunted for captures and profit. The Greenlandmen spent around six weeks capturing seals and shooting or clubbing them to death as the scientists sought new discoveries. Dr Donald, sailing on *Active,* found a number of mosses, birds and eggs, and he preserved the skeletons of some penguins and the various kinds of seals they had captured. However, the scientists found the experience disappointing as they had expected more time for their researches. Many of the natural history items the scientists collected were handed to the museum of University College, Dundee, as it was then known,[15] so the city did benefit from the scientific involvement. Nevertheless, when the artist Burn Murdoch published his book about the expedition, *From Edinburgh to the Antarctic*, Captain Robertson slated the content, possibly reflecting the tension between the scientists and the whaling men that was evident throughout the expedition.

Despite a trio of desertions from *Balaena* at the Falkland Islands[16] and an outbreak of scurvy on *Polar Star*, the journey home was uneventful. *Balaena* was first back to Dundee, arriving in Camperdown Dock on Tuesday 30 May 1893, to find a crowd waiting to greet her. *Active* was next, arriving on 9 June with 3,700 sealskins and 160 tuns of oil.[17] On Friday 16 June *Polar Star* arrived with 1,908 sealskins and 47 tons of oil. *Diana*, beset with engine trouble, returned under sail through the Pentland Firth. She arrived in Dundee on 20 June with 3,700 skins and 160 tuns of oil. Overall, the four ships brought home an estimated 15,700 seals and nearly 500 tons of oil.[18] Within a few days of the first whaling ships returning, furriers from London had arrived to inspect the sealskins,[19] and the *Courier* carried the pithy comment: 'oil of the seals from the South Seas is as offensive to the olfactory organs as that of the Davis Straits species'.[20] In July sealskins from Newfoundland and the Antarctic were simultaneously displayed for sale in Liverpool; there were no buyers for the Antarctic skins.[21]

Once ashore, the various troubles that beset *Diana* came to court as David Turnbull brought his case against the company who had withheld his pay. Turnbull claimed the crew had mutinied because *Diana* had been unseaworthy and their actions had resulted in the arrival of Board of Trade officials to rectify matters. However, he also said the repairs were incomplete, and *Diana* sailed south against the will of the crew. Any deduction of wages, Turnbull claimed, should only have taken place if there was proof of theft. The defence denied Turnbull's story and claimed that drink had caused the mutiny.[22] It is unlikely that the full truth will ever be known, but *Diana* did return safely, albeit without steam power, so perhaps there was merit to both sides of the story.

On 11 August 1893 the owners and shareholders involved in the Antarctic expedition met in Mathers Hotel in Dundee. After a short discussion, they decided not to send any more ships south as there was apparently no interest in buying the skins of Antarctic seals.[23] Dundee had tossed its last dice in the gamble of whaling and had lost. As the shareholders left the hotel on that late summer evening, perhaps they were aware that their industry was dying.

Paradoxically, the Dundee industry faded as world interest stirred in Arctic exploration and nature. In the early years of the twentieth century, D'Arcy Thompson, the Dundee and St Andrews-based naturalist, was asked if he could supply the skins of Arctic animals or even living animals to the American Museum of Natural History.[24] However, the old days of Dundee whaling ships supplying the world's museums were gone: there might be a few more bright years in the gloom, but despite all their efforts, the Dundee and, with it, the Scottish Arctic whaling industry was finished

Antarctic whaling, however, was not. Although contemporary Arctic whaling tools and methods were unsuitable for the more powerful whales of the Antarctic, the Norwegian Svend Foyn was a leading light in devising new techniques for the far south. The Norwegians created a savagely efficient harpoon that contained an explosive heart within an array of barbs. They fired this weapon from the bows of steam powered whale catchers which could stalk even the largest of whales and thus began a new period of whale hunting that was a world away from the experience of the Dundee whalers.[25] The mantle of European whaling that had begun with the Basques, continued with the Dutch, passed on to the English and then to the Scots, passed finally to the Norse.

11

Farewell to the Whaling

The noble fleet of whalers went sailing from Dundee
Well-manned by British sailors to work upon the sea
The Balaena: traditional song

When in 1914 *Active* sailed to the whaling, her crew probably knew they were the last kick of a dying trade. It had been a long journey from the early days of *Bonnie Dundee* back in 1753, through the wars of the eighteenth century, the heady days of spectacular catches in the 1820s, the terrible losses of 1836 to the days of steam when Dundee had led the whaling world. From insignificant beginnings as just one of many whaling ports, Dundee made commercial whaling a success and thrived for decades after most other ports had left the industry. Dundee was an anomaly. There is still some conception of Dundee, like Hull, as a whaling port, while few think of London, Liverpool or Newcastle as being involved in the trade, although their fleets were at least comparable to and, in the case of London, far larger than Dundee's. In her prime, Dundee never floated more than 17 ships compared with the scores from London or Hull, but Dundee survived in the Arctic industry longer than any other British port. The whaling bounty had encouraged Dundee adventurers to send ships north and supported them in the days of poor catches. For most of the eighteenth century, the Dundee whaling fleet consisted only of one or two vessels. Dundee whaling men served from 1753 until 1815 throughout the wars of the eighteenth and early nineteenth centuries. Two ships were captured by the enemy and there was some resistance to the impress service, but compared to other ports, where there were gun-to-gun confrontations with men killed and wounded, Dundee came through relatively unscathed. There were good years with high catches, and disasters such as the terrible winters of 1836 and 1837 when the bulk of two crews died of scurvy and exposure. The whaling men could be truculent – there were a number of mutinies, as on *Fairy* in 1843 and *Diana* in 1892, a murder and the occasional drunken brawl – but overall, the Dundee whaling man was no worse than the average British seaman of the period.

There is no doubt the Dundee experience from the 1850s onward was distinct from mainstream British whaling. The combination of jute, corsets and steam kept the whaling alive as Dundee developed new expertise but in retrospect, it was the last flick of the dinosaur's tail. The constant search for new whaling grounds in ever more inaccessible locations created a breed of explorer shipmasters. The need for strong ships led to Dundee-built ships being sought after by Polar explorers and by sealing companies from across the world – the later Dundee vessels were undoubtedly the finest purpose-built Arctic vessels then available. However, Dundee remained loyal to old techniques of whaling and markets for whale oil when new technology took the industry south to Antarctic waters. The hunting grounds, the methods and the ships were already anachronistic at the time Dundee climbed to the apex of the whaling ladder, and the failure of the 1892 Antarctic expedition highlighted the problems of underpowered ships and outdated techniques.

From the early 1900s, the Norwegians took the lead in European whaling. They set up in business in Leith, the home of Scotland's first whaling industry, and worked from South Georgia, where the Dundee Antarctic Expedition had made their base. There were Dundonians in many of the vessels that sailed south, but Dundee no longer played a significant part in the industry.

Terra Nova, built in 1884, was the last whaling ship built in Dundee and whaling companies folded in painful succession. There was a tragic inevitability about the end that only a few diehards refused to acknowledge. Despite the efforts of a group of skilled whaling masters, catches were in a long term decline. The introduction of the modern brassiere around 1907 saw demand for whalebone plummet. Yet the demand for whale oil continued outwith Dundee; Norwegian whaling ships used new techniques and hunted in new whaling grounds. Rather than use the small boats with low powered whaling guns, the Norwegians used large calibre weapons that fired explosive charges into blue whales which were too large for Dundee vessels to handle. The Dundee entrepreneurs did not follow this route; perhaps that was a failure in imagination or a lack of enterprise. Maybe Dundee had invested so much into the precarious business of Arctic whaling over the preceding century and a half that there was no desire for further risk.[1]

In 1914 Dundee's hunting of Arctic whales ended. *Active* returned clean to Armageddon as Dundee men sacrificed themselves in the monstrosity of the First World War. After 150 years, the Dundee whaling industry ended not with a roar of triumph, but a weary whimper. In 1925 Professor D'Arcy Wentworth Thompson made one last statement about the Dundee Arctic fleet in a letter to Frederick Lucas of the American Museum of Natural

History: 'our Scottish whaling fleet (i.e. the old Greenland fleet) is totally extinct . . . the old Captains are gone, and the old crews.'[2] There could be no return to the North.

12

Twentieth Century Scottish Whaling

Whoever said that 'whaling's great', told a pack of lies

Tam Gordon, Antarctic whaler

Scottish whaling did not die with Dundee. Throughout the rise and fall of the Dundee whaling industry, the Scottish whaling connection continued on two separate fronts with shore-based whaling stations and Scottish whalers who worked in the Antarctic. Much of this activity was spearheaded by the firm of Christian Salvesen which, as the name suggests, had its origins in Norway. The Salvesen family's connection went back to the end of the eighteenth century when Ole Salvesen exported timber to Scotland. However, his grandson Theodor moved to Scotland in 1843 and, three years later, started his own company in Leith and Grangemouth. His brother Christian joined him and the company eventually took his name. In 1904, when Christian's three sons were running the company, they bought the Norwegian-built whaling ship *Thor* and opened a shore station in Shetland. This final chapter gives a very brief overview of Scotland's connection with shore-based and Antarctic whaling until its final demise in the 1960s.

In 1907 the Whale Fisheries Act (Scotland) prevented whaling without a licence but encouraged shore stations. The Norwegians had begun shore-based whaling in the 1860s and in 1903, established two shore stations in Scotland, both at Ronas Voe in Shetland. A Glasgow man, A. Dixon Rennie, owned 33 per cent of the shares of the first station, the Zetland Whale Fishing Company. The Leith-based Christian Salvesen owned 5 per cent of the shares of the second station, Norrona Whale Fishing Company, a figure that rose to around 15 per cent in 1908. The Norwegian-owned Alexandra Whaling Company opened at Collafirth the following year, as did Salvesen's Olna Whaling Company in the Olna Firth.

The Norwegian stations had Norwegian managers and imported Norwegian accommodation that was assembled on the site. The whalehunters had entirely Norwegian crews, but some local men were employed at the shore stations. The Norwegian stations only survived until 1914, the year that Dundee Arctic whaling finished. The First World War had intervened – Norwegians were now termed aliens and the war effort required the whale catchers for equally bloody business.

Christian Salvesen's Olna Station was Scotland's largest; Scottish owned, it had an intermittent life, closing in 1914 with the First World War but operating again in the 1920s with a Norwegian manager. In a letter to Ernest Holt of the Irish Department of Agriculture in October 1907, the naturalist D'Arcy Wentworth commented on the abundance of whales: 'I saw one day in Shetland sixteen whales at a single station.'[1]

In 1923 there were four steam powered whale hunters at Olna, and when a whale was killed, it was kept buoyant with air pumped into it, then towed back to the station. Unlike Arctic whaling in which only the blubber and baleen was kept, every part of the whale was used in shore based-whaling, with the meat sent to Norway for animal fodder and the bones used for fertiliser.[2]

There was also shore-based whaling at two stations in the Hebrides, at Bun Abhainn Eadar, or Bunavoneader, in Harris and at Great Bernera off Lewis. Again, there was heavy Norwegian involvement, with a Norwegian company, A/S Harpunen owning the Harris site, a Norwegian manager and some Norwegian staff. That station was successful, exporting baleen to the Paris fashion industry.[3] The Bunavoneader site was ideal for whaling, with a safe harbour and fresh water while there was access to the main road to Stornoway and Tarbert. At its peak it employed nearly a hundred people, mostly seasonal staff.[4] D'Arcy Thompson mentioned that they caught 24 Biscayan right whales in 1907 alone.[5]

In common with the other Scottish shore stations, Bunavoneader closed in 1914, reopened in 1920 but failed. Although Lord Leverhulme tried to revive it for the Lever Brothers margarine manufacture,[6] all whaling ended there in 1928. D'Arcy Thompson's *On Whales Landed at the Scottish Whaling Stations During the Years 1908–1914 and 1920–1927*, a published study of whales landed at Scottish whaling stations revealed that modern whaling methods had savagely reduced the number of whales in the North Atlantic. Between 1908 and 1914, 3,701 whales were caught from Scottish whaling stations: far more than the Dundee Arctic whalers managed. In 1927 only 312 whales were caught, a drop from 749 in 1920,[7] and two years later the company went into liquidation. There was a brief flurry again in the early 1950s, with a mixture of Hebridean and Norwegian staff, but by 1952 all shore-based Scottish whaling had ended.[8]

In 1905 scientists discovered that hydrogenating the oil of a baleen whale could harden it so it was useful for margarine and soap. Three years later Salvesen began Antarctic whaling,[9] with his New Whaling Company operating firstly from the Falkland Islands, with a prefabricated whaling station bought from Iceland and transported south,[10] and then from Leith Harbour, its station in South Georgia. Despite the Scottish name, Norwegian was the prevalent language.[11] After a few years, factory ships joined the shore stations and whale catchers as the Antarctic fishery developed. During the First World War, Norwegian competition withdrew and Salvesen became the main force in the area.[12] His whale oil was invaluable for margarine and soap making and the Antarctic whale fishery continued, with the slumps and booms common to the industry, until the final demise of British whaling in the face of economic pressure in 1963.[13]

This final phase of whaling in Britain had a strong Scottish slant; as well as the Leith base of Salvesen's, many of the crews were Scots, whether from Leith, Shetland or the Hebrides, but with a fair sprinkling of Dundonians as well. None of the ships, however, were Dundee built, and the men were only a part of much more varied crews than those that sailed in *Dorothy* or *Terra Nova*. The Dundee connection may have survived, but in a diluted form. The cable that connected Dundee and the whaling industry finally frayed and parted in 1963.

Appendix 1
Ships of the Dundee Fleet

This appendix describes all the known vessels that sailed in the Dundee whaling fleet from 1753 to 1914. The ships are listed in alphabetical order and details are provided, where known, about when and where they were built, their weight, the type of ship, their engines, known masters and owners while listed in the Dundee Register, their best catches and any further information about their careers as part of the fleet.

Achilles

When and where built: 1813 at South Shields, County Durham, England

Weight: 367 tons

Description: *Achilles* was a carvel-built sailing ship; two decks, three masts, ship rigged with standing bowsprit, square sterned, scroll figurehead. 101 feet 8 inches long by 29 feet 8 inches wide with a depth of 5 feet 6 inches.

Known masters in Dundee fleet: 1820 William Deuchars; 1821–28 William Valentine; 1829 James Hogg

Known owners in Dundee fleet: 1824 P. Smith and W. Newall; 1829 Dundee Whale Fishing Company

Registered in Dundee: from at least 1820 until 1830

Best catches: 1828 – 24 whales

Notes:
On 11 October 1821 *Achilles* was returning from the Arctic when she struck the powder magazine just outside Dundee Harbour. She broke her bowsprit but entered the harbour safely and with no casualties. According to the *Dundee Directory*, in 1824 *Achilles* had a crew of 52 men, slightly more than average. She fell victim to the ice on 25 June 1830, the same year 19 British vessels were sunk, and around 1,000 seamen camped out on the ice in an episode known as the Baffin Fair. At least one French vessel was also lost, for *Ville de Dieppe* was alongside *Achilles* when the ice claimed both. Both crews abandoned safely, set fire to *Ville de Dieppe* and removed enough stores to keep them alive on the ensuing 17-day journey across the ice to the Dundee ship *Horn*.

Active

When and where built: 1852 by Francis Robertson, Peterhead

Weight: Registered tonnage 348, net tonnage 236

Description: 117 feet by 28 feet 6 inches beam by 18 feet draught; one deck and three masts. *Active* was originally ship rigged but was altered to barque rig in February 1874. Carvel-built, as were all Dundee whaling ships, she had a wooden framework, a square stern and no gallery. Her figurehead was of a man in the dress of an early nineteenth-century seaman with white trousers and a hat. There is a photograph in Dundee Museum that clearly shows this figurehead.

Engines: *Active* was built as a sailing vessel but Hall Russell of Aberdeen later added engines. When she joined the Dundee Register, Gourlays of Dundee compounded her engines. They were two cylinder, 20 inches and 30 inches diameter with 21-inch stroke and 40 horsepower.

Known masters in Dundee fleet: 1874–78 Captain Alexander Fairweather; 1878–81 Captain James Fairweather; 1882 Captain Taylor; 1883 Captain Salmond; 1884–87 Captain Brown; 1894–97 Captain Thomas Robertson; 1900, 1904, 1908, 1911 Captain Murray; 1912 Captain James Bannerman; 1913 Captain Alexander Murray; 1914 Captain John Murray.

Known owners in Dundee fleet: 1874 Tay Whale Fishing Company, with George Welch as managing owner; 1882 privately owned, but still managed by Welch; 1884 Robert Kinnes bought all the shares in December, became the ship's husband in February 1886 and managing owner by 12 December 1888. After that date Kinnes retained the same position but shares were divided among a number of people.

Registered in Dundee: 1874–1916, No. 97100

Best catches: 1874 – 25 whales, 3,200 seals; 1878 – 5,500 seals

Notes: *Active* was built as a sailing ship in 1852 and was originally in the Peterhead fleet where she was commanded by Captain David Gray who was probably one of the most famous whaling masters of his day. She was sold to English owners in 1866 before coming to Dundee in 1873. Hall Russell and Co of Aberdeen added engines around 1870. Four years later Gourlay Brothers of Dundee compounded her engines. There is a nice little anecdote about her when Captain James Fairweather was her master in the mid 1870s. At that time the ship keeper was an elderly man with a white beard. The Board of Trade Inspector arrived to inspect the ship's provisions but he was obviously more used to the sleek clippers and steam liners of the Clyde so the stubborn shape of an Arctic whaler would come as a bit of a surprise. When he saw the white bearded man he commented he thought *Active* was like the Ark and the watchman was Noah himself.

For most of her Dundee career, *Active* hunted both seals and whales, with two trips to the Arctic each year; one to the Greenland Sea for seals and a second to Davis Straits. In 1881 one 30th share of her was sold for £225, giving her a very roughly estimated value of £6,750. In 1883, outward bound for Greenland, *Active* anchored off Broughty and was boarded by customs officers. During the obligatory inspection, they found a seal broken on the duty-free tobacco which led to some suspicion, but as the customs officers believed 'the master is a man of good repute, not known to have ever been engaged in any illegal practices', the matter blew over.

In 1892 *Active* was part of the Dundee Antarctic Whaling Expedition. During this expedition, her master, Captain Thomas Robertson, did a little exploring and found that Joinville Island to the north of Graham Land was split in two. He named the southern part Dundee Island. Although the vessels did not capture any whales, one of *Active*'s boats harpooned a blue whale, but the animal was so powerful it was said to have towed the boats and *Active* for fourteen hours before breaking free. After the excitement of the Antarctic Expedition, *Active* returned to the more mundane business of commercial hunting off Greenland and by 1898, in Hudson Bay. By 1900, with Arctic whaling declining, *Active* was also used to collect oil from Kinnes' shore station on Southampton Island. Five years later, she made an abortive expedition to try to rescue an exploring party at Lyons Inlet.

In 1914 *Active* made her last whaling voyage and only discovered the country was at war on 4 October when she met the United States vessel *Pelican* in Hudson's Bay; the Royal Navy also stopped her near Cape Wrath on her homeward voyage. *Active* was the last Dundee whaler to sail to the Arctic with a Dundee crew. Requisitioned by the government and altered to carry conventional cargo, she sailed from Leith with armaments for Russia in December 1915 but was lost with all hands. The first crew picked for that voyage refused to sail as they believed the ship was unseaworthy. Wreckage from *Active* was later washed ashore on Orkney, which was a sad postscript to a ship with such a distinguished history.

Advice

When and where built: 1785 at Whitby, England

Weight: 324 tons

Description: *Advice* had two decks and three masts. She was 97 feet 11 inches by 28 feet 1 inch, with height between decks of 6 feet 9½ inches; ship rigged with a standing bowsprit; square stern, carvel-built, no figurehead.

Known masters in Dundee fleet: 1805–07 James Webster; 1808 James Webster; 1809 either George Caithness or James Webster; 1810–12 William Adamson; 1815–18, 1820–25 Lanceman Webster; 1826–37 George Deuchars; 1837 Lanceman Webster; 1840 William Anderson Junior; 1843 Captain Deuchars; 1844 Alexander Deuchars; 1845 Captain Crammond; 1848 Captain Crammond; 1849 William Penny; 1851 Charles Reid; 1852 David Robb; 1854–59 George Simpson.

Known owners in Dundee fleet: 1809 David Brown, ship's husband; 1818 David Brown; 1824 John Hume. Together with John Sime, these gentlemen were trustees of the Tay Whale Fishing Company.

Registered in Dundee: from at least 1805 until 1859

Best catch: 1810 – 16 whales, 180 tuns oil, full ship (a record catch); 1823 – 23 whales, 210 tuns oil; 1828 – 29 whales, 140 tuns oil, full ship; 1832 – 24 whales, 240 tuns oil; 1833 – 29 whales, 270 tuns oil

Notes: *Advice* may be said to be an unlucky ship, although there is no mention of such a tag in her history. She certainly had one of the most colourful careers of any in the Dundee fleet, with a host of anecdotes and incidents. In 1806, while in the Tay, a boat coming to her overturned, with one man drowned. In 1807, on her return from a whaling voyage, the collector of customs found some mistakes in her logbook, as the master had forgotten to take soundings when he sighted land or a sail. The law required he do so if he was to claim the whaling bounty. *Advice* had a slight mishap in 1808 when one of her boats again capsized in the Tay with 15 men floundering in the water but no casualties. That same year she was licensed to trade to Merrimachi in what is now Canada, presumably for timber. In 1809, along with many other whaling ships, she had a licence to carry arms; the Napoleonic Wars were in full swing and northern waters were dangerous with privateers. However, the following year, His Majesty's brig *Pickle* boarded *Advice* off Thurso with the intention of pressing some of her seamen. Not surprisingly, many of *Advice*'s crew fought back, which led to trouble for her master, Captain William Adamson. By 1814 Lanceman Webster was her master, and took her to Riga when the whaling season was over. He was presumably after a cargo of flax as Dundee was experiencing a linen boom at the time.

Advice's greatest trial came in the winter of 1836, when she was beset in the ice of the Davis Straits for some months. The ice finally eased on 17 March 1837 and she made her slow way home with her crew dead or dying of scurvy, starvation and exposure. On 3 June *Grace* of Liverpool, en route from Glasgow to Virginia, sighted her drifting, leaking and with her sails in tatters. Only three of the crew of Advice were fit enough to go on deck. The others, including survivors from the foundered Dundee whaling ship *Thomas*, were either already dead or lying suffering below. *Grace* loaned her two men and some food, and brought some of her crew on board. *Advice* berthed in Sligo on 13 June, but of the 59 men on board, only 10 survived, including the masters of *Advice* and of *Thomas*. The *Advertiser* of 23 June 1837 reported: 'This vessel, for the safety of which the slightest hope had almost ceased to be entertained, has at last reached a port in the United Kingdom. The state in which she has arrived, however, is one of extreme distress, about six sevenths of her crew being dead and the remainder for the most part in a state of extreme weakness and debility.'

When *Advice* eventually returned to Dundee, crowds gathered to see this ship of the dead, and some commented, perhaps with disappointment, that she appeared no worse than many another vessel returned from the north. Strangely, even after centuries of fighting scurvy and the issue of lime juice to the Royal Navy, people blamed the deaths on 'reducing slumber' caused by not exercising while on board. *Advice* continued to sail north but there was more bad news in 1847 when two of her crew died of scurvy on board and four more died after their arrival in Orkney. Two years later there was another bad season as seven British ships were beset in the ice; this time *Advice* remained free. As none of the vessels carried sufficient provisions to last the winter, most of the men were distributed among the remainder of the whaling fleet. At one point there were more than a hundred men on board *Advice*, more than twice her normal crew of 48. That situation was only temporary as the ice eased and all the crews were returned to their own vessels.

In 1857 more bad weather damaged *Advice* when outward bound so she had to return home, and two years later, after an adventurous 55-year career, *Advice* was lost in the Davis Straits. She was anchored onto an ice field 30 miles off Broughton Head but on the morning of 23 July, the ice closed and nipped her. Two men died and the remainder of the crew spent two days on the ice before *Emma* of Hull rescued them.

Albert

When and where built: 1889 by H. Fellows and Sons, Great Yarmouth

Weight: 155 tons gross, 97 tons net

Description: 100 feet by 25 feet 6 inches by 11 feet 9 inches, *Albert* was a ketch-rigged auxiliary screw.

Engines: Oil powered, twin cylinders, 16 and 18 inches diameter, made by the famous Swedish engine company J. and C. G. Bolinders and Company of Stockholm.

Known masters in Dundee fleet: 1903–11 Captain James S. Mutch; 1914 Captain Beavan; 1916 John Murray; 1920 Captain Beavan

Known owners in Dundee fleet: Banks and Mitchell

In Dundee fleet: 1903 to at least 1908

Best catch: 1903 – 11 walrus; 1904 – two black whales, 19 white whales, 5 walrus, 686 seals, 16 bears, 10 tons oil, 5 cwt baleen, 54 foxes; 1906 – 684 seals, 29 bears, 150 foxes; 1907 – 21 walrus, 560 seal, 28 bears, 40 foxes, 17 tons oil

Notes: Built in 1889 for the Christian evangelist *Mission to Deep Sea Fishermen*, the medical missionary Wilfred Grenfell used *Albert* on his visit to the Inuit of Labrador. James Mitchell of Dundee bought her in 1902 to service the shore stations. In 1903 she sailed to the Davis Strait with barter goods for the Inuit and stores for shore settlements, and she became involved in the whaling industry. In 1903 he spent a winter at Erik Harbour but moved to what became Albert Harbour and founded a trading post at Igarjua. Five years later Mitchell sold *Albert* to a syndicate based in Peterhead that used her for whaling. From 1913 she was used by the Arctic Gold Exploration Syndicate Ltd in an abortive hunt for gold. A shipwrecked whaling man from *Our Queen* named Charles Smith claimed to have found the gold near Melville Sound in 1879. That was around the time of the great gold strikes of Witwatersrand in South Africa and before the Klondike rush, but unfortunately there was no gold in Melville Sound. In 1919 Captain John Murray of Wormit in Fife sailed *Albert* to Cumberland Gulf; Captain Murray broke his leg on the homeward voyage and survived three weeks without medical aid before *Albert* put into Tobermory on the island of Mull. In 1923 the Hudson Bay Company bought her and from 1935 to 1960 a Faroese Company owned her. *Albert* was wrecked off Lossiemouth in Moray, but she was salvaged and used for fishing off the Faroe Islands before finally sinking off Greenland in 1968. Nantucket Whaling Archive has a copy of her 1910 log and her 1914 Engineer's journal.

Alexander (I)

When and where built: 1811 at Hythe, County Durham

Weight: 324 34/94 tons

Description: Alexander had two decks and three masts, with a standing bowsprit. She was square sterned and carvel-built with no galleries and a male bust figurehead. She was shorter than most of her contemporaries at 68 feet 5 inches by 27 feet 10 inches by 6 feet 1 inch.

Known masters in Dundee fleet: 1831 David Ramsay Thoms; 1835 George Cameron; 1837 David Robertson; 1840 David Sturrock; 1843 Charles Reid;1845–57 James Donnet Sturrock. There is some doubt as to the master after that date. The *Dundee Register of Ships* claims Sturrock remained in charge, but the Ingram Records, state that Captain Tod was master in 1857, John Nicoll in 1858 and 1859 and 1860 and Pattison in 1861.

Known owners in Dundee fleet: The Dundee Whale Fishing Company owned *Alexander* from 1831, with the three major trustees being George Miln, shipowner; Robert Stirling, merchant and James Crockatt, merchant, all of Dundee. Possibly as early as 1837, and certainly by late February 1843, the Dundee and Union Whale Fishing Company owned *Alexander*. This company was in existence until at least 1858. In 1859 the Arctic Fishing Company bought *Alexander*.

Registered in Dundee: 1831–62

Best catch: 1832 – 26 whales, 210 tons oil, 13 tons baleen; 1845 – 27 whales, 170 tons oil; 1849 – 22 whales, 160 tons oil, full ship; 1856 – 10 whales, 200 tons oil

Notes: In 1831 *Alexander* was bought from Grangemouth owners to replace *Achilles,* which was lost in the Baffin Fair fiasco of 1830. In 1838 she lost a boat and a crewman while whale hunting. The boat had harpooned a whale that had trapped itself on an ice floe but when the boat approached, the whale capsized it with a flick of its tail. One man drowned and others were injured. In 1848 two men died on board through disease and two years later *Alexander* caught fire while in King William Dock, Dundee, luckily with minimal damage, although her cabin was scorched. In 1852 a gale drove away three whales she had captured and the following year another of her boats capsized and two men were drowned when a harpooned narwhal fought back. On the credit side, that same year she rescued six shipwrecked Hull seamen from an ice floe.

In 1855 William Gilchrist, the tide surveyor at Broughty Ferry, charged Captain James Sturrock for smuggling rum and tobacco. Sturrock was fined £50. That same year *Alexander* was valued at £2,500. In January 1859 *Alexander* was sold to the Dundee Arctic Fishing Company for £1,750, apparently for use as a coal tender for steam whalers as well as for the Davis Straits whaling. That same year Captain Nicoll was also caught smuggling and in 1862 *Alexander* was lost in the Davis Straits.

Alexander (II)

When and where built: Launched 24 December 1865 by Mrs Gilroy of the famous textile company Gilroy, Sons and Co. at Alexander Stephen and Sons of Dundee.

Description: *Alexander* was a screw steamer and sailing craft. She was 157 feet 1 inch by 29 feet 3 inches by 18 feet 4 inches depth in hold from tonnage deck to ceiling at midships. She had two decks, three masts and was ship rigged with a square stern; carvel-built with no gallery, a scroll figurehead and a wooden framework.

Engines: *Alexander's* engine room was 26 feet 3 inches long and held two engines with 80 horsepower in total. The engines were built by Key of Kinghorn.

Known masters in Dundee fleet: 1864 George Deuchars; 1865–69 J. Walker

Known owners in Dundee fleet: When *Alexander* was registered, Captain Deuchars had two of the 64 shares, but he sold them in 1865 and the Gilroy Brothers became the sole owners.

Registered in Dundee: 1864–69, No. 45821

Best catches: 1865 – 18 whales, 170 tons oil; 1868 – 6 whales, 100 tons whale oil, 5.5 tons baleen, 11,408 seals, 140 tons seal oil

Notes: In July 1869 she was with *Erik, Ravenscraig* and *Esquimaux* in Melville Bay in the Davis Straits when a gale blew up and trapped her between two ice floes. At nine at night on the 18th, her 58 strong crew abandoned her and she sank at six o'clock the next morning. All her crew were rescued, with most being landed at the Danish settlement at Leively on Disco Island.

Apollo

Description: Sailing vessel

Known masters in Dundee fleet: 1789 Captain Greenaway.

Registered in Dundee: around 1789

Best catches: 1789 – 8 whales (full ship)

Notes: Very little is known about this vessel, which sailed from Dundee in 1789.

Arctic (I)

When and where built: Launched 7 February 1867 at Alexander Stephen and Sons of Dundee.

Weight: 625 tons gross (in 1874 the *Advertiser* recorded her weight as 567 tons gross).

Description: *Arctic* had one deck with three masts. She was ship rigged with a square stern. *Arctic* was carvel-built with no gallery, a scroll head and a wooden framework. She was 158 feet by 29 feet 4 inches broad by 19 feet 6 inches in depth.

Engine: *Arctic* had an engine room 26 feet long. She had two engines with 70 horsepower.

Known masters in Dundee fleet: 1867 Captain Wells; 1868–75 Captain William Adams

Known owners in Dundee fleet: Alexander Stephens and Sons; Alexander and William Stephen had 32 shares each.

Registered in Dundee: 1867–74, No. 52578

Best catch: 1871 – 37 whales, 17,800 seals (reputed to be the largest cargo ever brought into Dundee from the Arctic); 1874 – 45,000 seals

Notes: *Arctic* was one of the most successful vessels of the Dundee fleet, given her relatively short life span. Under the command of Captain Adams senior she achieved some spectacular catches. In 1871 she brought nearly 260 tons of oil into Dundee, with a value of £13,000 which was huge money for the time and nearly as high a value as the ship herself. It was said to be the largest whaling cargo landed in Dundee. In 1873 Captain Markham of the Royal Navy sailed with Captain Adams to learn about ice navigation for a forthcoming Arctic expedition. His subsequent book, *A Whaling Cruise to Baffin's Bay and the Gulf of Boothia*, was published in London the following year and contains a great deal of information about the voyage. In 1874 *Arctic* was caught in a gale off Cape Garry in Cresswell Bay, in the north west of Davis Straits; Captain Adams nosed into a natural harbour in the ice and she survived the first squeeze but subsequently ran into trouble. Adams reported:

> On the morning of the 7th August a very strong gale, blowing from the S.S E. was experienced. The ice ran very fast and squeezed the vessel heavily. At 8.30 AM the ice brought up on Cape Garry, causing it to crush more strongly round the *Arctic*. Her timbers creaked in an alarming manner but

she made no water. At 9 AM the ice took a fearful sally, heaving the vessel completely on her beam ends. It was then discovered that she was making water rapidly.

The ship caught fire at six in the evening with the flames from 185 tons of whale oil soaring spectacularly hundreds of feet skyward. *Arctic* slid stern first through a hole in the ice, surrounded by a cloud of steam. The crew abandoned and lived in tents made from the ship's sails on the ice for days, before Captain Deuchars of *Victor* rescued them.

Arctic II

When and where built: Launched 22 January 1875 by Miss Edith Stephen, daughter of William Stephen of Alexander Stephen and Sons, Dundee

Weight: Gross tonnage 828.18, registered tonnage 522.31

Description: One of Stephen's famous wooden-built auxiliary screw steamers, *Arctic II* was different from most other whaling ships as her engine room and funnel were amidships – forward of her mainmast. *Arctic II* was also distinctive as she had a 35-foot-long raised quarter deck. Her masts and yards were varnished, while her hull was painted black and her whaleboats were contrasting white. Her figurehead was equally unique; an Inuit with a lance, while the motto 'Do or Die' was painted in gold across her stern. *Arctic II* was 200 feet 7 inches by 31 feet 7 inches by 19 feet 6 inches in depth. She had two decks, three masts and was barque-rigged. She had a square stern, as did most Dundee whaling ships, no gallery and a wooden framework.

Engines: Made in 1875 by Alexander Stephen and Sons of Linthouse; compound inverted engines, two cylinder with 27 and 54 inch diameter and 33-inch stroke; 98 horsepower.

Masters while in the Dundee Register: 1875–83 William Adams (senior); 1884–87 Guy; 1887 Robertson

Known owners in Dundee fleet: William Stephens of Alexander Stephens and Sons, Dundee, managing owner with all 64 shares

In Dundee fleet: 1875–88

Best catches: 1875 – 8 whales, 120 tons oil, 7 tons bone, 13,000 seals, 130 tons oil; 1878 – 1 whale, 17 tons oil, 24 cwt bone, 33,000 seals, 300 tons seal oil, plus 1,100 seals on her second trip

Notes: *Arctic II* cost £24,000 to build; she carried an impressive 10 whaleboats, and her storage tank could hold 350 tons of oil. When she first arrived at Newfoundland, things looked black for *Arctic II*; the Newfoundland sealers were hostile, she broke her screw and was trapped in the ice for nearly three weeks but, when she rescued a group of Newfoundlanders from an ice floe and employed others as sealers, things improved. In 1879 she joined in the abortive search for survivors of the Tay Bridge disaster and two years later the Arctic ice squeezed her so badly a hydraulic jack had to be used to straighten her up. The following year Charles Hendry, chief engineer, died on board and in 1884 she rescued seven survivors of the missing US Greely

Expedition. Two years after that, she had a small adventure when she was whaling in Hudson's Bay and became trapped in floating ice off Resolution Island. A 10 knot current carried her 80 miles off her route before she extricated herself. In 1887 her adventurous career came to an end when she was abandoned near Foxe Channel in Cumberland Gulf.

Aurora

When and where built: Launched 30 December 1876 by Miss Henderson of Ganthorpe, Yorkshire, at the building yard of Alexander Stephens and Sons, Marine Parade, Dundee.

Weight: Gross tonnage 579.95, registered tonnage 386.23

Description: *Aurora* had one deck with three masts; she was square sterned and barque- rigged. Wooden framed and carvel-built, *Aurora* had no gallery and a female bust figurehead. She was 165 feet 3 inches long with a breadth of 30 feet 7 inches and a hold depth of 18 feet 10 inches. In common with many Arctic vessels she had a cutaway stem.

Engines: two engines, direct acting surface condensing compound engines, made in 1877 by Cunliffe and Dunlop of Port Glasgow. The cylinders had a diameter of 25 and 48 inches, with a 30-inch stroke; the combined horse power was 98.

Known masters in Dundee fleet: 1877–79 James Bannerman; 1880–82 Alexander Fairweather; 1883–88 James Fairweather; 1889 Harry McKay

Known owners in Dundee fleet: 1877–93 William Stephen of Alexander Stephen and Son, appointed Managing Owner in February 1877.

In Dundee Registry: 1877–94

Best catches: 1880 – 20 whales, 190 tons whale oil, eight tons baleen, 12,999 seals, 170 tons seal oil; 1888 – 24,693 seals, 243 tons oil

Notes: *Aurora* was involved in the 1882 attempt to rescue the American explorer Adolphus Greely who was trapped on Ellesmere Island in the Arctic. However it was not until 1884 that the Dundee built *Bear* and *Thetis* rescued the few survivors, amid tales of execution and cannibalism. *Aurora* was nearly crushed against an iceberg in 1886 and the crew abandoned her, staggering alongside as she drifted on a 4-knot current. The men nearly saw their ship sail away without them but Captain Fairweather and first mate Mr Davidson reboarded her after a couple of hours and the hands followed a few hours later. There were 300 men in the crew and one drowned; he had refused to drop his gear, so he lagged behind and fell into a pool in the ice. *Aurora* was anchored to an iceberg and when that berg collided with another the ice splintered and she was free again. Some of the 300 man crew walked 10 miles to get ashore and reported *Aurora* lost, so a rescue party was nearly ready to search for survivors when she turned up at Carolina Harbour, leaking and with her shaft bent, but still afloat.

In December 1893 Captain Harry McKay was fined a guinea for not issuing lime juice, an omission that resulted in one man catching scurvy. Ever since the 1854 Merchant Shipping Act, it was obligatory for British merchant seamen to have a daily quota of lime juice. Captain Mackay claimed it was customary for whaling masters to issue a month's supply of lime juice to the men and make them responsible for their own medication. In December 1894 *Aurora*'s passage to St John's was delayed by gales and several men were injured. In 1895, under Bowring ownership, *Aurora* was again stuck in the ice; she was also damaged in 1908 and reported lost two years later. In 1911 she was the main vessel in the Australian explorer Douglas Mawson's Antarctic expedition that discovered Clairie Land and confirmed the existence of Termination Land; on that expedition *Aurora* steamed 30,000 miles in Antarctic and sub Antarctic waters. When acting as support vessel for Shackleton's 1913 expedition, she was blown out to sea and drifted 500 miles in ten months. Four years later she disappeared while carrying coal from New South Wales to Chile. The only trace was a buoy with her name on it, carried by the tide to a New South Wales beach.

Balaena

When and where built: 1872, by Jorgensen & Knudsen, Drammen, Norway

Weight: Gross tonnage 415.61, registered tonnage 247.65

Description: *Balaena* had two decks, three masts and was barque-rigged. Unlike the majority of British whaling vessels, she had an elliptical stern. She had a wooden framework and was carvel-built with no galleries, a fiddle head, one bulkhead and no water ballast tanks. Her vital statistics were: length 140 feet 10 inches; breadth 31 feet 7 inches and depth 16 feet 7 inches.

Engines: *Balaena*'s engine room was 27 feet 3 inches long. Her engines were compound; two cylinders, 20 inches and 40 inches in diameter, with a 24¾-inch stroke; 66 horsepower. They were built by Nylands Engine Company, Christiansand, Norway.

Known masters in Dundee fleet: 1892–96 Captain Alexander Fairweather; 1897–1901 Captain Thomas Robertson; 1902 James Bannerman; 1903–08 Captain Guy; 1909–11 Captain J. Murray; 1917 Captain W. Adams

Known owners in Dundee fleet: 1890 Robert Kinnes; 1892 Kinnes sold various shares but retained management status; 1916 all shares sold to Liverpool owners.

In Dundee Registry: 1891–1917

Best catches: 1892 – 2 whales, 2,156 seals, 32 tons seal oil, 10.5 tons whale oil, half ton baleen; 1899 – 20 musk ox, 13 whales, 7 walrus, 9 seals, 3 narwhals, 11 bears, 41 tons oil, 2 tons baleen; 1902 – 640 white whales, 14 walrus, 4 seals, 17 polar bears, 65 tons oil

Notes: *Balaena* is one of the best remembered of the Dundee whaling ships, but ironically she was built in Norway and her original name was *Mjolne*. In 1891 she was added to Dundee register when Robert Kinnes bought her. In July next year *Balaena* rescued some of *Chieftain*'s crew from the ice in the Arctic and later she sailed south as Captain Alexander Fairweather commanded her on the Dundee Antarctic Whaling Expedition. She was part of a four-ship expedition together with *Diana*, *Active* and *Polar Star*, but the trip was abortive as they did not catch any whales. The costs were met by the number of seals they brought back. For the next two years *Balaena* worked in the Davis Straits and in May 1896 Captain Alexander Fairweather died on board when they were off Spitsbergen. In 1897 the crew of *Balaena* caused some trouble in Lerwick by fighting amongst themselves, but there were no serious casualties or damage caused. Four years later Captain Thomas

Robertson was fined for concealing tobacco in his cabin: Dundee whaling masters were not all angels! *Balaena* endured 80 days trapped in the Melville Bay ice in 1903, only being freed on 14 August. In 1917 she was sold to Liverpool owners, who in turn sold her to Norwegian owners, and in 1929 she was reported to be a hulk.

Calypso

When and where built: 1787

Weight: 306 tons

Description: Sailing vessel

Known masters in Dundee fleet: 1810–16 William Christopher; 1817–22 George Thoms

Known owners in Dundee fleet: 1810 Alexander Anderson was one of the owners; 1818 Powrie and Russell

In Dundee Registry: 1810–22

Best catches: 1810 – 14 whales, full ship; 1816 – 17 whales, 100 butts oil

Notes: *Calypso* came to Dundee from London owners and made an immediate impression. While entering the Tay on the homeward voyage, it was the custom for whaling vessels to indicate their catch by firing cannon. In 1810 one of *Calypso*'s guns misfired and the flash exploded the powder horn held by a seaman named David Lorimer, who was badly injured. In 1817 a wounded whale flicked its tail and smashed a whaleboat drowning one man and, four years later, the same thing happened, with two men drowned. *Calypso* was lost on 27 July 1822; her crew launched the boats over an icy sea and were picked up by others whaling vessels.

Camperdown

When and where built: 1860 by Alexander Stephen and Sons, Dundee.

Weight: Gross tonnage 541.03, registered tonnage 424.01

Description: *Camperdown* was a screw steamer. She was three-masted and ship-rigged with a square stern. She had a wooden framework and was carvel-built with no gallery and a scroll figurehead. 154 feet 6 inches in length, she was 30 feet in breadth and 18 feet 8 inches deep.

Engines: 70 horse power

Known masters in Dundee fleet: 1864–71 William Bruce; 1872–78 John Gravill

Known owners in Dundee fleet: 1860 David Duncan of Arbroath (27 shares), Alexander Stephen (25 shares), James Yeaman (7 shares), Peter Christie (3 shares), William Bruce (2 shares). All seem to have been part of the Dundee Seal and Whale Fishing Company which ran the vessel under the management of James Yeaman. From February 1876, David Bruce became the manager.

In Dundee Registry: 1860–78, No. 27496

Best catches: 1865 – 9 whales, 85 tons oil, 20,000 seals, 220 tons seal oil; 1866 – 5 whales, 60 tons oil, 22,500 seals, 260 tons seal oil; 1871 – 12 whales, 140 tons oil, 9.5 tons baleen, 2,500 seals; 1872 – 25 whales, 160 tons oil, 3,200 seals; 1874 – 32 whales, 175 tons oil, 9 tons baleen, 2,300 seals, 50 tons seal oil

Notes: *Camperdown*'s signal letters were P.R.M.B. Her career perhaps lacked the drama of some other vessels, with few recorded incidents. However, in January 1863 she had the misfortune to run aground in Earl Grey Dock in Dundee. She was also damaged while seal fishing in 1874 and had to be repaired before going back to the whaling. *Camperdown* was lost in the Davis Straits on 10 October 1878.

Chieftain

When and where built: 1868 by Jack of Lossiemouth.

Weight: Gross tonnage 193.54, registered tonnage 168.93

Description: *Chieftain* was a sailing vessel when built but was converted to steam late in 1890. She was 106 feet 10 inches by 23 feet 10 inches by 13 feet ¾ inch. She had one deck and was schooner rigged with three masts and a square stern. Carvel-built, *Chieftain* had a wooden framework, with no galleries and a male figurehead.

Engines: After conversion, *Chieftain* had a 25 foot 3 inch long engine room with two inverted compound engines. Gourlay Brothers of Dundee built the engines while Clark, Chapman and Co. of Gateshead made the boilers. The engines were 2 cylinder, 12 and 20 inches, with an 18-inch stroke. They were of 25 horsepower and gave *Chieftain* a speed of 6.5 knots.

Known masters in Dundee fleet: 1883–84 Thomas Ferrier Gellatly; 1885 Captain Malcolm; 1886–87 Captain Watson (the Ingram Records say Watson commanded until 1888); 1889–91 Captain Kilgour.

Known owners in Dundee fleet: 1883 John Fraser Birrell of 123 Murraygate, Dundee was managing owner for a short time; shares divided among a number of individuals who bought a small number of shares each; by the end of 1889 Robert Kinnes was managing owner with all 64 shares.

In Dundee Registry: 1883–93

Best catches: 1885 – 7 tons oil, 3 bottlenose whales, 36 walrus; 1890 – 2 whales, 30 tons oil, 25 cwt baleen; 1892 – 300 seals

Notes: *Chieftain* was brought to Dundee from Inverness, specifically for the bottlenose whaling. The best remembered incident in *Chieftain*'s career was in summer 1884 when she had four whaleboats out hunting in a fog. They were 200 miles off Iceland and lost the ship. One boat was rescued by a Norwegian vessel after a week. The other three tried to sail to Iceland. Two reached safety but the last ran into difficulties and all on board died except for James 'Toshie' McIntosh, who lost both legs through frostbite. This incident received much publicity and McIntosh became something of a local celebrity, although there were alternative, and darker, versions of the story. *Chieftain* was lost off Greenland on 14 July 1892.

Columbia

When and where built: 1835 by Blackwall, London

Weight: 324.92 tons

Description: *Columbia* was a sailing vessel with one deck and three masts. She was barque-rigged with a square stern. She had a wooden framework, was carvel-built with sham quarter galleries and a male figurehead. Her vital statistics were: length: 102 feet 9 inches by breadth 25 feet 9 inches by depth 17 feet 9 inches.

Known masters in Dundee fleet: 1867 John Reid

Known owners in Dundee fleet: Dundee Seal and Whale Fishing Company with David Bruce as joint manager

In Dundee Registry: 1867–68

Notes: *Columbia* was purchased as a store ship in 1867, costing £750. She carried coal to Stromness for *Narwhal* and was lost on her later voyage to Davis Straits. The crew blamed the master, who had no experience of sailing in Arctic conditions. She was lost on 31 July 1868, with master and crew saved. When the crew returned to Dundee, one member, Alexander Walker, attempted a court case against the owners for hiring an incompetent master but lost.

Cornwallis

When and where built: 1862 by Ritson at Maryport, Cumberland, England

Weight: 394 tons

Description: *Cornwallis* was a wooden built barque 131 feet 6 inches by 25 feet 6 inches by 18 feet. She was originally a purely sail-powered vessel but was converted to steam by A. Shanks and Sons in 1883.

Engine: *Cornwallis* had a compound horizontal three cylinder engine with 18, 18 and 36 inch diameter and a 20-inch stroke.

Known masters in Dundee fleet: 1884 John Nicoll

Known owners in Dundee fleet: 1884 W. S. Croudace; 1885 included Mr Nicoll

Best catches: 1884 – 1 whale, 13 tons whale oil, 0.5 tons baleen

In Dundee Registry: 1884–85

Notes: *Cornwallis* was not the most successful Dundee whaling ship and is barely remembered. In 1884, as her cargo was not landed at Dundee within the specified time, *Cornwallis'* owners had to pay the customs officials an extra fee. She was lost in the ice off Cape Kater in the Davis Straits in 1885.

Diana (I)

When and where built: 1871 by J. Jorgansen at Drammen, Norway

Weight: Gross tonnage 357.29, registered tonnage 271.7 (The *Dundee Advertiser* of 2 January 1895 states 212 tons net)

Description: *Diana* was a steam screw vessel with two decks and three masts. She was barque-rigged with an elliptical stern; she had a wooden framework and was carvel-built with no galleries, a scroll head and no bulkheads. Her vital statistics were: length 135 feet 6 inches; breadth 29 feet and depth 16 feet.

Engines: With an engine room 36 feet in length, *Diana* had engines of 45 horse power. Her inverted compound engine was built by Nylands Engine Company, Christiania. If steaming at full speed, she could burn 7 tons of coal in 24 hours.

Known masters in Dundee fleet: 1892–96 Robert Davidson; 1899–1904 William Adams; 1905–09 Harry McKay; 1910 William Milne: 1911 William Adams

Known owners in Dundee fleet: 1892 Robert Kinnes, but sold many shares to various people, who owned small numbers of shares, with Kinnes remaining in overall management control. In 1898 *Diana* was owned by W. F. McIntosh of Dundee with Kinnes as manager. In 1912 James Mitchell was manager.

In Dundee Registry: 1892–1915, No. 99211

Best catches: 1892 – 150 seals, 1.5 tons oil; 1893 – 3,700 seals (Antarctic); 1899 – 10 whales, 140 tons oil, 5.5 tons baleen; 1900 – 6 whales, 54 walrus, 24 bears, 76.5 tons oil, 77 cwt baleen; 1902 – 5 black whales, 1 white whale, 6 walrus, 17 seals, 30 bears, 70 tons oil, 91 cwt baleen; 1908 – 1 black whale, 217 white whales, 3 walrus, 5 seals, 24 bears, 33 tons oil, 4.5 cwt baleen

Notes: Bought by Robert Kinnes in 1892 and sailed to the Newfoundland seal fishing that same year. She was also one of the four vessels that took part in the Dundee Antarctic Expedition of 1892–93. In May 1895 she was laid up during a slump in the whaling industry and the following year she broke her propeller shaft off Greenland and returned early to Dundee. During a gale in 1901 *Diana* rescued members of crew of *Nova Zembla* and two years later her rudder was damaged while she was beset in Melville Bay. She was stuck in the ice for 17 days. In 1913 *Diana* was sold to a Liverpool company but remained in the Dundee registry. In 1915 she was sold to Russia.

Diana (II)

When and where built: 1869 by Alexander Stephens, Glasgow

Weight: 104 tons net, 179 tons gross **Description:** A steam yacht, *Diana* was modified to become a sealing vessel around 1870. She was described as a three-masted screw steamer schooner with a compound iron frame. She was 115 feet 5 inches in length, 21 feet 6 inches in breadth and 12 feet 5 inches deep.

Engines: *Diana* had 30 horse powers; compound inverted two cylinders, 13.25 by 26 inch engines with an 18-inch stroke, built by J Howden of Glasgow.

Known masters in Dundee fleet: 1885 Captain Allan

Known owners in Dundee fleet: *Diana* was a Glasgow vessel owned by J. Lamont of Knockdhu, but she operated from Dundee and in December 1880 she was sold to the Hudson Bay Company.

Dorothy

When and where built: 1812 at Jarrow, County of Durham, England

Weight: 368 64/94 tons

Description: *Dorothy* had two decks and three masts. She was ship-rigged and square sterned, carvel-built with neither figurehead nor gallery, but a standing bowsprit. Her vital statistics were; length: 99 feet 3 inches; breadth: 29 feet 5 inches; and height between decks 5 feet 8 inches.

Known masters in Dundee fleet: 1821 James Deuchars; 1822–24 William Deuchars(when he died on board, the mate, James Deuchars, took command); 1826 James Deuchars; 1827–34, 1837–38 Thomas Davidson

Known owners in Dundee fleet: 1824 Peter Thomson; 1829 Dorothy Whale Fishing Company (a Joint Stock Company), Thomas Nicoll of Hawkhill Place with various others: 1829 Thomas Davidson, shipmaster

In Dundee Registry: 1821–40

Best catches: 1828 – 37 whales, 280 tuns, full ship; 1829 37 whales, 290 tuns oil (this was a record catch); 1832 – 34 whales, 290 tuns oil, 18 tons baleen

Notes: As *Dorothea*, in 1818 *Dorothy* took part in the Great Northern Expedition which was intended to sail over the North Pole. She was strengthened inside and out, with the cabin windows doubled and sliding doors placed at the bottom of each hatchway. Copper pipes carried steam from the galley to heat the interior of the ship and box beds were fitted in place of hammocks. *Dorothy* carried 100 chaldrons (about 26 tons) of coal and a large stock of food and warm clothing. A chaldron was a unit of measurement for coal, but there were regional variations. A London chaldron was roughly 1422 kilograms. Captain David Buchan was her master with John Duke, previously working at Montrose, as surgeon. The four vessels of the expedition left Lerwick on 27 May, a good deal later than contemporary whaling ships would have departed and headed north. Not surprisingly, the expedition failed and when they met the Nairn whaling ship *Princess of Wales* in August, *Dorothea* had reached only as far north as 80 degrees 30 minutes. She was also badly damaged when caught between two icebergs that nipped her clean out of the sea. The London *Morning Post* of 19 October 1818 reported 'her irons forced, her ribs broken and it was with great difficulty she . . . reached the coast . . . put into Smeerenburg Bay in Spitsbergen to refit'.

By 1821 *Dorothy* was a whaling ship in Dundee but that same year she grounded on a rock just outside Dundee harbour and the steam ferry *Union* towed her off. Three years later Captain Deuchars died on the homeward voyage and in 1828 one of the harpooners, David Blyth, fell overboard and drowned in the Tay. That same year Captain Davidson got himself in trouble when he arrived in Dundee with a cargo of blubber but no manifest. Davidson had previously commanded a Kirkcaldy whaling vessel and claimed there was no requirement for a manifest in that port. In the following year the mate, a different Thomas Davidson, was found smuggling. Ice damaged *Dorothy* in the bad year of 1830, and in 1838 she was also used to carry timber to Dundee from Nova Scotia. Her owners withdrew her from whaling and put their whale fishing yard up for sale. In 1840, still a timber carrier, she foundered in the North Atlantic. The packet ship *Penguin* found her waterlogged but still afloat in May, and rescued a dog that had been left on board. There is no mention of an attempt at salvage so presumably *Dorothy* was left to sink in her own time. There is a copy of her 1834 log in Nantucket Whaling Museum.

Dundee (I)

When and where built: British built before 1752

Weight: 1773 – 364.5 tons, 1777 – 365.5 tons, 1788 – 338 tons

Known masters in Dundee fleet: 1752–56 William Cheyne; 1761–62 Robert Finlay; 1763–1765 William Cooper; 1766–68 Andrew Spink; 1769 James Archer; 1775, 1776, 1780 and 1782 Captain Robson

Known owners in Dundee fleet: In 1770 two of the owners were Messrs Russell and Syme, merchants in Dundee.

In Dundee Registry: 1752–82

Best known catches: 1765 – 6 whales; 1769 – 6 whales; 1775 – 2 large whales; 1780 – 11 whales; 1781 – 9 whales

Notes: Regular voyages to Greenland 1752 onward, with some additional trips to Newcastle. In 1760 she was supplied with salted pork and beef from Ireland. In 1770 she had a crew of 46 but in 1777 she had 48 men on board. *Dundee* was lost in the ice in June 1782 and Captain Robson left an account of the aftermath, a copy of which is held by Dundee Museum. She left the Tay on 4 May and sailed northward with the whaling ships from Dunbar. Reaching the ice on 1 June, *Dundee* was holed on the 4th and began taking on water fast. Captain Robson decided to abandon and the crew left in all six boats, heading for Charles Island or Fair Foreland, some 17 leagues (about 51 miles) away over the ice. They carried beef, ham, biscuits and 12 gallons of whisky as well as lemon, thyme, sage and balm which might have helped prevent scurvy, although Captain Robson believed that tea was better. A northerly gale prevented progress so they huddled on the ice for a week. They burned the wreckage of *Dundee* for warmth and sheltered within the boats with the sails as cover. They drank melted snow and fired muskets to keep prowling bears at bay. On the 11th they launched the boats and rowed through passages in the ice. Some of the men were sick after shooting and eating a bear, and on 23 June they shot ducks for food. The next day they were rescued by *Manchester* of Hull and *Young Eagle* of London. The crew all survived, which suggests excellent leadership by Captain Robson.

Dundee of Dundee (II)

When and where built: before 1786 at Bristol

Weight: 338 tons

Description: A sailing vessel with a length of 93 feet 9 inches, breadth 28 feet 10 inches

Known masters in Dundee fleet: 1787–91 William Souter.

Known owners in Dundee fleet: In 1795, Ebenezer Anderson was the agent for the owners. In the mid 1790s this vessel passed to the London Register.

Best catches: 1786 – 7 whales;[1] 1787 – 5 whales, 1,500 seals (*St James's Chronicle* claims 3,250 seals); 1794 – 3 whales

Notes: In 1789 her figurehead was damaged when in a collision with another ship. In July 1794 she had her most dramatic moments when the 44-gun French frigate *Brest* captured her off Duncansby Head, but the Royal Navy sloop *Kingfisher* recaptured her off Bergen four days later. Most of *Dundee's* crew were taken prisoner to France; the mate Peter Nicator and an apprentice called Alexander Robertson evaded capture. It seems that *Kingfisher* pressed Robertson into her crew but allowed Nicator to remain on board *Dundee* as navy seamen took her into the *Tay*. In 1797 the vessel was sold outside Dundee.

Dundee (III)

When and where built: Calman and Martin of Marine Parade, Dundee. She was launched on 22 January 1859 by Miss Bell, the daughter of Dr Bell, one of the shareholders.

Weight: gross tonnage 499.65, registered tonnage 339.76 tons

Description: *Dundee* was a steam screw vessel. She was ship rigged with three masts and a traditional square stern. She was 149 feet 9½ inches long by 29 feet 1 inch in breadth and 19 feet in depth.

Engines: Her 70 horsepower engines were built by Gourlays of Dundee.

Known masters in Dundee fleet: 1859 Captain Deuchars; 1861 Captain Sturrock

Known owners in Dundee fleet: in 1859 she was owned by a group of people including William Clark, William Ogilvie Taylor and James Kennedy Martin. By 1861 the Arctic Fishing Company owned her.

Registered in Dundee: 1859–63

Best catches: 1859 – 19 whales, 130 tons oil, no seals

Notes: Built in just three months and five days, in 1859 *Dundee* towed *Alexander* through Melville Bay and rescued 34 men from the Peterhead ship *Inuit*. However she returned clean from her initial sealing voyage. *Dundee* was reputedly the first vessel built in Dundee specifically for seal and whale fishing, although *Narwhal* may dispute that claim. In May 1863 heavy ice damaged her as she entered Davis Strait. The weather remained stormy and *Dundee* was leaking badly, reportedly taking in 21 inches of water an hour. Captain Sturrock took her into Holsteinborg, a small settlement in Greenland, beached her and effected temporary repairs. Captain Sturrock again sailed into the Strait but once more encountered thick ice. On 3 June her false keep was lost; Captain Sturrock ordered the men into the boats as a precaution. When the ice eased, they returned on board and sailed to Melville Bay but in July the ship lost a blade of her screw. More ice ripped through her hull and into the engine room on 6 July, and she was again nipped and further damaged. On 15 August the crew refused to stay on board and abandoned her. Together with some survivors from the Dundee ship *Jumna*, they took their boats and struggled over hummocks of ice for three days before reaching open water. A three-day sail took them to the Danish settlement of Upernavik on the Greenland coast.

Earl of Mar and Kellie

When and where built: 1856 at Alloa

Weight: 430 tons gross, 278 tons net

Description: *Earl of Mar and Kellie* was a barque, wooden built with auxiliary steam engine; she was 144 feet 4 inches in length by 25 feet 9½ inches broad and 16 feet 7 inches in depth.

Engines: This vessel was re-engined by W. B. Thomson, Dundee, in 1885 with a compound two cylinder, 20 and 40 inch diameter with 24-inch stroke creating 70 horsepower.

Known masters in Dundee fleet: 1885 Thomas Mackie; 1888 Walker; 1889 Fairweather; 1890 Captain Davidson; 1898–1901 James Fairweather

Known owners in Dundee fleet: 1888 John Duthie, Peterhead, managing owner and Alexander Smith of 29 Dock Street, Dundee, agent; 1891–92 A. E. Kinnear, London

In Dundee Registry: at least 1886 to 1890

Best catches: 1888 – 1,100 seals, 42 tons oil; 1890 – 5 whales, 317 white whales, 7,400 seals, 127 tons oil, 65 cwt baleen

Notes: *Earl of Mar and Kellie* did not make much of an impact in Dundee. She was damaged in a storm off Cape Farewell at the southern tip of Greenland in May 1888 and there is an oil painting of her in Simonstown Museum near Capetown, South Africa.

Earnest William

When and where built: 1879 by W. McCann of Hull

Description: *Earnest William* was a sailing vessel. She was carvel-built with no galleries, one deck and two masts. Ketch-rigged, she was square sterned and had no figurehead. Her statistics were: 75 feet 7 inches by 20 feet 5 inches by 10 feet 3 inches.

Known masters in Dundee fleet: 1910 Cannon; 1911 Lindsay

Known owners in Dundee fleet: Robert Kinnes but in 1911 sold all 64 of his shares to John Cooney of Wormit, who in turn sold them to Walter Kinnes. By late 1912 John and James Allison were part owners.

Registered in Dundee: No. 79483

Best catches: 1910 – 80 walrus, 200 foxes; 1911 – 160 walruses, 22 tons oil; 1913 – 4,500 seals, 30 tons oil

Notes: *Earnest William* was lost in Kikerton, Cumberland Gulf, 23 August 1913 after the crew had been 40 days pumping out water. *Earnest William* drifted ashore and a missionary helped the crew. There is a brief logbook of hers in the Central Library in Dundee.

Easonian

When and where built: 1918 at Astilleros de Passages in Spain; originally named *Nistra Senora de Arantzaza*

Weight: Gross tonnage: 250.45: registered tonnage: 175.40

Description: *Easonian* was a three-masted ketch with a schooner rig. She had an auxiliary engine. She was 119 feet 1 ¼ inches by 24 feet 1 ¼ inches by 12 feet 4 inches deep, with a single deck and semi-elliptical stern. *Easonian* was carvel-built with no galleries.

Engine: The engine room was 21 feet long with engines built in Newbury in 1920. They were two cylinder with 13 3/16 inch diameter and a stroke length the same, creating 90 horsepower and giving *Easonian* 5 knots.

Known masters in Dundee fleet: 1922 Captain Taylor

Known owners in Dundee fleet: Cumberland Trading Company, 33 Dock Street, Dundee; managed by Robert Kinnes

In Dundee Registry: 1921–22

Notes: *Easonian*'s owners were the Cumberland Trading Company Limited, but the shares were mortgaged to the Royal Bank of Scotland in 1922. She was reputedly the last Dundee trading vessel to go to the Arctic. *Easonian* sailed from Dundee in the summer of 1921 for the trading posts at Blacklead and Kekerton in the Cumberland Gulf. She carried a cargo of ammunition and provisions and intended to bring back furs. With the First World War a recent memory, ammunition was scarce and indispensible for the Arctic hunters. *Easonian* damaged her propeller in the ice and although a local blacksmith repaired her, she broke down again. Her master took her ashore for repairs but a fire started in her engine room above the fuel tanks and she burned. The ketch *Albert* rescued the crew and brought them to Peterhead.

Ebor

When and where built: While the *Dundee Register of Ships* gives *Ebor*'s construction date at 1815, the 1834 *Dundee Directory* states 1822, and the Ingram Records say 1819; of the three, the *Register* is probably most to be trusted. She was built on the River Hull.

Weight: 278 3/94 tons

Description: Barque-rigged, square sterned and carvel-built, *Ebor* had a standing bowsprit and no figurehead, no galleries, two decks and three masts. She was 96 feet long by 26 feet 6 inches broad and 5 feet 8 inches deep.

Known masters in Dundee fleet: 1831–33 George Cameron; 1835–36 Alexander Cook; 1837–39 Captain Cumming; 1843 Captain Cumming

Known owners in Dundee fleet: The Dundee Union Whale Fishing Company, with the three principal trustees as John Blair Miller, merchant; John Thain, merchant, and John Calman, shipbuilder. When John Miller died, his wife Mary Arnott, with David Milan of the Dundee Union Bank, took over his position.

Registered in Dundee: 1831–40

Best catches: 1832 – 22 whales, 165 tons oil, 8 tons baleen

Notes: Bought from Newcastle owners in 1831 to replace *Three Brothers*, after the 1830 disaster, *Ebor* was also used as a timber carrier. She was sold from Dundee in 1839 and wrecked off Montrose in 1845.

Eclipse

When and where built: 1867 by Alexander Hall & Co., Aberdeen

Weight: 434 tons gross, 296 tons net

Description: Auxiliary steamer, black painted topside with her lower masts white and a black bowsprit, yards, jib-boom and tops. She had a white line along her covering board and her poop bulwarks were also white. Her mizzen was protected from the funnel heat by copper sheathing. *Eclipse* was 141 feet 6 inches long by 29 feet 5 inches by 16 feet 4 inches.

Engines: *Eclipse* had compound inverted two cylinders, 23 and 40 inch diameter; 27-stroke engines creating 72 horsepower. There was a new boiler installed in 1903 and the engine was undated in 1909, at just 69 horsepower.

Known masters in Dundee fleet: 1893–1908 Captain Milne

Known owners in Dundee fleet: 1892 James Mitchell

Registered in Dundee: 1902–09

Best catches: 1868 – 7,800 seals; 1869 – 4 whales, 5,000 seals; 1881 – 14 whales; 1886 – 1 large whale; 1898 – 5 whales, 23 walrus, 4 seals, 13 bears (one alive), 72 tons oil, 4.5 tons baleen (estimated value £7,000).

Notes: Before she came to Dundee, Captain David Gray of Peterhead was her master. In 1886 *Eclipse* caught what was supposed to be the largest whale ever recorded in the Arctic, with a 22 foot long lower jaw. In 1900 she carried Dr Leonard Kamm back from the Arctic; he was an explorer who had overwintered on Ellesmere Island.

In 1902 *Eclipse* ran aground near Disco Island on the west coast of Greenland but was repaired at Holsteinborg; later that year she helped rescue the crew of *Nova Zembla*. In 1909 she was sold to a Norwegian company, Fangstaktieselsk Saelen of Christiania, and later to Russia, where she remained until at least 1936 under the name *Lomonessov*.

Emma

When and where built: 1809 at Calcutta.

Weight: As a steamship, gross tonnage 404.61, registered tonnage 306.72.

Description: *Emma* was originally a sailing vessel. She was 109 feet 8 inches by 31 feet 6 inches by 18 feet 6½ inches. Three-masted and barque-rigged, she was square sterned and carvel-built with wooden framework and a female bust figurehead. However, an engine was added in 1864.

Engine: *Emma*'s engine room was 21 feet 1½ inches long. Gourlays of Dundee fitted two engines with a combined horse power of 50.

Known masters in Dundee fleet: 1863 Captain Nicoll; 1864 Captain Gravill

Known owners in Dundee fleet: 1863 George Gilroy, Robert Gilroy and Alexander Gilroy, merchants

Registered in Dundee: 1863–64

Best catches: 1863 – 1 whale, 2 tons blubber; 11 cwt whale fins; 1864 – 350 seals

Notes: Captain Nicoll of the whaling ship *Tay* travelled to Hull with a crew to bring *Emma* to Dundee in January 1863. On voyage in the Davis Straits she lost one man, William Gray, but rescued four boats filled with men from the Aberdeen whaling ship *Pacific*. *Emma* had an engine fitted for 1864 season but she was lost in April, thankfully with no casualties.

Erik

When and where built: Launched 12 January 1865, built by Alexander Stephen and Sons, Marine Parade, Dundee.

Weight: 650 tons (Ingram says 533 tons gross, 412 tons net)

Description: Screw sailer, her statistics were: 158 feet 3 inches long by 19 feet 6 inches in breadth by 19 feet 6 inches deep

Engine: *Erik's* engines were fitted by Gourlay Brothers of Dundee. They were compound, 2 cylinders, 23 and 44 inches in diameter, with 24-inch stroke and 80 horsepower.

Known masters in Dundee fleet: 1866–69 Captain Jones; 1870–82 Captain John. B. Walker

Known owners in Dundee fleet: Anthony Gibb and Sons of London, but managed by David Bruce.

In Dundee Registry: *Erik* sailed from Dundee from 1866 to 1883 but she never seemed to have Dundee owners.

Best catches: 1869 – 8,300 seals, 80 tons seal oil; 1870 – 17 whales, 190 tons whale oil, 11 tons bone, 9,570 seals, 110 tons seal oil; 1871 – 21 whales, 210 tons oil, 10 tons baleen, 3,350 seals

Notes: Named after Erik the Red, discoverer of Greenland, *Erik* seems to have had the reputation of a lucky ship.[2] In May 1871 she was voyaging to Greenland and rescued the crew of the Danish barque *Frederick VII of Rome*. *Erik* dragged the survivors on board by ropes and carried them to the Danish settlement of Lively on Disco Island, Greenland. The Danish government awarded Captain John Walker with a pair of binoculars in gratitude. The *specktioneer* Peter Ramsay died on board in 1874; he was aged around seventy and had sailed under Captain Walker for 17 years; the Greenlandmen could really love their job. In 1876 *Erik* rescued the crew of the American exploration ship *Polaris* in the Arctic but in 1883 she left the Dundee Register and was sold to Peterhead owners for £10,200.
Later sold to Newfoundland owners, *Erik* became a supply vessel for Peary's exploration expedition, was transferred to the Hudson Bay Company and probably also used on the Grand Banks seal fishery. She collided with *Aurora* in 1908. She was finally sunk by the submarine U-156 in August 1918, with the German crew boarding her and laying explosives.

Esquimaux

When and where built: 1865 by Alexander Stephens and Sons, Dundee

Weight: After 1866 592.60 tons gross, less engine weight 126.85 tons, registered tonnage 465.75.

Description: Wooden built, *Esquimaux* was designed to be fitted with a screw. She had one deck and three masts, with a scroll figurehead and was 160 feet long by 30 feet broad with a depth of 19 feet 6 inches. She was altered in January 1879 when a forecastle was added. It is possible she was originally ship rigged but altered to a barque in 1883.[3]

Engines: two engines with 70 horse power in an engine room 25.3 feet long

Known masters in Dundee fleet: 1866–79 Captain Charles Yule; 1880–82 Captain John Edwards; 1883–89 Captain William Milne; 1892–95 Captain Jeffrey Phillips; 1896–97 Captain Adams; 1900 Captain Harry McKay.

Known owners in Dundee fleet: 1865 Alexander Stephen and William Stephen were joint owners but they transferred some shares next year; 1867 Dundee Seal and Whale Fishing Company; 1895 Dundee Arctic Fisheries Company Limited. From February 1876, David Bruce was manager.

In Dundee Registry: 1865–1900

Best catches: 1871: 16 whales, 200 tons oil, 13 tons baleen, 14,300 seals; 1873: 19 whales, 130 tons whale oil, six tons baleen, 9,840 seals, 110 tons seal oil; 1891: [Newfoundland] 4 whales, 135 tons oil, 2.5 ton baleen, 20,600 seals

Notes: *Esquimaux*'s maiden voyage was as a merchant vessel to Archangel, but she was soon adapted to be a whaling ship. In 1895 bad weather drove her ashore at Disco in the Davis Straits and two years later there were 43 stowaways out of a Newfoundland sealing crew of 375. That same year she also steamed through a shoal of seals seventy miles in extent, but the weather was so poor she only managed to capture 2,000. There was a bitter tragedy in 1884 when a bottlenose whale dragged a man overboard. His name was Alan Smith and his father had been a crewman in the same ship and had drowned in the same manner.[4]

In 1898 *Esquimaux* was sold to Liverpool owners for £1,800, but was fitted out at the Dundee Shipbuilding Company as a yacht. In April 1899 she was sold to the USA and again refitted in Dundee, this time for an Arctic expedition. There were 20 stowaways on board but they were discovered before she left the Tay. *Esquimaux* was renamed *America*. Used for a Swedish expedition to Greenland in 1900, the following year she took part in an abortive North Pole expedition with the American William Ziegler. The explorers argued and *America* was wrecked in Franz Josef Land in 1903. *Terra Nova* rescued the survivors in 1905.

Estridge

When and where built: 1777 at Shorehouse in Sussex

Weight: 316 68/94 tons (Ingram says 312 tons)

Description: *Estridge* was a three-masted, two-decked vessel, ship-rigged with a standing bowsprit. (Ingram says she was a schooner.) She was carvel-built and square sterned with no figurehead. Her measurements were 98 feet by 27 feet 5 inches and she was 5 foot 8 inches between decks.

Known masters in Dundee fleet: 1800–02, 1805–07 Robert Webster; 1808–12 Adam Christopher; 1815–16 John Binnie; 1818 Robert Coupar or George Deuchars; 1819–25 George Deuchars

Known owners in Dundee fleet: 1809 David Ramsay; in 1810 David Jobson was one of the owners and in 1824, John Hume was mentioned. All presumably had shares in the Tay Whale Fishing Company, who owned *Estridge*.

In Dundee Registry: at least 1800 until 1825

Best catches: 1802 – 7 whales; 1810 – 12.5 whales; 1821 – 18 whales, 210 tons oil; 1823 – 28 whales, 193 tons oil

Notes: *Estridge* had a reported crew of 40 in 1800 and 1801, but 50 in 1824. When she applied for the whaling bounty in 1807 the customs collectors found various discrepancies in her logbook, such as failing to make observations when she found a dead whale off Cape Elizabeth. Such irregularities were sometimes used as an excuse not to pay the Bounty. In 1809 *Estridge* also worked as a cargo ship sailing to New Brunswick, possibly for timber.

In 1823 the Dundee customs records mention *Estridge* was allowed two puncheons of British plantation rum with her stores, which appears quite normal for the period. The following year she was mentioned in the Police Courts, when two young boys broke into her cabin when she was in Dundee harbour; they were caught and sent to jail for four days on bread and water. *Estridge* was lost in May 1825, but her crew was saved.

Fairy

When and where built: 1801 at Thorn, Yorkshire

Weight: 247 67/94 in 1824, 290 tons *c.*1837

Description: *Fairy* had two decks and three masts. She was ship rigged with a standing bowsprit, but in March 1827 she was altered to barque-rigged. As with most British vessels of the period, she was carvel-built and square sterned, and had no figurehead. Her statistics were: 95 feet 6 inches in length, 24 feet 10 inches beam, while her height between decks was 5 feet 6 inches.

Known masters in Dundee fleet: 1818 John Fyffe; 1820–25 William Thoms; 1826–32 John Welch; 1833 David Ritchie; 1837 Captain Ritchie; 1838 David Davidson; 1839–40 David Thoms; 1840 George Peters to March 1841; 1841 John Nicoll; 1842 Buttars; 1843–45 Captain Davidson; 1847–49 Captain Kerr; 1856 Captain Taylor; 1857 Captain Abernethy.

Known owners in Dundee fleet: 1818 Andrew How; 1824 James Soot; 1826 New Whale Fishing Company (presumably James Soot was involved with the New Whale Fishing Company); 1840 Fairy Whale Fishing Company; 1842 New Whale Fishing Company of Dundee (George Fyffe, shipowner seems to have been the major shareholder).

Registered in Dundee: at least 1818 to 1849

Best catches: 1823 – 18 whales, 150 tons oil; 1827 – 19 whales; 1832 – 20 whales, 170 tuns oil, 10 tons baleen; 1847 – 7 whales, 90 tuns oil, 5,500 seals

Notes: *Fairy* was stranded at Unst in Shetland in 1819 and bought for the whaling. She had a crew of 46 in 1824, a year in which she was allowed three puncheons of rum in her stores. In spring 1834 she sailed to Quebec for timber and to Archangel in the autumn. In 1840 she was again acting as a general cargo vessel, sailing to Memel after the whaling season had finished. The following year she was valued at £1,500 when her owners tried to sell her; that year she carried a parcel of emigrants from Cromarty to Quebec, with a return cargo of timber. In 1842 *Fairy* was whaling again.

There was a mutiny that year when she had an inexperienced master named John Buttars, and her crew refused to go into the ice without sufficient stores. *Fairy* returned to Dundee. The crew were landed without wages or their clothes, and had to stay the night in the police station. That was not uncommon in the nineteenth century. Peter Twatt, one of the Shetland men, took the whaling company to court for his wages. When he won his case and was awarded £7 5s 2d, others followed suit. Next year Captain Davidson took over command of *Fairy*. In 1845 *Fairy* lost three of her crew. Four years later *Fairy* was advertised for sale at £800, a price that included boats, stores and oil casks. For a while she sailed for the Arctic under English owners, but was sold to Peterhead and was finally lost in 1860.

Friendship

When and where built: Built before 1803, possibly at Hamburg but more likely in one of the Dutch colonies; her original name was possibly Zeeluft (Sea Breeze).

Weight: 304 45/94 tons.

Description: *Friendship* had two decks and three masts. She was ship rigged with a standing bowsprit; square sterned and carvel-built with no figure head. Her vital statistics were: length: 102 feet, 7 inches; breadth 26 feet 8 inches and height between decks 6 feet 2 inches.

Known masters in Dundee fleet: 1810–24 James Ireland (died on board); 1825 James Ireland, Jnr; 1826–31 James Chapman; 1832–34 David [?] Davidson; 1837 Captain Sturrock; 1839–40 Captain Davidson

Known owners in Dundee fleet: 1818 David Jobson (possibly as a partner in the Friendship Whale Fishing Company); 1824–26: David Jobson senior; 1824 Friendship Whale Fishing Company; 1829 Dorothy Whale Fishing Company

In Dundee Registry: from at least 1810 to 1840

Best catches: 1821 – 17 whales, 160 tons oil, 9 tons baleen; 1832 – 29 whales, 185 tons oil and 10 tons baleen; 1833 – 29 whales, 197 tons oil and 11 tons baleen; 1838 – 18 whales, 12 tons oil and 8 tons baleen; 1840 – 2,467 seals, 22 tons oil

Notes: When *Friendship* was sailing under enemy colours, HMS *Chiffone* captured her and brought her into Leith. She was sold as a prize of war. *Friendship* became what was known as a 'prize made free'. For a while she had London owners, but in 1809 they sold their shares to David Ouchter-lony of Dundee, with each one-eighth share valued at £475. The following year *Friendship* was granted a licence to carry arms in case of attack by the French. A new foremast was also fitted that year. She was whaling from Dundee from 1810, but also seems to have been trading to Charleston, South Carolina. In 1815 Captain Ireland took her to Petersburgh for flax. Seven years later, when the rest of the fleet returned, she lingered on the whaling grounds and captured a further eight whales. In 1825 Captain Ireland died on board and his son, the mate, brought *Friendship* back to the Tay. On 26 March 1830, *Friendship* was in Dundee Roads and a boat capsized, tipping five men into the Tay. The men seem to have been drunk at the time, but all were rescued. *Friendship* was sold to Newcastle owners that year, with an asking price of £800.

Grandtully

When and where built: British built, sometime before 1757

Weight: 249 tons

Known masters in Dundee fleet: 1757 Captain McCur or Maceur?; 1761–62 William Cheyne; c 1780 Robert Mawer

In Dundee Registry: at least 1757 to around 1780

Notes: Known to have sailed for Greenland in 1757 and 1762.

Heroine

When and where built: 1831 by John Calman of Dundee

Weight: 387 12/94 tons

Description: *Heroine* was carvel-built with one deck; she was square sterned with three masts and a standing bowsprit. She had no galleries but a figure-head of a female bust. She was 105 feet 9 inches in length by 29 feet 6 inches in breadth and 19 feet 6 inches in depth to the foot of her hold.

Known masters in Dundee fleet: 1831 Captain Lamb; 1832 John Noval Smart; 1834–37 John Welch; 1853–55 Captain David Sturrock; 1856–57 Captain George Deuchars

Known owners in Dundee fleet: 1831 John Calman, then the Dundee Banking Company; 1832 Dundee New Whaling Company; December 1837 William Duthie of Aberdeen; 1851 Dundee and Union Whale Fishing Company.

Registered in Dundee: 1831–37; 1853–58

Best catches: 1833 – 36 whales, 240 tons oil; 1856 – 19 whales, 185 tons oil

Notes: *Heroine* was built as a cargo vessel and possibly as a speculative venture rather than to a contract. She seems to have made a single voyage to Canada before she was strengthened for Arctic whaling. She had two spells in Dundee ownership with a period when she worked from Aberdeen. While in Aberdeen, *Heroine* was used for the Australian emigration trade. In 1853 she came back to Dundee to replace the elderly *Horn*, which had been lost off Fife. While outward bound to the whaling grounds in 1854, Captain David Sturrock was drowned and the mate, Mr Swankie, took command. The same wave that swept Captain Sturrock overboard also mortally injured his nephew, James Sturrock. In July 1858 she was sheltering in an ice dock which the crew had carved by means of the huge ice saws but the ice collapsed. The crew scrambled to save what they could before they escaped. The crew on *Eclipse* of Peterhead, who shared the same dock, lost everything. There were no casualties and the crew was rescued by a Danish vessel.

Horn

When and where built: 1783 in Sunderland

Weight: In August 1810 was 291 and twenty one ninety-fourths of a ton, but the customs records in Dundee stated she was to 'proceed in a short time to Hull in order to be lengthened'.

Description: *Horn* was two-decked, three-masted and ship-rigged. In common with most British ships of the period, she had a square stern and was carvel-built with a standing bowsprit and no figurehead. The customs records give her as 168 feet 7 inches long by 28 feet 10 inches broad and a height of 6 feet 7 inches between decks, presumably after she was lengthened in Hull.

Known masters in Dundee fleet: 1806–20 William Valentine; 1821–29 William Jeffers; 1830–34 Captain (John?) Stevenson; 1835 David Ramsay (according to customs records) 1835–1838 Captain Thomas; 1843–52 Captain D. Sturrock

Known owners in Dundee fleet: 1806 Dundee Whale Fishing Company; 1809, 1818 Walter Newall; 1829 Dundee Whale Fishing Company; 1842–52 Dundee and Union Whale Fishing Company

Registered in Dundee: approximately 1806 until 1852

Best catches: 1820 – 17 whales, 236 tons oil, 14 tons baleen; 1823 – 33 whales, 238 tons oil, 14 tons baleen; 1827 – 18 whales, 171 tons oil; 1832 – 25 whales, 226 tons oil, 11 tons baleen; 1845 – 33 whales, 225 tons oil, 14 tons baleen; 1849 – 19 whales, 170 tons oil

Notes: When *Horn* was built in Sunderland, she was named after her owner, Thomas Horn, a local grocer. She was first used as a whaling ship in 1787 with owners from north east England. In 1794 she was sold to a London owner. *Horn* came to Dundee in 1809 and was licensed to carry arms during the Napoleonic Wars. In 1830, when much of the British whaling fleet was destroyed, she rescued the crew of a stricken whaling ship, squeezing 90 more men. on board. *Horn* was lengthened in 1839 and by 1852 she was the second oldest ship in the Dundee fleet; she captured her last whale on 9 October that year and shortly afterward returned to Scotland.

On 5 November *Horn* was off the Tay in a night of poor visibility when Captain Sturrock apparently thought he was four miles off shore. *Horn* struck the land between Kingsbarns and Boarhills in Fife at two in the morning in an ebb tide. Sturrock ordered the crew to ready for abandonment. One seaman swam ashore with a line, and the surgeon landed and obtained a gig from the local farmer. By six in the morning the crew had landed ashore with no casualties. Some of the crew took the time to rescue some of the animals on board the ship – sheep, hens, a goat and two cats – but *Horn* was too badly damaged to sail again.

Intrepid

When and where built: Launched 5 November 1851, built by Francis Robertson of Peterhead.

Weight: 425.57 tons gross, registered tonnage 326.34

Description: *Intrepid* was carvel-built with a square stern, two decks and no gallery. She was barque-rigged with a standing bowsprit and a female figurehead. Her statistics were: length 122 feet 9 inches; breadth 30 feet 2½ inches and depth of hold, 9 feet.

Engines: It is unknown when *Intrepid* was first converted from sail to auxiliary steam, but it was before April 1866, when the Dundee *Courier* termed her 'the steam whaler *Intrepid*'. Gourlay Brothers of Dundee fitted new engines in 1874; a compound two cylinder, 23 and 24 inch diameter, engine with 22-inch stroke engines creating 70 horsepower. Her engine room was 21 feet long.

Known masters in Dundee fleet: 1866 Alexander Deuchars; 1869 Captain Allan; 1872/1874/ 1875–76 Captain Soutar; 1877–80 Captain Nicoll; 1881–83 Robert Davidson; 1885 Robert Davidson

Known owners in Dundee fleet: February 1866 George Welch was the sole owner, but next month he sold some shares to George Whitton and John Sharp. He remained the manager while the vessel was owned by the Tay Whale Fishing Company.

Registered in Dundee: 1866–85

Best catches: 1868 – 15 whales, 115 tons oil; 1871 – 24 whales, 160 tons oil, 9 tons bone; 1872 – 16 whales, 176 tons oil, 3,000 seals, 38 tons seal oil,full ship; 1874 – 24 whales, 185 tons whale oil, 10 tons baleen, 2,208 seals, 25 tons seal oil

Notes: The Tay Whale Fishing Company of Dundee owned *Intrepid* from 1866. In 1883 there was a minor mutiny when *Intrepid* called at Reykjavik to recoal. Captain Davidson went ashore to drop off a sick seaman. The two men who had rowed him ashore got drunk and requested permission to return. Davidson refused and the ensuing confrontation only ended when the captain threatened to put the mutineers in irons. The mutineers later stole a boat and rowed ashore anyway, followed by some others. When the second mate attempted to bring them back, the men stoned him. Five men returned on board when *Intrepid* sounded the steam whistle to say they were leaving; three were left behind. The men refused to accept their blame in this situation and took the whaling company to court to refund the cost of their passage home to Scotland.

In 1885 *Intrepid* ran aground at the entrance to Bressay Sound in Shetland and leaked for the duration of her voyage. She was crushed by ice off Greenland on 21 July that year and two Norwegian vessels rescued the crew.

Jan Mayen (I)

When and where built: 1873 at Bremerhaven

Weight: Gross tonnage 468.97, registered tonnage 318.90

Description: A carvel-built steam ship with three masts, *Jan Mayen* was barque-rigged. She had a round stern, no gallery and a scroll head. Her measurements were: 138 feet 9½ inches by 29 feet 5 inches.

Engines: *Jan Mayen's* engine room was 12 feet 5 inches. She had two compound surface condensing, direct acting engines, made by Hansa of Rostock in 1873. The cylinders were 23½ inches and 39 inches, with a length of stroke of 2 feet 3 inches and combined horsepower of 90.

Known masters in Dundee fleet: 1875–82 Captain Deuchars but the *Courier* said Captain Salmond in 1882; 1883 Captain Guy; 1884–85 Captain Deuchars

Known owners in Dundee fleet: 1875 William Ogilvie Taylor and James Luke; in March that year shares were transferred to the Dundee Polar Fishing Company with William Ogilvie Taylor as managing owner; Robert Valentine Scroggie became manager in June 1885.

Registered in Dundee: 1875–86

Best catches: 1875 – 7 whales, 75 tons oil, 3 tons baleen, 10 seals; 1876 – 6 whales, 70 tons whale oil, 3 ton baleen, 5,587 seals, 65 tons seal oil; 1878 – 2 whales, 42 tons oil, 2 tons baleen, 7,800 seals, 78 tons oil; 1880 – 14 whales, 108 tons whale oil, 5 tons baleen, 3,700 seals, 50 tons seal oil

Notes: *Jan Mayen* was crushed by ice in 1886 at Cape Atholl, Davis Straits.

Jan Mayen (II)

When and where built: Launched 29 August 1859 at the yard of Francis Robertson, Peterhead.

Weight: Gross tonnage 337.34, registered tonnage 233.42

Description: *Jan Mayen* was a screw steamer with one and a half decks. She was carvel-built, barque-rigged with a square stern, a scroll head and no galleries. Her statistics were: 119 feet by 29 feet 2½ inches by 17 feet 5 inches depth in her hold.

Engine: *Jan Mayen's* engine room was 23 feet 4 inches long. She had two engines, direct acting condensing, with 20 inch diameter cylinders, 24-inch stroke and 40 horse power. They were built in 1867 by John Scott of Inverkeithing.

Known masters in Dundee fleet: 1878–81 William Salmond.

Known owners in Dundee fleet: 1878 George Thomson the younger of Pitmedden; in December 1878 George Welch bought 56 shares. He sold the shares in small packets to a variety of people and became managing owner.

Registered in Dundee: 1878–82

Best catches: 1878 – 4,600 seals, 100 tons oil; 1880 – 4,400 seals, 100 tons seal oil

Notes: *Jan Mayen* was abandoned off the Greenland coast on 21 April 1882.

Jane

When and where built: 1783

Weight: 279 33/94 tons

Known masters in Dundee fleet: 1805–09 William Christopher

Known owners in Dundee fleet: 1809 John Dunn

Registered in Dundee: from at least 1795 until 1809

Best catches: 1805 – 7 whales, 100 casks oil; 1806 – 10 whales, 140 casks oil; 1807 – 10 whales

Notes: *Jane* was licensed to carry arms in 1809, during the Napoleonic Wars. When she was wrecked on the Banks of Tay in 1810, her wreckage and sundry items of material from the ship was put up for sale.

Jumna

When and where built: 1853 by Thomas and John Brocklebank, at Bransty, Whitehaven, England

Weight: Gross tonnage 363.05, net registered tonnage 280.07

Description: *Jumna* was a three-masted, ship-rigged vessel with a square stern. She was carvel-built with no gallery and a wooden framework. Her statistics were: 107 feet 6 inches in length by 26 feet breadth and 18 feet 10 ¼ inches in depth.

Engines: The Dundee Register of Shipping states *Jumna* was converted to steam in 1857. She had a 19 foot long engine room with two 18 horse power engines. However, the Dundee *Courier* states that Gourlay Brothers of Dundee gave her two engines of 'about 35 horse power' in 1863.

Known masters in Dundee fleet: 1857–58 Captain A. Deuchars; 1859 Captain Hay; 1861 Alexander Deuchars; 1863 Captain Deuchars

Known owners in Dundee fleet: 1856 Tay Whale Fishing Company; 1859 Tay Whale Fishing Company

Registered in Dundee: 1856–63

Best catches: 1857 – 4 whales, 58 tons oil, 3.5 tons baleen; 1860 – 3 whales, 40 tons oil; 1861 – 19 whales

Notes: She came to Dundee in 1856 and was converted to steam. In 1863 ice crushed her in Melville Bay.

Mary Ann

When and where built: 1784

Weight: 292 79/94 tons

Known masters in Dundee fleet: 1803 William Deuchars; 1805–12 William Deuchars; 1814–19 William Deuchars

Known owners in Dundee fleet: 1806 Dundee Whale Fishing Company; in 1809 Walter Newall was the ship's owner or 'husband'.

Registered in Dundee: 1803–19

Best catches: 1804 – full ship, all casks filled and two whales carried on deck, her pumps were also choked with oil; 1808 – 9 whales, 140 butts oil,full ship; 1810 – 14 whales, full ship; 1812 – 13 whales, 170 butts oil

Notes: After she returned from the whaling in 1809, *Mary Ann* sailed to Charlottetown in North America, presumably for timber; in February 1811 *Mary Ann* was allowed to carry arms. In 1817 she was up for sale. She was crushed by the ice in July 1819. There is a Mary Ann Lane near Seagate in Dundee, where the boiling yard for this ship was once situated.

Maud

When and where built: 1865 by Thomas Turnbull and Sons, Whitby.

Weight: 298 tons gross

Description: When first built, *Maud* was a sailing vessel. She had a deck and a break deck, three masts and was barque-rigged. Carvel-built, she had an elliptic stern with no galleries and a shield figurehead. Her statistics were: 116 feet 8 inches by 25 feet by 15 feet 9½ inches. She was converted to steam in March 1886.

Engine: *Maud* had a 35-foot engine room. She had two inverted compound engines, 15 and 27 inch diameter cylinders with 18-inch stroke and a combined 35 horsepower, built by Whyte & Cooper of Dundee.

Known masters in Dundee fleet: 1884 Watson or James Bannerman; 1886–90 William Adams; 1892 Milne

Known owners in Dundee fleet: 1884 Captain Watson; 1884–90 William Adams; 1891–92 Andrew Scott

Registered in Dundee: 1883–92

Best catches: 1884 – 56 bottlenose whales, 70 tons oil; 1885 – 1,400 seals, 45 tons seal oil, 4 bottlenose whales, 36 walrus; 1886 – 100 seals, 35 tons oil, 6 white whales, 220 walrus, 23 bears, 27 narwhal; 1887 – 60 tons oil, 1.5 tons baleen

Notes: In 1883 Captain Adams bought *Maud* from William McCulloch of Inverkeithing and converted her to a steam whaling ship. He sent her north in 1884 under Captain Watson but from 1886 to 1890 he commanded her in person. She was wrecked in October 1892 in Coutt's Inlet, Davis Strait.

Mazinthien

When and where built: 1850 in Merrimachi, New Brunswick, Canada

Weight: Gross tonnage 397.10: registered tonnage 307.91

Description: *Mazinthien* had one-and-a-half decks. She was three-masted and square-rigged, carvel-built with a square stern, with no galleries. She was 130 feet by 28 feet by 16 feet 1½ inches depth.

Engines: *Mazinthien* had a 24-foot-long engine room with two 40 horse power engines built by Mitchell and Sons of Peterhead. The engines were condensing with cylinders of 1 foot 8 inches, 2-stroke.

Known masters in Dundee fleet: 1878 William Loffley; 1879–82 Captain Soutar

Known owners in Dundee fleet: 1878 William Croudace, but he sold various shares in February of that year.

Registered in Dundee: Although *Mazinthien* sailed from Dundee from 1874, she was not officially transferred from Peterhead until 1878. No. 15934

Best catches: 1879 – 5,800 seals, 95 tons seal oil; 1880 – 10 whales, 50 tons whale oil, 2 tons baleen; 1882 – 11 whales, 95 tons whale oil, 4 tons baleen

Notes: Peterhead owners sold *Mazinthien* to W. S. Croudace of Dundee in 1878 for a reported £3,850. She was wrecked in Peterhead Bay on 17 March 1883.

Morning

When and where built: 1871 at Tonsberg, Norway with the name *Morgenen*

Weight: 444.45 tons gross, 226.87 tons net

Description: *Morning* was a steam ship, single screwed, with three masts. She was barque-rigged with an elliptical stern, carvel-built with a billet head, flush decks and no bulkheads. Her statistics were: 140 feet by 31 feet 5 inches by 16 feet 7 inches.

Engines: *Morning's* engine room was 29 feet 1½ inches long. She had one compound, surface condensing engine with two iron boilers with 70 pounds pressure. The cylinders were 23 feet 4 inches and 46 feet 4 inches; 27-inch stroke 85 nominal horse power (NHP) and 400 indicated horse power (IHP). Nylands of Christiania made both engine and boilers.

Known masters in Dundee fleet: 1905–14 Captain Adams; 1914–15 Captain Fairweather; 1915 Captain Smith

Known owners in Dundee fleet: Robert Kinnes managed *Morning* in 1902, by 1906 he owned her, and remained as managing owner during her time in Dundee. As usual, there were a number of shareholders who held one or more shares of the vessel but even when the British government commandeered her during the First World War, Kinnes remained her official owner.

Registered in Dundee: 1905–14

Best catches: 1905 – 3 whales, 9 white whales, 42 walrus, 12 seals, 24 bears, 46 tons oil, 2.25 tons baleen (Davis Straits); 1908 – 2 whales, 218 white whales, 68 walrus, 45 seals, 37 bears, 71 tons oil, 1.75 tons baleen (Davis Straits); 1910 – 7 whales, 3 walrus, 12 seals, 37 bears, 90 tons oil, 1.25 tons baleen (Jones Sound)

Notes: The famous Svend Foyn of Tonsberg, Norway, owned *Morning* from 1871 to 1902, at which date the British Government bought her to help in the *Discovery* Relief Expedition. Foyn was the inventor of an improved harpoon gun, whose design lasted until the demise of Scottish whaling. *Morning* was an Antarctic relief ship from 1902 until 1904. In 1905 Robert Kinnes of Dundee bought her and in 1906 the lecturer and photographer Sandon Perkins sailed on her and took many images, which can be seen in the collection of Dundee Museum. In 1907 *Morning* rescued the crew of the Dundee whaling ship *Windward*, wrecked on the Carey Islands. *Morning* was also in the 1911 British Antarctic Expedition to search for *Discovery*, but in December 1915 she foundered with most of her crew while carrying arms to Russia. Captain Smith and the second mate survived.

Narwhal

When and where built: 1859 by Alexander Stephen & Sons, Dundee

Weight: 532.73 tons gross, registered tonnage for steamer as 362.26 [The *Post Office Directory* for 1869 gives her weight as 434 tons]

Description: *Narwhal* was a screw steamer with two decks and three masts. She was carvel-built and ship rigged with a square stern, no galleries and an unusual fish head for a figurehead.

Engines: *Narwhal* had two engines; built by Gourlay Brothers of Dundee: inverted cylinders, direct acting compound and surfacing condensing. The cylinders were 23 and 44 inches in diameter with a 2-foot stroke creating 75 horsepower.

Known masters while in Dundee register: 1859–61 George Deuchars; 1863 George Deuchars; 1864 Captain Wells; 1865 Captain Sturrock; 1866 James Sturrock; 1867 Alexander Deuchars; 1868 George Deuchars; 1870–82 John McLennan; 1883–84 Jeffrey Phillips

Known owners while in Dundee register: When first registered a group of Dundee merchants owned *Narwhal*: James Soot, Robert McGavin, Thomas Smith, William Gibson and Alexander Stephen, shipbuilder, but David Bruce managed her. From April 1867 the Dundee Seal and Whale Fishing Company were owners, still with David Bruce as Manager.

Registered in Dundee: 1859–84

Best catches: 1861 – 30 whales, 220 tons oil, 3.3 tons baleen; 1870 – 14,000 seals, 140 tons seal oil; 1871 – 8 whales, 80 tons oil, 4.5 tons baleen, 5,700 seals; 1878 – 1 whale, 18 tons oil, 1 ton baleen, 17,000 seals, 200 tons oil; 1879 – 7 whales, 60 tons oil, 3 tons baleen, 8,500 seals, 9.5 tons seal oil; 1880 – 6 whales, 55 tons whale oil, 3 tons baleen, 13,769 seals, 143 tons seal oil; 1881 – 1 whale, 15 tons oil, 0.75 tons baleen, 31,557 seals

Notes: Captain Penny of Aberdeen is alleged to have supervised the construction of what was to be the forerunner of many successful steam whaling ships. In her first trip in 1859, *Narwhal* caught 3,000 seals in two days, and despite losing part of her stem in the ice, helped rescue the crew of the steel whaling ship *Empress of India*. In that same eventful year a fire on board caused £1,000 of damage and prevented her sailing to the Davis Straits whaling. The following year she rescued 65 men from the Hull whaling ship *Chase* in Pond's Bay, now Pond Inlet, Baffin Island. In 1872 Surgeon McDonald successfully dealt with a smallpox outbreak on board but, not surprisingly,

Narwhal was not permitted to disembark her crew at Dundee until they had been officially examined and the ship cleared from quarantine.

In 1880 *Narwhal* had 12,000 captured seals on board when she became icebound in Conception Bay on the northeast coast of Newfoundland. Despite being there for some weeks, she escaped without serious damage. Three years later, there was a police case when Alexander McKenzie, the steward, was caught smuggling duty free tobacco to Dundee. *Narwhal* was finally abandoned when damaged by ice off Cape Searle, Davis Straits in September 1884. She sank shortly after.

Nova Zembla

When and where built: 1873 by Wencke of Bremerhaven

Weight: Gross tonnage 375.46, registered tonnage 255.31

Description: *Nova Zembla* was a one-decked, three-masted screw steamer with a barque rig and a round stern. She was carvel-built with a scroll head and no gallery. Her statistics were 140 feet 8½ inches by 27 feet 9 inches by 15 feet 8½ inches in depth.

Engines: With an engine room 29.4 feet long, *Nova Zembla* had a single compound engine built by Hansa Company of Rostock. The engine could create 58.5 horsepower and had 21 and 36 inch cylinders with a 23-inch stroke.

Known masters in Dundee fleet: 1875–77 William Loffley; 1878–82 Captain Guy; 1883–85 Kilgour; 1886–87 William Allan; 1889Jeffrey Phillips; 1893–1900 Captain Guy

Known owners in Dundee fleet: 1875 Dundee Polar Fishing Co, managing owner William Ogilvie Taylor; 1883 manager was William Valentine Scroggie

Registered in Dundee: 1875–1902

Best catches: 1875 – 7 whales, 75 tons oil, 3 tons baleen, 65 seals; 1876 – 2 whales, 35 tons whale oil, 1.5 tons baleen, 11,300 seals, 132 tons seal oil; 1880 – 7 whales, 95 tons whale oil, 5 tons baleen, 2,000 seals, 26 tons seal oil; 1882 – 8 whales, 65 tons oil, 3 tons baleen, 9,800 seals, 125 tons seal oil; 1884 – 8 whales, 105 tons whale oil, 0.55 tons bone; 1898 – 75 tons oil, 530 white whales, 10 walrus, 4 bears; 1899 – 8 whales, 160 tons oil, 6 tons bone; 1900 – 2 whales, 12 walrus, 4 bears, 38.5 tons oil, 2 tons baleen; 1901 – 1 black whale, 418 white whales, 43 tons oil, 3 cwt baleen

 Notes: *Nova Zembla* was originally named *Novaya Semblya* but in 1875 the Board of Trade authorised a change of name. In 1895 she lost a Shetlander named William Lawrensen in the Davis Straits. She brought back a live polar bear that trip. She was abandoned sinking after striking a rock in Dexterity Fjord in September 1902. Captain Cooney had ordered the pumps manned, but water poured in faster than they could cope and the crew took to the boats. *Diana* and *Eclipse* took the crew home.

Ostrich

When and where built: before 1800

Description: Sailing ship

In Dundee Registry: *c.*1800

Best catches: 1800 – 9 whales, 50 butts blubber

Notes: Not much is known about this vessel, which made a brief appearance in 1800. It is entirely possible that the newspaper was mistaken about the name, and Ostrich is the same vessel as *Estridge.*

Our Queen

When and where built: 1860 in Liverpool

Weight: 461.57 tons gross, 424 tons net

Description: *Our Queen* was a single decked, three-masted vessel. She was barque-rigged with a round stern, carvel-built with a wooden framework and a female bust as a figurehead. Her statistics were: 136 feet long by 26 feet 6 inches broad.

Engines: *Our Queen* was built as a sailing ship, but in 1879 double acting compound engines were added. Gourlay Brothers of Dundee built the engines which had 23 and 24 inch cylinders and a 2-foot stroke. They totalled 80 horsepower.

Known masters in Dundee fleet: 1879 Alexander Fairweather

Known owners in Dundee fleet: June 1874 George Welch but many transactions of small numbers of shares after that date, including to James Yeaman MP. In March 1879 George Welch was appointed as Managing Owner.

Registered in Dundee: *c.*1874–79

Best catches: 1879: 14 whales, 120 ton whale oil, 6 tons baleen, 2,500 seals, and 36 tons seal oil

Notes: This vessel seems to have made no impact at all in Dundee and is barely remembered. She was built in Liverpool and transferred to Dundee in 1873 or 1874. In 1879 the Tay Shipbuilding Company converted her to a steam whaling ship. She had her trial trip in March that year. Despite wild weather, the voyage was a bit of a pleasure cruise, with some of the directors of the company on board to enjoy lunch and drinks as they cruised to St Andrews Bay and back. However the vessel had only a short life as a Dundee whaling ship. She made a successful sealing trip to the Greenland Sea, returned to Dundee and was refitted for the whaling. She picked up men at Lerwick and captured a good cargo of whales, but was crushed between two ice fields on 18 July 1879 in the opening of Admiralty Inlet, Lancaster Sound, Davis Straits. She sunk very quickly. The ice broke her in half and the crew hardly had time to scramble clear. As with so many ships that sank in the ice, there were no casualties.

Polar Star

When and where built: 1857 at Stephen & Forbes, Peterhead

Weight: registered tonnage 215.65

Description: *Polar Star* was a three-masted barque with a single deck and a shield for a figurehead. She was square sterned and carvel-built, while her statistics were: length: 104 feet 9 inches, breadth 24 feet 2 inches and depth 14 feet 7 inches.

Engines: *Polar Star* was built as a sailing vessel but engines were added at a later date.

Known masters in Dundee fleet: 1882–89 Captain Thomas Robertson; 1892–96 James Davidson; 1897 Captain Murray; 1898 Captain Davidson; 1899 Captain Robert Davidson

Known owners in Dundee fleet: 1882 privately owned but Robert Kinnes was the manager. He had originally bought the ship but sold many of the shares while retaining his position as managing owner. In 1889 Kinnes still owned 11 shares.

Registered in Dundee: 1881–99

Best catches: 1882: 67 bottle nose whales, 76 tons oil; 1884, 3,500 seals, 110 tons oil, 10 bottlenose whales;1885: 6 whales, 60 tons oil, 2 tons baleen, 4 bottlenose whales, 36 walrus; 1892: 440 seals, 6.5 tons oil; 1893, Antarctic, 2,000 seals; 1899: 130 walrus

Notes: The Tay Whale Fishing Company originally bought *Polar Star* from Peterhead in December 1881 after being laid up the previous year. She cost less than £520. She took part in the Dundee Antarctic Expedition of 1892 and subsequently worked in the Greenland Sea but was lost in the ice at Cumberland Gulf in 1899. *Active* rescued her crew.

Polynia

When and where built: Launched 9 February 1861 at Panmure Yard of Alexander Stephen and Sons, Dundee.

Weight: 472.33 gross tonnage; 358.96 tons net

Description: *Polynia* was a two-decked, three-masted and barque-rigged vessel. She was square sterned and carvel-rigged with no gallery, a wooden framework and a scroll head. Her statistics were: 146 feet 2½ inches by 29 feet by 18 feet 1 inch.

Engine: *Polynia's* engine room was 24.8 feet in length. Her engine was of 60 horse power according to the Register of Shipping, although the *Dundee Directory* for 1867 and 1869 claim the engine was of 70 horsepower.

Known masters in Dundee fleet: 1861 Captain Penny; 1864 Captain Gravill; 1865–67 Captain Nicoll; 1870–71 William Walker; 1874–80 Captain David Kilgour; 1881–82 Captain Yule; 1883–85 John B. Walker; 1886 Captain Burnett; 1888–90 Captain William Guy

Known owners in Dundee fleet: When she was first registered in Dundee, there were various owners but James Yeaman and William Stephen were majority shareholders. In 1861 James Yeaman was the manager. After a number of share transactions, in 1867 the Dundee Seal and Whale Fishing Company of East Whale Lane was the owner. This company continued to own the vessel, with David Bruce the manager from February 1876.

Registered in Dundee: 1861–91, No. 25491

Best catches: 1861:13 whales, 90 tons oil; 1864: 11,232 seals, 123 tons seal oil; 1865: 8 whales, 70 tons oil, 15,000 seals, 190 tons seal oil; 1873: 15 whales, 125 tons whale oil, 8 tons bone, 25 seals; 1874: 18 whales, 155 tons oil, 8 tons baleen, 2,254 seals, 25 tons seal oil; 1882: 11 whales, 110 tons oil, 5 tons baleen; 1884: 6 whales, 65 tons whale oil, 3 tons baleen, 1,000 seals; 1885: 6 whales, 60 tons seal oil, 2 tons baleen, 1 ton seal oil; 1886: 3 whales, 50 tons whale oil; 2.25 tons baleen, 12,080 seals; 1889: 19,350 seals, 195 tons oil

Notes: *Polynia* was another of those vessels that caught the imagination and is still remembered in Dundee. In 1862 she was beset in an area known as the Maiden Patch, presumably off Newfoundland or Labrador, as she rescued the crews of other vessels. Her propeller was damaged and she had to return to St John's in Newfoundland for repairs. In the 1864 hunting season she killed 22 polar bears, which was not her usual prey. In 1874 Captain Kilgour took her into Batty Bay in the Davis Straits for fresh water and the crew found material deposited by Captain Kennedy of *Prince Albert* in 1852. *Prince Albert* had been engaged in the search for the missing explorer Franklin. There was tragedy in the 1891 season when a huge wave struck *Polynia*, killing one man and injuring ten others and on 11 July that year *Polynia,* was crushed by ice in Lancaster Sound. Her crew abandoned and she sank not long afterward. The Dundee ships *Maud* and *Aurora* rescued her crew, some of whom arrived in Wick on the 3 October.

Princess Charlotte

When and where built: 1814 at South Shields, County Durham

Weight: 359 48/49 tons

Description: *Princess Charlotte* was a two-decked vessel with three masts. She was ship-rigged and square sterned with a standing bowsprit. Carvel-built, she had no galleries or figurehead. Her statistics were: 105 feet 4 inches by 28 feet 6 inches by 6 feet 3¼ inches height between decks.

Known masters in Dundee fleet: 1820–37 William Adamson; 1838–44 George Deuchars; 1845–56 Captain Alexander Deuchars

Known owners in Dundee fleet: *Princess Charlotte* was owned by the Tay Whale Fishing Company; when first registered, the three trustees were: David Brown, John Sime and John Hume.

Registered in Dundee: from at least 1820 until 1856

Best catches: 1821 – 27 whales, 210 tons oil; 1823 – 26 whales; 230 tons oil; 1827 – 21 whales, full; 1828 – 33 whales, full; 1838 – 23 whales, 270 tuns oil (total value £10,000)

Notes: *Princess Charlotte* is all but forgotten, but she had a career full of incident. On a Saturday evening in October 1829, *Princess Charlotte* had returned from the whaling and was lying inside Dundee harbour and near the entrance. A sloop, *Peggy,* came into harbour and collided with her, so *Peggy* lost her mast 3 feet above the deck. *Peggy's* rigging fell to the deck, knocking down Captain Paton, her master. Shortly after, a second sloop, *Prompt,* also collided with *Princess Charlotte* and lost her top gallant mast. There were two reasons for these accidents: *Princess Charlotte* had no lights to mark her position and Dundee dock was tidal and did not have enough water for her to berth properly.

In 1831 a man fell from the mainyard and died as *Princess Charlotte* sailed to the whaling ground. Of all the events in her life, the high point came in early 1837. The ice had been bad in the Davis Straits the previous year and six British whaling ships, including *Thomas* and *Advice* of Dundee, were trapped over the winter. Bowing to pressure from the whaling ports, the government offered a bounty of £300 if any ship left port before 5 February 1837 to rescue the trapped vessels; £500 to any vessel that actually gave assistance to the trapped ships; and £100 to any vessel that rescued them. Two Dundee vessels, *Horn* and *Princess Charlotte,* sailed in early March. *Thomas* had already sunk and the other vessels had eased free except for *Swan* of Hull.

The crew of *William and Ann* of Hull sighted *Swan* but refused a rescue, so Captain Adamson of *Princess Charlotte* organised a rescue that involved many other Dundee vessels and a massive amount of sawing through the ice. *Princess Charlotte* earned £700 salvage and £500 government award.

Next year, 1838, *Princess Charlotte*'s catch was one of the largest then landed in Dundee, being bested only by *Dorothy* in 1828 and 1829. Four years later, *Princess Charlotte* was en route to the whaling grounds when she began to leak and had to sail back to Dundee for repairs. In 1847 she came back with five of her crew riddled with scurvy and others shaking with lack of food and fatigue; it had been an abnormally long season and British merchant ships were not obliged to carry antiscorbutics until after the 1854 Merchant Shipping Act. *Princess Charlotte* was finally crushed between two ice floes and lost in Melville Bay on 14 June 1859 with no casualties. The ship sank in 15 minutes and the master scrambled down from the crow's nest just as she went down with all her sails still set.

The crew worked for 18 hours solid to haul her hull into a suitable position for Captain Deuchars to blast it open to retrieve their clothes. They also broke open the sprit locker, rescued 63 gallons of rum and spent the next 30 hours drinking. After that there was a general fight with some of the crew of *Truelove* of Hull, who had joined in the festivities. It was a sad, but perhaps fitting, end for a splendid ship.

Problem

When and where built: 1899 at Yarmouth

Weight: 66 tons

Description: Possibly a smack but the Ingram records call her a ketch.

Known masters in Dundee fleet: 1901 Captain Ogsten

Known owners in Dundee fleet: Robert Kinnes

Notes: *Problem* was used to carry stores from Dundee to the shore stations in the Arctic. She had a short career. In 1901 she sailed from Dundee with stores for Southampton Island but hit bad weather in the North Atlantic. *Problem* lost her sails and when the crew had been weeks at the pumps, the tanker *Oilfield* rescued them. The smack was abandoned to the waves on 13 September 1901.

Queen Bess

When and where built: 1886

Weight: 72 tons

Description: Sailing ketch

Known masters in Dundee fleet: 1904, 1908 Captain Stephen

Known owners in Dundee fleet: 1910 Robert Kinnes

Catches: 1904 – 4 white whales, 2 walrus, 350 seals, 12 bears, 1 ton oil; 1905 – 15 seals, 25 bears, 268 foxes; 1906 – 8 walrus, 450 seals, 17 bears, 531 foxes; 1908 – 7 white whales, 82 walrus, 260 seals, 6 bears, 14.5 tons oil

Ravenscraig

Weight: 500 tons

Engines: 70 horse power

Known masters in Dundee fleet: 1866, 1870, 1872–73 Captain Allan; 1874–77 Captain Bannerman; 1878 Captain David West; 1879 Captain Adam

Known owners in Dundee fleet: in 1866 Ninian Lockhart of Kirkcaldy owned *Ravenscraig*. She was managed by Taylor and Miller of Dundee until 1876 when W. O. Taylor took control of her management. She was Kirkcaldy-owned until 1879.

Best catches: 1870 – 8 whales, 125 tons whale oil, 6 tons baleen, 9,570 seals, 110 tons seal oil; 1872 – 10 whales, 80 tons whale oil, 4,000 seals; 1874 – 16 whales, 130 tons whale oil, 6 tons baleen, 7,800 seals, 75 tons seal oil

Notes: Although she was Kirkcaldy owned, when *Ravenscraig* was newly built she operated from Dundee. She was converted to a steamer in 1866 and her figurehead was removed in 1867. In 1873 she brought home a small boat built by the shipwrecked crew of the US exploration ship *Polaris*. This vessel had been attempting to reach a new 'Furthest North' but had run into trouble. *Ravenscraig* and *Arctic* helped save the survivors; the US Navy awarded Captain Adams of *Arctic* a generous $800 for his trouble, plus money for a chronometer, with a further $1,000 for the owners and $25 for each member of the crew.

The following year a fire damaged the engine room and, in a separate incident, a seaman named Sinclair Thomson of Sandness was killed. He had been flensing seals when the master shot him by accident and he bled to death. In May 1879 *Ravenscraig* returned to Dundee leaking heavily; with the vessel in such a dangerous state the crew refused to sail to the Davis Straits. When she arrived in the Tay and anchored off Carnoustie, the master, Captain West, committed suicide by stepping overboard. He had only been a ship master for a couple of years, having previously sailed as mate of *Intrepid*. *Ravenscraig* was repaired in dock and sailed back to the Davis Straits under Captain Adam but was wrecked off Cape Austin on 8 October that same year. No lives were lost.

Resolute

When and where built: 1880 by Alexander Stephens & Sons, Dundee

Weight: 624.17 gross; 424 registered tonnage

Description: *Resolute* was a three-masted, barque-rigged screw steamer. She had a wooden framework, was carvel-built with a square stern, no galleries and a male figurehead. Her statistics were: length 175 feet 6 inches, breadth 30 feet 8 ¼ inches and depth 18 feet 7 inches from the tonnage deck to the hold.

Engine: with an engine room 31 feet long, *Resolute* had two inverted compound engines made in 1880 by Pearce Brothers of Lilybank Foundry, Dundee. They had cylinders 27 inches and 52 inches in diameter with a 33-inch stroke and a combined horsepower of 98.

Known masters in Dundee fleet: 1880 Charles Yule; 1881–82 David Kilgour; 1883 W. Deuchars; 1884–85 Arthur Jackman; 1886 Charles Yule or Arthur Jackman

Known owners in Dundee fleet: Until at least 1884 Dundee Seal and Whale Fishing Company with David Bruce as manager

Registered in Dundee: 1880–86

Best catches: 1880 – 6 whales, 60 tons whale oil, 2.5 tons baleen, 497 seals, 6 tons seal oil; 1883 – 20,124 Newfoundland seals, 237 tons seal oil, 1,497 Greenland seals, 28 tons seal oil; 1884 – 435 seals; 1885 – 4 whales and 200 white whales, 48 tons whale oil, 1.5 tons baleen, 38,800 seals, 4,009 tons seal oil

Notes: *Resolute* was crushed in ice off Ireland Rocks, Fogo Island, Labrador, on 27 March 1886. At the time there were 348 men on board, mainly Newfoundland sealers, and when she struck the ice, the men below decks were close to panic. They were trapped in a sinking ship with the access ladders destroyed. Captain Jackman took charge and calmed everybody down. Although the keel had been torn off, the pressure of the ice kept the ship afloat until everybody was safely off. Some of crew walked the 20 miles to the Dundee built SS *Mastiff* while most tramped 70 miles across the ice to the shore. Nobody was lost.

River Tay

When and where built: 1868 by John Key, Kirkcaldy and Kinghorn

Weight: 600 tons gross; 439 tons net

Engines: 70 horse power

Known masters in Dundee fleet: 1868 Captain Birnie

Best catches: 1868 – 2,800 seals, 30 tons oil

Notes: *River Tay* was Dundee's first and last iron whaling ship. She was very strongly built, with her bow extra strengthened for sailing through the ice, and there was a rumour some people considered her unsinkable. The blubber tanks were integral to the vessel's construction, with a supposed advantage of having 42 separate watertight compartments within the hull and a hold beam for every frame so she was able to endure the pressure of ice. She was launched in the Forth on 10 February 1868, but even her launch was not without incident as she was immediately damaged and a tug, *Atlas*, towed her to Granton to be repaired. Unfortunately, *River Tay* did not last long in the Arctic. She had made five captures but on 17 August 1868, on a calm sea, she hit an ice floe and sank in 16 hours. The crew had time to salvage food and stores and were rescued by other Dundee whaling ships. Dundee did not try any further experiments with metal hulled whaling ships.

Rodney

When and where built: 1766, 'plantation built', possibly in North America

Weight: 176 tons

Description: Sailing brig

Known masters in Dundee fleet: 1790–93 Cornelius Frogget; 1797–1801 Cornelius Frogget (Frogget may well have been in command from 1790 to 1806); 1806–09 Captain James Ireland (possibly William Christopher in 1807); 1810 Captain Finlay or more likely Captain Mills, as mentioned in Dundee customs records.

Known owners in Dundee fleet: 1801 David Jobson; 1809 David Jobson senior

Registered in Dundee: at least 1789 until 1810

Best catches: 1781 – 6 whales; 1794 – full ship; 1800 – 9 whales, 150 butts oil; 1803 – full ship; 1804 – 11 whales; 1808 – 12 whales, full ship

Notes: *Rodney* worked as a whaling ship from Dundee from at least 1789 but in 1799 was also employed in the Baltic trade. There was a whaling vessel of the same name in Dunbar in 1788, and it is possible this was the same vessel. In 1800 *Rodney* had a crew of 32 men and was allowed a longboat; while in 1808 she carried a crew of 36. In 1807 she was sold at the Exchange Coffee Rooms by public roup, and in 1808 she returned to Dundee as a full ship. She had fished the Greenland Sea that year, while the other Dundee ships had operated in the Davis Strait. In the Howff graveyard in central Dundee there is a gravestone erected by the master of *Rodney* to commemorate his children. *Rodney* sunk on 31 May 1810 in the Greenland Sea but all her crew were saved. The boiling yard and equipment belonging to the Rodney Whale Company were sold by public roup later that year.

Scotia

When and where built: 1872 by Johansen & Holman, or possibly Jorgensen & Knudsen, Drammen, Norway.

Weight: Gross tonnage 357.02; registered tonnage 238.66

Description: *Scotia* was a wooden-built auxiliary screw barque. She had two decks, three masts and a square stern. Carvel-built with no galleries, she had a billet head and no water ballast tanks. Her statistics were: 139 feet by 29 feet by 15 feet 10 inches.

Engines: Compound direct acting vertical inverted cylinders, 15 and 32 inches diameter, with 24-inch stroke creating 55 horsepower. Steel boiler with 180 pounds pressure; both built by Muir & Houston of Glasgow.

Known masters in Dundee fleet: 1905–14 Captain T. Robertson

Known owners in Dundee fleet: 1904–14 Robert Kinnes, Dundee but with various share transactions to a number of other people including Charles Yule, ex-whaling master and Dundee harbourmaster, and a number of people from Ireland, Dundee, Fife, England, Glasgow and other places.

Registered in Dundee: 1904–14

Best catches: 1906 – 4 whales, 2 walrus, 8 seals, 16 bears, 40 tons oil, 2 tons baleen (Greenland and Davis Straits); 1908 – 6 whales, 131 seals, 13 bears, 53 tons oil, 2.75 tons baleen (Greenland); 1909 – 8 whales, 4 seals, 10 bears, 69 tons oil, 3.75 tons baleen (Greenland)

Notes: *Scotia* was built in Norway in 1872 with the name of *Hekla* or *Hecla*. While under the Norwegian flag she took part in various Arctic exploration expeditions. In 1902 William Speirs Bruce bought her for his Scottish Antarctic Expedition. Robert Kinnes bought her in 1904 and she was a whaling ship until 1913, when she became an ice patrol vessel in the wake of the *Titanic* disaster. In 1905 *Scotia* rescued the crew of the Norwegian sealer *Idraet* after they had been shipwrecked for 17 days at sea. The Norwegian government gave Captain Thomas Robertson a silver cup for his efforts. In 1915 the Hudson Bay Company bought *Scotia* and later chartered her to the French government. She was used as a cargo vessel in the First World War but proved unsuitable as she was unseaworthy when her blubber tanks were removed. She caught fire in the Bristol Channel in January 1916 and was destroyed.

Seduisante

When and where built: 1878 at Hecquet, Dunkirk, France

Weight: Gross tonnage 115.40; registered tonnage 66.91

Description: *Seduisante* was a sailing vessel with an auxiliary screw and a petrol motor. She was 93 feet 1½ inches by 21 feet 3 inches by 11 feet½ inch deep from the top of her keel to the top of beam amidships. *Seduisante* had a single deck with two masts, was schooner-rigged with a square stern. She was carvel-built with no galleries but a female figurehead and one bulkhead.

Engines: *Seduisante* had an engine room 13 feet 7 inches long. She had an inverted, direct acting internal combustion petrol engine built in 1907 by Globe Gasoline, Eddystone, Pennsylvania. This engine had four 7-inch cylinders with 10-inch stroke and created 35 horsepower. *Seduisante* could motor at 4 knots.

Known masters in Dundee fleet: 1910 Captain Brown

Known owners in Dundee fleet: Osbert Clare Forsyth Grant of Ecclescraig, near Montrose

Registered in Dundee: 1910–11

Best catches: 1910: 433 walrus, 630 seals

Notes: Captain Forsyth Grant bought *Seduisante* and had her fitted out in King William Dock, Dundee. In 1912 she was lost at Nottingham Island, Hudson Bay, along with her master and all the crew.

Snowdrop

When and where built: 1886 at Scarborough

Weight: 62 tons

Description: Ketch

Engines: There was an engine fitted in 1905.

Known masters in Dundee fleet: 1905 Captain Ogsten; 1906 Captain Walter J. Jackson; 1907 Captain Brown.

Known owners in Dundee fleet: 1905 – managing owner was Mr Robert Ferguson.

Best catches: 1905 – 1 black whale, 2 walrus, 17 bears, 15 tons oil, 18 cwt baleen; 1907 – 184 walrus, 190 seals, 23 bears, 50 foxes, 10.5 tons oil.

Notes: Built and owned in Scarborough for the first few years of her life, *Snowdrop* came to Dundee in 1905. She was wrecked in Frobisher Straits in 1908, and a young harpooner named Alexander Ritchie and his Inuit guide crossed 500 miles to find help. In July 1909 the vessels *Paradox* and *Justin Agatha* sailed to rescue the stranded crew but both vessels were lost. However the Peary expedition vessel *Jeannie* rescued the survivors although one man died of frostbite. The book *Arctic Adventurer* by Fraser and Rannie features *Snowdrop* and Dundee Museum holds one of her signal flags.

Spitzbergen

When and where built: Before or in 1876 in Germany

Description: Whaling ship, doubled all over, tripled forward.

Engine: Built by Penn of Greenwich and capable of creating 60 horse power.

Known masters in Dundee fleet: 1876 Captain Adam

Known owners in Dundee fleet: 1876 Cox Brothers and Mr Yeaman

Notes: *Spitzbergen* was German built and when the Dundee owners bought her from Hamburg, they intended her to join the Dundee whaling fleet. Unfortunately she sank before she even reached Norway where she was to have her blubber tanks fitted, so took no part in the Dundee whaling trade.

St Hilda

When and where built: 1875 at Woolston in Hampshire

Weight: 97 tons gross, 63 tons net

Description: Ketch

Known masters in Dundee fleet: 1908–11 Captain Cooney

Known owners in Dundee fleet: 1910 Robert Kinnes

Best catches: 1908 – 238 walrus, 1,938 seals, 20.5 tons oil; 1909 – 1 whale, 240 walrus; 1910 – 390 walrus, 24 tons oil; 1911 – 1 whale, 0.5 ton baleen, 26 white whales, 50 seals, 20 bears

Notes: *St Hilda* had been a yacht in Cowes. She was over 30 years old when she came to Dundee and was claimed to be very ornate and easy to sail. She was rumoured to be able to travel at 12 knots with all her sails set and could steam at 7 knots but required major work before she was fit to sail to the Arctic. On 2 September 1886 she sunk after running onto a reef in Cumberland Gulf.

Star

When and where built: 1855 in Dundee

Weight: 288 tons gross, 229 registered tonnage

Description: *Star* was a one-decked, barque-rigged sailing vessel. Two-masted, she was square sterned and carvel-built with no gallery, a scroll head and a wooden framework. Her length was 102 feet 8 inches, her breadth 24 feet 1½ inches and her depth was 14 feet 10½ inches from the tonnage deck to the ceiling at midships.

Engine: When registered, this vessel had no engines although Dundee University Archives have an entry where she is mentioned as a brig with a 20 horsepower engine.[5]

Known masters in Dundee fleet: 1883 Captain McLennan; 1885 Captain Salmond

Known owners in Dundee fleet: Dundee Seal and Whale Fishing, manager George Welch; 1882 Robert Kinnes appointed managing owner. In 1884 and 1885 this vessel was privately owned by a group of shareholders but Robert Kinnes managed her.

In Dundee Register 1883–86

Best catches: 1883 – 40 bottle nosed whales, 41 tons oil; 1885 – 900 seals, 55 tons seal oil, 27 bottlenose whales

Notes: *Star* struck a reef in the Cumberland Gulf on 2 September 1886. The crew abandoned her and it is presumed she sank.

Success

When and where built: before 1763

Weight: 175 tons

Description: *Success* was 86 feet 1 inch long by 25 feet 1 inch in breadth. She was purely sail powered with no engines.

Known masters in Dundee fleet: 1788–91 James Lundie, according to Customs and Excise records, but the Ingram Files say James Sinclair was her Master in 1790.

Registered in Dundee: 14 September 1763 to 9 December 1794

Best known catches: 1767 – 2 whales; 1787 – 2 whales

Notes: *Success* operated in the Greenland Sea; in 1787 she left the ice on 8 July and arrived at Dundee on the fifteenth with 112 butts blubber.

Tay (I)

When and where built: Before 1786

Weight: 284.5 tons

Description: *Tay* was a purely sail powered vessel. She was 89 feet 6 inches long by 27 feet 1/4 inch in breadth.

Known masters in Dundee fleet: 1787–98 Captain Robert Webster

Registered in Dundee: 1786–99

Best catches: 1787 – 1,400 seals; 1788, 8 whales (*London Chronicle* 10 July 1788); 1791 – 11 whales (*St James's Chronicle* says 10); 1799 – 9 whales, full ship

Notes: When she was on the Bristol Register, *Tay* was known as *Phoenix*. She arrived in Dundee in June 1786 and operated in the Greenland Sea. In 1788 Captain Webster said the weather was 'very stormy' on the whaling grounds (*London Chronicle* 10 July 1788). On 30 June 1799, while off Kinnaird Head and returning from the Greenland Sea, *Tay* was captured by the French privateer *Le Resolve*, who took her to Bergen. *Le Resolve* had already captured five British vessels including *Martha Cranstoun* of Dundee, but when they saw *Tay*, the privateer's crew were apprehensive, believing her to be a warship. Two of *Le Resolve*'s crew were British including the second mate. *Tay* and her cargo of nine whales were valued at £6,000. The crew were returned to Scotland, landing at Aberdeen on 28 July.

Tay (II)

When and where built: 1812

Weight: 364 tons

Known masters in Dundee fleet: 1814–19 William Adamson

Best catches: 1816 – 11 whales; 1818 – two whales

Notes: Not much known about this vessel. The custom and excise records mention she obtained a yawl in 1814 and she was crushed in the ice in July 1819.

Tay (III)

When and where built: 1850 at Dundee

Weight: 560.46 tons gross; 455.04 registered tonnage as a steamer i.e. without engines

Description: *Tay* was a two decked vessel with a square stern. She was carvel-built with three masts, ship rigged with two quarter galleries, a wooden framework and a female figurehead. She also had a quarter deck. *Tay* was 141 feet 7 inches long by 19 feet 7 inches broad and 19 feet 7 inches deep. Launched as a sailing ship, she was later converted to steam and boasted a telescoping funnel.

Engines: 75 horse power. Her engines were bought from M. J. P. Almond in North Shields but fitted up, together with boilers, by Neish and Pearce of Dundee.

Known masters in Dundee fleet: 1858 George Deuchars; 1859 Captain Deuchars or Captain Sturrock; 1860 Captain Sturrock; 1861 Captain Nicoll; 1864 Captain Sturrock; 1865–67 Captain Birnie; 1868–69 Captain Spence; 1872 Captain Greig; 1873 Captain Greig; 1874 Captain Loffley

Known owners in Dundee fleet: 1850 William Clark, William Ogilvie Taylor, James Martin, George F. Alison and William Strong; from November 1857 The Dundee Arctic Fishing Company

Registered in Dundee: 1858–74

Best catches: 1859 – 15 whales, 155 tons oil, no seals; 1861 – 14 whales, 84 tons oil; 1865 – 7 whales, 40 tons oil, 14,000 seals, 150 tons seal oil; 1866 – 1 whale, 9 tons oil, 17,000 seals, 210 tons oil

Notes: *Tay* shares the honour of being one of the first two vessels in Britain to be converted from a sailing ship to a screw whaler, with *Diana* of Hull being her rival. Before becoming a whaling ship, she was an Indiaman. The Dundee Arctic Whaling Company owned her from November 1857 onward, the date of her conversion. Although there were major advantages in being steam powered, there were also negatives, as the engine room required so much space that *Tay*'s cargo – or blubber – carrying capacity was reduced by 160 tons. *Tay* had a retractable screw to help cope with the ice and carried 300 tons of coal. On a good day she could steam at 7 knots.

Unusually for Arctic whalers, *Tay* had a blubber boiler on board so she had no need to return to port to convert blubber to oil. Although her engines needed repair after her first sealing trip, the experiment still proved a success, so other steam whaling ships followed in *Tay*'s wake. On her initial whaling voyage, Captain Deuchars helped *Diana* of Hull by transferring coal and gave *Chase*, also of Hull, her spare rudder. *Tay* was lost on 16 June 1874 at the entrance to the North Water in Melville Bay, Davis Straits. Sliced by ice, she sank in 45 minutes and only her figurehead floated to the surface. Dundee Museum has a model of *Tay* when she had a full complement of guns so presumably she was then operating as an Indiaman.

Terra Nova

When and where built: 1884 – built by Alexander Stephen and Sons, Dundee, and launched by Miss Stephen, presumably the daughter of the owner.

Weight: 744 tons gross, 450.28 registered tonnage

Description: There is a great deal known about *Terra Nova*, the last whaling ship built at Dundee. She was 187 feet by 31 feet by 19 feet deep in the hold. She was three-masted and barque-rigged, carvel-built with a square stern, a wooden framework and the figurehead of a demi woman. She had oak or elm planking between 4¼ and 5¼ inches thick, strengthened on the exterior with up to three inches thick greenheart or bark. While her hull averaged 12 inches thick, there was further strengthening with iron bark, steel plates and pitch pine at the bows to make them nearly 32 inches thick. There were also logs and heavy knees, right angled bars used to strengthen the internal structure, which gave *Terra Nova* more support against the ice. She had 34 blubber or oil tanks and two steam winches, with berths for a crew of 300 during the sealing season at Newfoundland. Overall she cost £16,000 to build.

Engines: *Terra Nova* had a 31 foot 2½ inch long engine room, with a 120 horsepower engine made by Gourlay Brothers and Company of Dundee. The engine was a two cylinder compound engine with cylinders of 27 and 54 inches in diameter with a 33-inch stroke. The Ingram files claim the engine was 94 horsepower. *Terra Nova* could use 14 tons of coal in 24 hours hard steaming at full speed.

Known masters in Dundee fleet: 1885–88 Captain Alexander Fairweather; 1889–93 Charles Daw; 1894–1903: Captain A. Jackman; 1903 Captain Harry Mackay (sealing only); 1904 Captain A. Jackman (exploration); 1905–08 Captain Harry McKay (whaling only); 1906–08 Captain A. Kean, Newfoundland (sealing only); 1909 Captain Edward Bishop, Newfoundland; 1910 Captain R. Scott; 1914–15 Captain W. Bartlett; 1916 Captain S. Windsor; 1917–18 Captain Kennedy; 1919–23 Captain A. Kean

Known owners in Dundee fleet: Alexander Stephen and Sons built, owned and operated *Terra Nova* as a whaling ship. When she was first registered, William Stephen, senior, owned *Terra Nova*. In December 1893 David Bruce bought her for £11,060 but five years later, he sold her to C. T. Bowring and Co of St John's, Newfoundland. In 1903 the British Government bought her as a relief ship for Captain Scott who was trapped in the Antarctic in the

Dundee built *Discovery*. Scott also used her for his second, 1910 Antarctic expedition. By 1914 she was back in Newfoundland hands, and remained a working vessel until 1943 when a German vessel sunk her.

Registered in Dundee: 1884–98

Best catches: 1885 – 21,844 seals, 195 tons oil (Newfoundland); 8 whales,62 tons oil, 3 tons whalebone (Davis Straits); 1887 – 25,134 seals, 297 tons oil (Newfoundland), 1 whale, 580 white whales, 110 tons oil, 0.5 ton bone (Davis Straits); 1889 – 25,734 seals, 256 tons oil (Newfoundland); 1890 – 18,075 seals, 180 tons oil (Newfoundland); 1891 – 35,239 seals, 370 tons oil (Newfound-land); 1892 – 12,369 seals, 128 tons oil (Newfoundland), 1 whale, 221 white whales (Davis Straits)

Notes: Known familiarly as 'Novey', *Terra Nova* was the last Dundee built whaling ship and arguably the best. She was built to replace the successful whaling ship *Thetis*, which had been sold to the United States Government. All the skill and experience of the previous two decades of whaling ship construction created what was undoubtedly a superb example of an Arctic-worthy hunting vessel. However it is not for her whaling exploits that she is best remembered, but for her use in exploration. As well as her famous appearance in the 1902–03 *Discovery* Relief Expedition, *Terra Nova* also sailed in the 1894 Harmsworth Expedition, the 1905 *America* Relief Expedi-tion and the 1910–11 British Antarctic Expedition.

Terra Nova was a fast ship, with a record passage of 11 days on her maiden voyage from Dundee to St John's in February 1885. In 1887 76-year-old James Cummings died while on board: he had sailed in 57 Arctic trips during the previous 60 years. In 1894 one of her harpooners killed a huge whale which had survived a previous attack, for there was already a harpoon inside her. The harpoon had belonged to the Bo'ness whaling ship *Jean* which had sunk 37 years before.

In 1901, no longer in Dundee ownership, *Terra Nova* caught a record 40,000 whales, creating 800 tons of oil. In 1903, before she sailed to the Antarctic, the Dundee Shipbuilding Company refitted her in an amazing three weeks work that employed 300 men including those from Gourlay Brothers. On this trip, Harry McKay was the master and Ernest Shackleton supervised *Terra Nova's* loading. The Royal Navy towed her part of the way south, and with the experience of Captain McKay, she was able to help free *Discovery* from the ice. Captain Scott used her again in 1910, when she flew the flag of the Royal Yacht Squadron.

The Glengall ironworks company refitted her to Scott's requirements, re-rigged her as a barque and erected an ice house on her upper deck, with the capacity to hold 150 frozen carcasses. Her galley was refurbished, her wardrobe modernised and a lamp room, chronometer room and instrument room added. The saloon was enlarged so that Scott's 24 officers could live in comfort, while the accommodation for the warrant officers was reduced. When all the blubber tanks were removed, *Terra Nova* could no longer be classified as a whaling ship, but with that expedition complete, she was recoverted and returned to sealing in the Arctic. She was sunk in 1943, with no casualties to the crew.

There is a fine model of *Terra Nova* in the museum in Dundee.

Thetis

When and where built: 1881 by Alexander Stephen and Sons Ltd

Weight: 805 tons

Description: *Thetis* was a screw steamer, barque-rigged with two decks and a square stern. She was carvel-built with a demi female figurehead and no galleries. Her statistics were: length 181 feet 1½ inches, breadth 30 feet 10½ inches and depth 19 feet 1½ inches in hold from the tonnage deck to ceiling at midships.

Engines: With a 30.6 feet engine room, Thetis had two direct acting, compound surface condensing engines made by W. B. Thompson of Tay Foundry, Dundee. The cylinders were 27 and 54 inches in diameter with a stroke of 2 feet 9 inches which together created 98 horsepower.

Known masters in Dundee fleet: 1881 Captain Brown; 1882 Captain J Fairweather; 1883–84 Captain A. Fairweather

Known owners in Dundee fleet: When registered, Alexander Stephen & Sons owned all 64 shares; on 9 February 1881 William Stephen was appointed managing owner. In 1884 the United States Government bought *Thetis* for the Greely Relief Expedition and then in 1916, she was owned by the Thetis Steam Ship company, St John's, Newfoundland, and later owned by Job Brothers, St John's.

Best catches: 1881 – about 8,000 seals (Newfoundland), 300 seals, 12 bottlenose whales (Greenland); 1882 10,500 seals (Newfoundland), 3,300 seals, 8 bottlenose whales, 95 tons oil (est.) (Greenland); 1883 25,000 seals, 5 whales, 700 porpoises, 2 bears (Newfoundland)

Notes: On her first voyage in 1881, *Thetis* broke her propeller and lost two of her men which did not auger well for her success. The following year, she was trapped in the ice for some weeks in March and April, alongside other vessels from Dundee. Her adventures continued in 1883 when she was sealing from St John's Newfoundland and lost two of her crew. A boat's crew got fast to a bottlenose whale; the line became tangled and overturned the boat. In February 1884 Alexander Stephen & Sons sold her to the United States Government for a sum reported to be £27,000 or £31,500 as a relief ship for the lost Greely Expedition. When the Dundee crew arrived to join *Thetis* for the whaling expedition, they were not pleased to be told the ship had been sold. *Thetis* had the 31 Dundee men in her crew when she sailed, although the Master was Lieutenant Commander Reamey of the US Navy. On that trip she worked alongside *Hope* of Peterhead and *Bear*, which had also been built in Dundee and sold to United States owners. *Loch Garry*, also Dundee built, acted as store vessel.

Thetis remained in US ownership until 1916, when she was sold to the Thetis Steam Ship Company of Newfoundland. Later Job Brothers of St John's owned her; she worked from Newfoundland until she was scrapped in 1937.

Thomas (I)

When and where built: 1809 at Paull in Yorkshire.

Weight: 356 28/94 tons

Description: *Thomas* was a purely sail powered vessel. She had two decks and three masts with a square stern and a standing bowsprit but no figurehead. When she was originally registered, she was barque-rigged but was altered to ship rig in March 1831. Her statistics were: length 107 feet by breadth 29 feet 10 inches with 5 feet 10 inches between decks.

Known masters in Dundee fleet: 1823–34 George Thoms but, according to the Directory of British Shipping in Dundee Archives, Alexander Cook was master in 1834; 1835 John Stevenson; 1836–38 David Davidson

Known owners in Dundee fleet: 1824 John G. Russell, John Blair Miller and John Calman, trustees of the Dundee Union Whale Fishing Company; 1829 Dundee Union Whale Fishing Company; 1837 Dundee and Union Whale Fishing Company

Registered in Dundee: 1823–36

Best catches: 1823 – 37 whales, 240 tons oil; 1828 – 19 whales; 1833 – 28 whales, 273 tons oil

Notes: According to the customs records, in 1824 *Thomas* was allowed three puncheons of rum as part of her stores, with the owners stopping the allowance of beer in return. Three years later the owners, Dundee Union Whale Fishing Company, was charged for 40 days customs tidesman's wages as she was 40 days late in unloading her cargo and the tidesman, a minor official, had to remain with her for that length of time. In 1829 *Thomas* and the Peterhead whaling ship *Traveller* were in dispute over who had best claim to a whale that both vessels had harpooned. Although the harpooner from *Traveller* struck the whale first, the Dundee ship claimed the whale had escaped and was therefore a legitimate target. The Peterhead boat said the Dundee men had stolen the whale by weight of numbers. The case reached the High Court in Edinburgh and *Traveller* won. The owners of *Thomas* had to pay £600 compensation.

In the terrible season of 1830, *Thomas* was damaged by ice, but worse came when she was lost in the ice on 13 December 1836, with two of her crew being killed. The 48 survivors were distributed among various ships including *Advice* of Dundee, *Grenville Bay* of Newcastle and *Dee* of Aberdeen. Most died of scurvy over the next few months as the ships remained trapped in the ice. Very few of the crew of *Thomas* made it back to Dundee.

Thomas (II)

When and where built: before or in 1911

Best catches: 1911 – 5 white whales, 30 walrus, 2500 seals, 10 bears, 27 tons oil

Notes: This vessel operated from Dundee in 1911 and is one of the forgotten Dundee whaling ships.

Three Brothers

When and where built: 1811 at Jarrow, County of Durham

Weight: 339 28/94 tons

Description: *Three Brothers* was a two decked sailing vessel with three masts. She was barque-rigged with a standing bowsprit, a square stern and was carvel-built with no figurehead. Her statistics were: length 98 feet 1 inch; breadth 29 feet and height between decks 6 feet 8½ inches.

Known masters in Dundee fleet: 1815 Alexander Thomas; 1816–24 Robert Foreman; 1827–30 William Steven [or Stephen]; from 1830 George Cameron

Known owners in Dundee fleet: 1818, 1824 Thomas Powrie and J. G. Russell; 1829 Union Whale Fishing Company. The Dundee Register of British Ships says: 'Owners – John Blair Miller, merchant; John Calman, shipbuilder; John Gabriel Russel, insurance broker – three of the trustees of the Dundee Union Whale Fishing Company'.

Registered in Dundee: From at least 1813 to 1830

Best catches: 1813 – 7 whales; 1820 – 18 whales, 195 tuns oil; 1823 – 28 whales, 220 tuns oil; 1827 – 20 whales, 210 tuns oil

Notes: According to the Dundee customs records, in 1824 *Three Brothers* was allowed three puncheons of rum as part of her stores. In return the owners stopped issuing beer to the hands. On 3 April 1830 *Three Brothers* was struck by a north-north-easterly gale that carried away her foremast and main topmast, leaving her partly crippled. She had to return to Stromness in Orkney to replace them, making her late for the start of the whaling. However, her bad year was just beginning. On 30 July she carved out an ice dock in Melville bay and survived for days, only to be crushed in July alongside the Hull vessels *William, Gilder* and *North Briton* and *Alexander* of Aberdeen. Her master composed the following letter:

> Davis's Straits, September 21 1830
> Ship 'Traveller'
> Sir – it is not without feelings of the deepest regret that I now take up my pen to address you at this moment as this has been a season which will long be remembered by those employed in the Whale-fishery on account of the number of vessels which have fallen a sacrifice to the ice this year - and it will be seriously felt by those whose misfortune it was to be deprived of the comfort and support of their vessels and when it is considered that their sole dependents are chiefly placed upon the success of their voyages. I am sorry to say that we are included amongst the number of vessels which have been

cut off by the merciless edge of the ice.

After having remained about a fortnight at the South-west, and whilst plying to the northward for the space of three weeks in clear water [the wind prevailing from the eastward during that time] we fondly indulged the hope of not being interrupted in our progress by barriers of ice, and of getting an easy and speedy passage across to the West Land. But alas! Other scenes of a truly lamentable nature were yet reserved for us to experience and behold.

After having got in among the floes in Melville Bay, we met with several interruptions of a trivial kind which would have been easily surmounted had we not been overtaken by a most violent gale from the south west upon the 2nd of July, which set the ice in among us so furiously that we were obliged to cut out a dock for the safety of the vessel, which was accomplished without loss of time; but we found it impossible to clear it as the ice was then so rapidly setting in upon us. So prodigious was the compression that it laid four vessels, then lying beside us, quite on a level with the surface of the ice before it had the same effect upon us; and it was not until the last shock, which came with irresistible force, that we joined the rest.

It is now a little better than two months since we got out of Melville Bay, leaving behind us the ships Thomas, Friendship, Dorothy, Advice, Princess Charlotte and Horn [with the exception of the Fairy] closely beset amongst the ice; and it is to be apprehended they are still remaining in the same situation as they have not been seen by any vessel that we have inquired at since, the ships that we spoke came out of the Bay. I am sorry to add, the ships in general are but poorly fished this season.

Signed GEORGE CAMERON

Tilly

Notes: There is not much information about this vessel. She was not strictly part of the Dundee whaling fleet but was involved in the very last stages of the industry in Dundee. Robert Kinnes chartered her during the First World War when the whaling industry had ended in Dundee. She sailed from Dundee in August 1915 with a crew from the neutral nations of Norway and the United States as well as from Nova Scotia. The intention was to take supplies to Blacklead Island whaling station and return with their produce. Unfortunately, on 13 October *Tilly* ran into a storm that drove her onto rocks near the island where she sank. Her master, 70-year-old Captain Stephens, drowned but all the rest of the crew survived.

Triune

When and where built: 1869 at South Hylton, Durham, by Gibbon and Nichol

Weight: February 1884, gross tonnage 385.09, registered tonnage 261.86

Description: When first registered in Dundee in 1883 she was a sailing vessel with one deck and three masts. She was barque-rigged and carvel-built with an elliptical stern, a billet head and a wooden framework. Her statistics were: length 129 feet; breadth 28 feet 1½ inches and depth 17 feet 4 inches. On 4 February 1884 she was re-registered as a screw steamer.

Engine: On registration as a screw steamer she had a 25 foot 9½ inch long engine room. She had two engines made by J. & H. Whyte and Cooper of Dundee; they were inverted compound with cylinders of 21 and 39 inches and a 24-inch stroke, creating 65 horse power.

Known masters in Dundee fleet: 1884–86 Captain David Souter

Known owners in Dundee fleet: At the time of first registration in Dundee, the sole owner was William Storey Croudace, but he sold several of his shares in small numbers to a number of people from different parts of the United Kingdom.

Registered in Dundee: 1883–86

Best catches: 1884 – 11 whales, 93.5 tons oil, 4.5 tons bone; 1885 – 1 whale, 40 white whales, 15 tons oil, 0.5 ton baleen

Notes: This vessel was originally built for the copper ore trade but was converted into a whaling ship. In June 1886 she was first driven ashore and suffered slight damage at Sukkertoppen and then squeezed by ice off Cape Atholl and began leaking at the rate of five inches an hour. After being surveyed by the master and officers of *Maud*, she was declared unseaworthy and abandoned on 12 August. Her crew were distributed between *Maud* and *Nova Zembla*.

Vega

When and where built: 1872 at Wencke, Bremerhaven

Weight: 405.47 tons gross, 299.58 registered tonnage

Description: *Vega* was a single screwed barque with two decks and three masts. She had an elliptical stern and was carvel-built with a billet head but no galleries or bulkheads. Her statistics were: length 138 feet 6 inches; breadth 27 feet 8½ inches and depth 15 feet 8½ inches.

Engines: With an engine room 31 feet long, *Vega* had a single compound engine and a single boiler. The engine was built in 1872 and had two cylinders of 21⅛ inches and 36 inches, with a 21- inch stroke, creating 36 horsepower and a top speed of 7 knots.

Known masters in Dundee fleet: 1903 Captain John James Cooney

Known owners in Dundee fleet: On registration, the owner was given as Robert Ferguson of 39 Dock Street, Dundee. He became the managing owner at the end of March 1903. However, he also sold many of his shares to various people including Captain Cooney.

Registered in Dundee: 1903, No.110998

Notes: In 1878 the Swedish explorer Baron Nordenskjold took her from the North Cape to the Bering Strait, the first successful navigation of the North East Passage. *Vega* came to Dundee in 1903 but was wrecked on her maiden voyage as a whaling ship. She had been beset for a week off Wilcox Point in Melville Bay in late May, but on 31 May the ice stove in her hull and she sank in just a few minutes. The 44-man crew crossed 30 miles of ice before sailing 160 miles to safety in Upernavik in Greenland, where they arrived on 5 June.

Victor

When and where built: 1847 at Peterhead

Weight: 360.64 tons gross, less 82.38 tons for engine, 278.26 tons net

Description: *Victor* was a screw steam ship, with dimensions of 106 feet 1½ inches in length, 28 feet 8½ inches in breadth and 18 feet 5 inches in depth of hold from the tonnage deck to the ceiling at midships. She had two decks, three masts and was square sterned and carvel-built. From 1869 she was barque-rigged. She had no gallery and when she was first built probably had a figurehead of a female bust, although this was later altered to a simple scroll.

Engines: With an engine room 19 feet long, *Victor* had two direct acting condensing engines. Gourlay Brothers of Dundee made the engines in 1873. They had 18 and 34 inch diameter cylinders and a 1½ inch stroke giving 50 horsepower.

Known masters in Dundee fleet: 1864–65 Alexander Deuchars; 1868–70 Captain Gravill; 1872 Captain Bruce; 1874 Captain Edwards or Captain Deuchars; 1875–77 Captain Nicoll; 1878 Captain Adams; 1879–80 Captain Robert Davidson; 1881 Captain Burnett

Known owners in Dundee fleet: 1864 Tay Whale Fishing Company, with the manager being George Welch. He remained one of the main shareholders and was appointed managing owner in February 1876. In 1868 Thomas Hunter Cox and George Ower became shareholders in the company.

Best catches: 1865 – 11 whales, 110 tons oil; 1866 – clean of whales, 12,000 seals, 130 tons oil; 1871 – 8 whales, 70 tons oil, 1,402 seals, 15 tons oil; 1874 – 24 whales, 135 tons whale oil, 8 tons baleen, 850 seals, 7 tons seal oil

Notes: In 1863 the Tay Whale Fishing Company bought *Victor* from Peterhead to replace *Jumna* which was lost in the ice. *Victor* was fitted with an engine soon after she came to the Dundee Register. In 1867 her figurehead was removed and in 1877 she was alleged to have caught a whale 81 feet long. On the 17 July 1881 she was crushed by ice 8 miles south of Elwin Inlet in the Davis Straits.

Wildfire

When and where built: 1854 in Quebec, Canada

Weight: 406.14 tons gross; 346.39 tons net

Description: *Wildfire* was a sail-powered vessel with two masts and, unusually for a whaling ship, a poop deck. She was square rigged on all her three masts, with a square stern and a topgallant forecastle used for stores. Ingram claims she was later converted to steam.

Known masters in Dundee fleet: 1860–61, 1864 Captain John Walker; 1865–68 Captain David Souter

Known owners in Dundee fleet: 1860 Mr George Welch of Dundee but on the 13 February 1860, he sold all his 64 shares to William Harris, corn merchant; John Cunningham, wine merchant; and George Welch, manager of Tay Whale Fishing Co. Welch remained as the manager while the Tay Whale Fishing Company owned the vessel.

Registered in Dundee: 1860–68

Best catches: 1861 – 19 whales, 160 tons oil; 1864 – 5 whales, 68 tons oil; 1865 – 7 whales, 70 tons oil; 1866 – 6 whales, 60 tons oil; 1867 – clean of whales, 5,522 seals, 80 tons oil

Notes: After the loss of *Advice* in 1859, *Wildfire* was bought from Hull as a replacement. She lasted until 1868. Dundee City Archives holds a letter from George Welch that stated: 'the vessel was seriously stove in Davis Straits by heavy ice and was abandoned full of water on the 18th July last' (CE 70.11.10).

Windward

When and where built: 1860 by Stephen and Forbes, Peterhead

Weight: 355.95 gross; 157.17 registered tonnage

Description: *Windward* had two decks and three masts. She was a clinker built, square sterned vessel with a wooden framework, and had neither a bulkhead nor water ballast tank. She was barque-rigged and had a break deck. Her statistics were: length 118 feet; breadth 28 feet 11½ inches and depth 16 feet 8 inches.

Engines: With an engine room 27 feet 2½ inches long, *Windward* had a compound tandem engine with a single steel boiler of 100 pounds pressure. The engine had two cylinders 14 and 28 inches, with a 2-foot stroke and created 35 horsepower and a top speed of 6 knots. While the *Register of British Shipping* in Dundee City Archives states the engine was foreign built, Alexander Buchan in his splendid *The Peterhead Whaling Trade* says that in 1866, Gourlay Brothers of Dundee fitted *Windward* with double acting steam engines. Possibly the original engines were replaced that year.

Known masters in Dundee fleet: 1904–06 Captain J. Cooney

Known owners when in Dundee Register: On registration in Dundee *Windward* was owned by Robert Ferguson of 39 Dock Street, Dundee. However, Ferguson sold shares to many people, usually in small numbers of between one and eight at a time. On 21 February 1906 Robert Kinnes of East Whale Lane became the manager.

Registered in Dundee: 1904–07, No. 27527

Best catches: 1905 – 2 black whales, 2 walrus, 38 bears, 40 foxes, 37 tons oil, 2 tons baleen; 1906 – 1 white whale, 50 walrus, 13 seals, 13 bears, 4.5 tons oil

Notes: *Windward* had been originally built as a whaling ship, but she was later converted to an Arctic exploration craft. Between 1894 and 1903, first Captain Wiggins, the Siberian explorer, and then the Jackson-Harmsworth Arctic expedition used her. In 1904 she came to Dundee and was again used as a whaling ship. *Windward* was wrecked on the Carey Islands on 26 June 1907, but most of the crew were saved. Unfortunately the engineer and one crewman died of exposure.

Appendix 2
Dundee Ship Masters

Adams, William

William Adams senior is one of the big names in Dundee whaling history. According to his gravestone in Barnhill Cemetery, he was born in Dundee on 15 September 1837 and died on 6 August 1890. He began his career with the Dundee Perth and London shipping company but completed his apprenticeship elsewhere. His early voyages were to the Baltic and the Far East and it was not until 1850 that he first sailed on the whaling where he was to make his name. From 1869 onwards he worked for Alexander Stephen and Son as master of *Arctic* and, when that vessel was lost in the ice at Cresswell Bay, he commanded *Arctic* II from 1875 to 1883. He retired in 1883 and shortly afterward bought the vessel *Maud* from Fife owners, converted her to a whaling ship and returned to the Arctic. He was master and owner of *Maud* from around 1884 until his death in 1890.

Captain Adams had a good name within the whaling fraternity. The Lord Mayor of London invited him to a dinner to honour the Leigh-Smith Arctic Expedition and he was reputed to be the first whaling master to enter Lancaster Sound when he took *Arctic* there in search of whales in 1868. In 1879, when the Tay Bridge collapsed into the firth taking a train full of passengers with it, he commanded *Arctic* in the search for survivors. In 1885 he was asked to go to Canada to advise on creating trade links between Winnipeg and Port Nelson, and between 1887 and 1889, he commanded *Maud* on the Livingstone-Learmonth exploring expedition. He was seriously ill on the return journey and was put ashore at Thurso, but died on the journey south.

Captain Adams' home life was equally fruitful. He lived in 8 James Place, Broughty Ferry, from 1874 to 1878. In 1879 he lived in 12 Duntrune Terrace, West Ferry, also known as Disco after the island off western Greenland. He married twice and had a number of children, with his second wife surviving him.

Adams, William (junior)

The son of William Adams senior, this ship master was also from Dundee. He was born in 1869 and died in September 1942. In a long and successful career, Captain Adams junior commanded the whaling vessels *Diana, Morning* and *Esquimaux*. First travelling to the Arctic as a member of his father's crew, he was first mate of *Balaena* during the 1892 Dundee Antarctic Expedition and two years later commanded *Esquimaux*, following that by *Terra Nova, Diana* and finally *Morning*. Leaving the dying whaling industry, Captain Adams took command of twelve vessels in a trade mission to the Kara Sea and Obi River in Siberia as well as charting part of Canada. Finally, he transferred to the Brocklebank Line as a pilot.

When he left the sea, Captain Adams lived at Gordon House in Colinsburgh in Fife. He was married with a family, but his son, also William, was killed at sea in 1939, early in the Second World War. Captain Adams died in Crail in Fife aged 73.

Adamson, William

Captain William Adamson had a long and eventful career spanning war and peace. As a whaling master he commanded *Horn, Advice, Tay* and *Princess Charlotte* and was notable both as a successful whaler and a mariner.
Captain Adamson commanded *Horn* from July 1808 to February 1809, thereafter moving to *Advice* in 1809 and *Tay* in 1814, finishing his career with a long spell as master of *Princess Charlotte* from 1820 to 1838. Captain Adamson worked in the whaling industry for 40 years, and for 29 years he was a whaling master. He was also one of the original partners of the Tay Whale Fishing Company.

As a young seaman, he served on board HMS *Monmouth* at Admiral Duncan's victory at the Battle of Camperdown and was sent on board one of the captured Dutch ships as a member of the prize crew (seamen from a victorious vessel who took control of an enemy ship). While commanding *Advice* he got into trouble when his crew defended themselves against a Royal Navy press gang that boarded them off the north coast of Scotland. In 1837 he was influential in rescuing the Hull whaling ship *Swan* from the ice and saving most of her crew.

Captain Adamson may be the same William Adamson who lived in Crichton Street in Dundee in the 1820s. He also lived in Erichtside Cottage in Blairgowrie in 1859, the year of his death aged 82.

Allan, William

Born in Peterhead in 1823, Captain Allan had a long and useful career as a ship master, although his name is barely remembered in Dundee. His certificate was numbered 9211 and he commanded the whaling ship *Ravenscraig* between 1866 and 1873, *Nova Zembla* between 1886 and 1887 and *Chieftain* in 1887 to 1888. He was also mate of *Polar Star* in 1892. In between times, he commanded the non-whaling vessels *Helen West* in 1879, *Catherine* in 1881, *Alert* (1884-1885) and *Heedful* in 1886.

Bannerman, James

One of the most interesting of Dundee's whaling masters, James Bannerman was born in Dundee in 1846 and alternated between master and mate. His master's certificates were numbered 87322, 013496 and finally 016899. He was mate of *Arctic* between 1872 and 1873 and master of *Ravenscraig* from 1874 to 1876 and of *Aurora* from 1877 to 1879. In 1881 he was mate of *Esquimaux* and the following year master of *Kara* when she was searching for survivors of the *Eira* disaster. In 1884 he was master of the Dundee whaling ship *Maud*, but after that he stepped down to become mate of the trading vessel *Blue Cross*. He remained as mate for a few years, sailing on *Maud* in 1888 and *Terra Nova* between 1889 and 1893. He was master of *Aurora* in 1894 but reverted to mate in *Balaena* in 1895, followed by *Esquimaux* between 1896 and 1897 and *Diana* until 1901. He was mate of *Diana* in 1903 and 1904, of *Morning* from 1905 to 1907; of *Eclipse* in 1908, *St Hilda* in 1909 and of *Morning* 1910 and 1911. He was second mate of *Morning* when she sank carrying military supplies to Russia in 1915.

In the 1870s Captain Bannerman rescued two Inuit who were starving to death on either Ellesmere or Devon Island. On the voyage south to Ponds Lake (now Pond Inlet), the Captain and one of the Inuit became so friendly that next year she gave birth to a daughter, Ulajuq or Jessie Bannerman, one of the many Dundee-Inuit children of the Arctic. While in Scotland, Captain Bannerman once lived at Leuchars in Fife, but there was also a shipmaster named James Bannerman at 74 Ferry Road.

Birnie, Robert

Master of *Tay* 1865–67 and of the ill-fated *River Tay* in 1868. He died of smallpox in Naples in June 1871 at the age of 51.

Buttars, John

Captain John Buttars had only one trip as a whaling master. In 1842 he was master of *Fairy*, but he lacked experience of the Arctic and did not carry sufficient stores for the voyage. *Fairy* was trapped in the ice for a month and had to borrow supplies from *Traveller* of Peterhead, but on *Fairy's* release, Butters still insisted on plunging deeper into dangerous waters. The crew, however, were more experienced and argued against the decision. Calling them mutineers, Buttars returned to Dundee and expelled them from the ship without pay, leaving 32 Shetland seamen destitute and far from home. Peter Twatt, one of the Shetlanders, took his case to court and won his wages back, whereupon the other seamen followed suit. Buttars did not command a Dundee whaling ship again.

Cheyne, William

William Cheyne was one of the very earliest Dundee whaling masters. He commanded the whaling ships *Dundee of Dundee* between 1753 and 1756 and *Grandtully* in 1761 and 1762. He may well have commanded more but details are scanty. Before coming to Dundee he sailed on the Leith whaling vessel *Tryal*, in the 1750 season, and commanded the Leith vessels *Royal Bounty* in 1751 and *Edinburgh* in 1752.

Cook, Alexander

Alexander Cook was Master of *Thomas* in 1834 and *Ebor* in 1836. The McManus Galleries and Museum in Dundee hold a copy of a fascinating journal written by Surgeon Wanless of *Thomas* in 1834 which provides great details of her voyage when Alexander Cook was in command.

Cooney, John

An Irishman from Wicklow, Captain John Cooney was known for his daring approach to whaling. After nine years as mate of *Nova Zembla*, he took command of her in 1903 but she was sunk on his first voyage in charge. He seems to have been an unlucky ship master as in 1907, *Windward* was also lost while under his command. He had been her master since 1904. When *Windward* was wrecked on the Carey Islands, there were no casualties. Captain Cooney died in 1912 on St Helena in the South Atlantic.

Davidson, James

James Davidson had a long and interesting career. Born in Peterhead, he was mate of *Hope* and *Eclipse* of Peterhead before working on Dundee vessels. In

1890, aged 40, James Davidson became master of *Earl of Mar and Kellie*. In 1893 he was master of *Polar Star* for the Dundee Antarctic Expedition and commanded *Diana* during the later expedition to Franz Josef Land. He also commanded *Polar Star* in 1896

Davidson, Robert

Peterhead born, Robert Davidson commanded a clutch of Dundee whaling vessels and became one of the most successful masters in the fleet. From *Arctic II* in 1879 and *Victor* the following year, Robert Davidson went on to command *Intrepid* in 1881, 1882 and 1885, *Polar Star* and then *Diana* during the 1893 Dundee Antarctic Expedition. He finished off in command of *Eclipse*.

Davidson was born around 1840 and first went to sea when he was 14 years old. He was associated with the whaling industry for the next forty years, and his captain's certificate number was C32589, later changed to 32598. In the 1888 *Dundee Directory* there was a Robert Davidson, shipmaster, who lived at 32 Ferry Road, and this may well be him. He retired in 1903 and died in January 1904 aged 63, leaving a widow and a grown up family. At that time he lived in Cunningham Street, Dundee.

Davidson, Thomas

Captain Thomas Davidson was another whaling master who started his career at a different port but ended in Dundee. It is possible that he was master of the Leith vessel *Dexterity* in 1814 and 1815, and he almost certainly commanded whaling ships in Kirkcaldy, but by 1828 he was working from Dundee. Thomas Davidson was master of *Dorothy* from 1828 to 1834 and again in 1837 and 1838. His first season in *Dorothy* was a particular success as he brought 37 whales into Dundee, which was the largest catch to date, but he got himself into trouble with the customs officers as he had no cargo manifest. He forgot the manifest again the next year, but that oversight paled into insignificance beside the behaviour of his mate, also named Thomas Davidson, who was prosecuted for smuggling and nearly consigned to the Royal Navy for five years. It is possible that Captain Davidson is the same Thomas Davidson, shipmaster, who lived in Seagate in 1829.

Deuchars, Alexander

One of the many Dundee Captain Deuchars, Alexander Deuchars had a long career in the Arctic. Born in Dundee around 1808, he had command of various vessels. He had three spells as master of *Princess Charlotte*: 1838–39, 1841–43 and 1845–56. Possibly he commanded *Achilles* from 1820 to 1824 and in 1828, and *Dorothy* in 1826, *Advice* in 1827, 1830–37 and in 1844. He commanded *Jumna* in 1857, 1858 and 1861 and was also in command of *Narwhal* in 1868, the last of his 48 Arctic voyages. In 1856, when *Princess Charlotte* was lost in the ice, he blasted open the hull with gunpowder to get at the crew's clothing and food. Alexander Deuchars died aged 62 at Ellenbank, Broughty Ferry, in June 1870 leaving a widow and a family.

Deuchars, George

Captain George Deuchars was another Deuchars with a long Arctic career. He seems to have commanded *Advice* between 1826 and 1838, but with gaps in 1835 to 1837. He is also associated with *Princess Charlotte* from 1838 to 1850 although Alexander Deuchars has also been quoted as her commander in those years.

Deuchars, George

Yet another of the many Captain Deuchars who sailed from Dundee, this Captain George Deuchars was one of the most admired in the whaling trade. He was master of both *Princess Charlotte* and, in 1864, *Alexander*. He was also master of *Narwhal* in 1859 and 1861 to 1863. He was employed by Gilroy Brothers, the jute manufacturers. In 1859 he helped rescue the crew of *Empress of India* when she sank in the ice. *Empress of India* was one of the very few Scottish iron hulled whaling vessels of the nineteenth century; none of them proved successful. Captain George Deuchars was mentioned in the journal of Alexander Smith, chief engineer of the whaling ship *Camperdown*.

George Deuchars lived in Broughty Ferry until paralysis forced his retiral from the sea at the early age of 40. He moved to Cuthlie, Arbirlot, in August 1865 and died there a few weeks later, leaving a widow and children. He had two shares in *Alexander* in 1864, but sold them in 1865.

Deuchars, William

Captain William Deuchars was one of the early Deuchars to command a Dundee whaling vessel. But as with most ship masters of his period, all that is known are the names of some of the vessels he commanded; ignorance blankets his private life. However, he commanded the whaling vessel *Mary Ann* from 1805 until 1807 and again from 1809 to 1819, as well as *Achilles* in 1820 and *Dorothy* in 1824. He died on the homeward voyage in 1824. There was a shipmaster named William Deuchars who lived in Seagate in 1818, who might be the same man.

Fairweather, Alexander

Captain Alexander Fairweather was a well-known Dundee whaling master who commanded some of the most famous ships of his time. His master's certificate of competency was number 84494. He was master of *Diana* and then *Active* from 1874 to 1876 and again in 1887 and 1888, and the well-known *Balaena* from 1893 to 1896, including her Antarctic expedition of 1893. In between times Captain Fairweather was in charge of *Our Queen* in 1879 and *Terra Nova* from 1885 to 1888. He was also on *Aurora* and *Thetis*.

Alexander Fairweather was Dundee born and went to sea aged just ten years old. After an apprenticeship on coasters and experience of some of the most difficult seafaring anywhere, he went north on *Tay* in 1863 but spent the following three years sailing to the Far East. In 1866 he was a harpooner, one of the most important positions, in *Camperdown*, and was back as her mate in 1870. By that time he was married to Helen Mitchell. He commanded *Diana* on an expedition to find Baron Nordenskjold, one of the many Polar explorers who got themselves into difficulties in that period. Fairweather was also master of *Our Queen* when ice sank her. He seems to have been a superstitious man, as many whaling seamen were. He was afraid of the number 13 and refused to sign on men on a Friday, while his cabin was decorated with a bunch of red herring. He died at sea off Spitsbergen on the last day of May 1896 aged just 52, leaving his widow and a family.

Fairweather, James

The younger brother of Captain Alexander Fairweather, James Fairweather had an equally interesting career. Born in Dundee in 1853, at the age of 14 he signed apprentice's articles as a ship's boy on *Stork*, a Dundee registered barque, sailing to the White Sea and the Baltic. In 1871 he was a fully fledged seaman on the whaling ship *Tay*, and eight years later had risen through the ranks to be master of *Active*, a position he held until 1882 when he transferred to *Thetis*. James Fairweather commanded *Aurora* in 1889 and *Earl of Mar and Kellie* from 1893 to 1897 but that was his last Dundee whaling command. From that date he worked on cargo vessels, first for E. P. Baptie of Glasgow, then A. and J. H. Mudie of Dundee. He spent a lot of time in Calcutta and Australia and retired in 1913. However, the outbreak of the First World War in 1914 brought him back as master of *Morning* and then as Chief Examination Officer of the Tay defences at a time when submarines and mines threatened the coast and the German Navy bombarded English coastal towns. In 1916 he commanded *Discovery* on the expedition to relieve Shackleton and the following year became a lieutenant in the Royal Naval Volunteer Reserve. James Fairweather died in 1933.

Frogett, Cornelius

Captain Frogget or Frogett (different records spell the name in different ways) was a whaling master at the turn of the eighteenth and nineteenth centuries. He commanded *Rodney* in 1790, 1791 and 1795, and from 1797 to 1799. He may have commanded her for the full period. Captain Frogett fished in the Greenland Sea and seems not to have entered the Davis Straits. He held shares in the whaling ship *Jane* which he left to his wife, Jean Thomson, when he died sometime before September 1808. Although he was successful in his professional life, Captain Frogett's personal life was tinged with tragedy as there is a gravestone to two of his children in the Howff in Dundee.

Guy, William

From 1878 to 1882 Captain Guy commanded *Nova Zembla*, and in 1883 he was master of *Jan Mayen*. From 1884 to 1887 he was in command of *Arctic II* and in 1892 *Eclipse*. Finally, from 1903 to 1907, he was master of *Balaena*. Strangely, for a man with such a distinguished career, there seems to be no folklore or anecdotes attached to him. He lost *Arctic II* in the Foxe Channel, Cumberland Sound, in 1887, *Polynia* in Davis Straits in 1891 and *Nova Zembla* in Dexterity Fjord in 1902 after nine years in command.

Mawer, Robert

Robert Mawer came from a seafaring family as his father was Robert Mawer, a Dundee shipmaster and the boxmaster of the Dundee Fraternity of Masters and Seamen. Robert Mawer junior was a seaman on board Dundee's first recorded whaling ship, *Dundee of Dundee,* in 1753 and 1754. By 1757 he was a burgess of Dundee and around 1780 he became master of *Grandtully.*

McKay, Harry

Captain Harry McKay deserves to be remembered as one of Dundee's finest whaling masters. Born in Dundee in 1857, his father was James McKay, a gas worker. Harry McKay obtained his master's certificate in 1882 and seven years later he was master of *Aurora.* That year, he caught 11,166 seals at the Newfoundland fishing. McKay remained in command of *Aurora* until 1894 when he took *Terra Nova* into Hudson Bay where, as well as hunting whales and seals, he helped in the search for two Swedish explorers, Bjorling and Kalenius. The Swedish Anthropological and Geographical Society awarded him a medal when he discovered the explorers' boat, *Ripple.* That same year, he caught 14 whales, which was excellent for the period.

In March 1896 Captain McKay was master of *Blencathra*, a luxury yacht in which he took the Coats family on an Arctic cruise to Spitsbergen. The Coats family were industrialists from Paisley who made their money in thread manufacturing. In 1902 McKay also commanded the iron yacht *Caterina*. However, McKay's finest hour came in 1903 when he was selected to command *Terra Nova* on the *Discovery* Relief Expedition. On this expedition he took *Terra Nova* out of Dundee in August 1903, sailed south to the Antarctic, helped blast Captain Scott's *Discovery* free and was back in the United Kingdom on 18 August 1904. The crew of *Terra Nova*, unfortunately, were not always on their best behaviour and half were thrown into jail for drunkenness in Hobart.

McKay himself was a handsome, cheerful man who seems to have made a good impression on everybody he met. Captain Scott of *Discovery* said he was 'excellent company for a depressed state of mind'. In the 1890s McKay had moved house from Strathmartine Road, Dundee, to Rockview, Tayport, and from 1905 to 1909 he took command of *Diana*. He retired from the sea in 1909 and died of cancer of the tongue and larynx in 1925. His wife and daughters survived him.

Milne, William

Captain William Milne is one of the better known Dundee whaling masters of the later whaling period. Born in Peterhead in 1851, William Fraser Milne first visited the Arctic as a 17-year-old seaman. Five years later, he moved from Peterhead to Dundee and sailed as a harpooner and boatswain on *Esquimaux*, a ship he commanded from 1883 until 1889. He passed his master's certificate at Dundee in 1879 with the certificate number 989944, and in 1890 he took command of *Maud*, where he remained until 1892 when the ship was driven ashore in Coutts Inlet in the Davis Straits; the Newfoundland sealer *Eagle* rescued his crew. However, it was with *Eclipse* that he made his name. He commanded her from 1894 until 1909, rescuing the crew of *Eagle* in his first year in command. He was master of *Diana* in 1915 and 1916 and master of *Albert* on the abortive gold exploration expedition.

Captain Milne was renowned for his knowledge of Inuit culture and life. He hoped to bring a missionary to the Inuit of Arctic Canada, as the Danes had done to the Inuit of Greenland. He also gave advice to the Norwegian explorer Roald Amundsen on his successful negotiation of the North West Passage. For his help, the Norwegian Government knighted him in December 1907. Captain Milne is reputed to have sailed to the Arctic 42 times in total, and to have caught 1,797 whales, 86,470 seals and 599 walrus. He was married for 55 years, with five daughters and five sons. He lived at 5

Tay Terrace in Dundee until he retired and moved to Tayport, then to East
Mains of Guthrie. He died in 1937 aged 85.

Murray, Alexander

Captain Murray was another Peterhead ship master who spent much of his
career in the Dundee whaling trade. After being apprenticed to his father
on the whaling ship *Windward*, he served on other Peterhead vessels before
becoming master of the Dundee ship *Active* in 1898. He was still in command
when he died at Ottowa Island, East Hudson Bay in 1913.

Murray, John

Captain John Murray was the brother of Captain Alexander Murray. He was
born in Peterhead in 1868 and died in 1950. He was the son of Peterhead
whaling Captain Alexander Murray with whom he sailed on his first whaling
voyage in the barque *Windward*. He was 16 years old. After a voyage that
lasted more than two years in the Dundee barque *Helenslea*, he was a fully
fledged seaman. He had also experienced jail, when he was locked up in
Caldetra, Chile, at New Year 1889. He sailed under Captain Milne in *Esquimaux*, and then gradually worked his way upward, sailing in *Alert*, *Perseverance* and *Hope* of Peterhead to become master of *Perseverance*. In 1899 he
was on Southampton Island creating a trading station for Robert Kinnes. At
that time, John Murray was the mate of *Active* of Dundee and then of *Scotia*
with the formidable Captain Thomas Robertson in command.

In 1907 the crew of *Scotia* got drunk at Reykjavik and temporarily took
control of the ship, showing that even with a strong master and mate, Dundee
whaling men were not to be taken lightly. Between 1908 and 1911 Murray
was master of *Balaena*, followed by command of the ketch *Albert* and finally
he commanded *Active* in 1914, the last whaling vessel to sail from Dundee.
Although there was no more whaling, Captain Murray continued to work in
the Arctic, sailing in various small vessels, rescuing the crew of *Easonian* in
1922 and finally retiring to Wormit where he died in 1948 aged 82.

Penny, William

Born into a Peterhead whaling family in 1809, William Penny first sailed
north in 1821 and became a mate when he was just 20 years old. Six years
later he was a ship's master. His career made him undoubtedly one of the
most respected and influential whaling masters in Scotland. From helping
in the search for the missing explorer Franklin to bringing an Inuit back to
Scotland, Penny was at the forefront of the industry, proving both innovative
and daring. Helped by an Inuit guide, he opened up Cumberland Sound for

whaling; he began the practice of overwintering in 1853; began floe whaling and attempted an ambitious holistic whaling venture that would have included a network of settlements across the Arctic Ocean from Eastern Canada to Nova Zembla. A man of infinite energy, Penny also brought a missionary to teach Christianity to the Inuit and helped stretch Canadian influence into the Arctic.

During his time in the Dundee whaling industry, Penny was master of *Advice* and *Polynia*. He commanded *Advice* in 1849 and in 1861 he took *Polynia* to the Davis Straits but fell out with the owners and lost command of the ship. However, he was said to have been crucial in the design of *Narwhal*, one of Dundee's early purpose-built steam whaling ships, and a vessel that influenced four decades of Dundee dominance in the Arctic. There is a rumour that the Dundee Greenlandmen were not over-enamoured with the first steam powered whaling ships and threatened to tar and feather Captain Penny,[1] but if so, his personality and skill won them over. His last whaling voyage was in 1864 and he died in 1892, having never lost a ship in his entire career.

Robertson, Thomas

In common with so many of Dundee's whaling masters, Thomas Robertson was born in Peterhead. He was master of *Arctic II* in 1889 and, at the age of 38, commanded *Active* during the 1892 Dundee Antarctic Whaling Expedition, when he became a minor but important explorer. From 1897 to 1901 he commanded *Balaena,* and in 1901 he fell foul of the law and was fined for hiding tobacco in his cabin. Although tobacco may have been a weakness, alcohol certainly was not: Basil Lubbock in his *Arctic Whalers* stated Robertson was known as 'Coffee Tam' because of his teetotal principles.

After *Balaena,* Robertson was master of *Scotia* in William Bruce's Scottish National Antarctic Expedition. Bruce had been a scientist in the Dundee 1892 voyage to the Antarctic and must have been impressed by Robertson's seamanship. Robertson gave examples of his experience on this expedition too, when in 1903 *Scotia* was searching for Lethewaite Strait north of the South Orkney Islands. After a period of squalls, the sea smoothed over and Robertson's experience told him there was an iceberg ahead. Bruce paid a handsome tribute when he wrote: 'nothing but the able handling of the ship by my officers and crew, and their long experience of navigating among ice could have saved us from a most deadly collision'.[2] On the return of *Scotia,* the Royal Scottish Geographical Society awarded Robertson a silver medal. He remained as master of *Scotia* until 1914, which included a period when she was an ice patrol vessel after the 1912 *Titanic* disaster. The archives of Dundee's McManus Galleries and Museum hold a photograph of this shipmaster.

Robson, Thomas

Captain Thomas Robson commanded *Dundee* between 1775 and 1782. In 1775 and 1776 respectively he captured two whales. In 1782 *Dundee* was lost in the ice and Robson left an account of the disaster. *Dundee* had sailed from Dundee on 4 May, teamed up with a few vessels from the Dunbar fleet and sailed north, passed Shetland five days later and soon after, struck out alone for the ice. At 78 degrees north, sailing at a steady six knots, *Dundee* slammed into an ice floe and began taking water. As the ship began to sink Captain Robson ordered all six whaleboats to be provisioned and sent them out to the ice. The crew survived for 21 days walking across the ice before being rescued off Magdalen Point by *Young Eagle* of London and *Manchester* of Hull.

The *Dundee Directory* has a shipmaster named Thomas Robson living in the Murraygate in 1782. This may well be the master of *Dundee*.

Sturrock, David.

Captain David Sturrock was Master of *Horn* from at least 1843 until 1852 when she ran aground at Kingsbarns near St Andrews in Fife. In 1846 he experienced a family tragedy when his son was accidentally killed while on a shooting expedition. In 1854 Captain Sturrock took over the whaling ship *Heroine* but on March 29 the following year, a wave swept him overboard while he was voyaging to the sealing. He drowned before he could be rescued. The same wave fatally injured his nephew, James Sturrock, who was also on *Heroine*. David Sturrock was the father of Captain James Sturrock of *Alexander*; he was 54 years old when he was killed.

Sturrock, James Donnet

The son of Captain David Sturrock, James Donnet Sturrock was master of *Alexander* between 1840 and 1847, and 1849 to 1855. In 1855 customs officers searched *Alexander* when she arrived off Broughty Ferry and found a number of items concealed including 13 bottles of wine and three bottles of brandy packed in straw around the water closet in his cabin, with 14 pounds of tea and 11 pounds of tobacco. The case came to the Justice of the Peace court where Captain Deuchars of *Princess Charlotte* spoke for Captain Sturrock, saying it was common practice to take stores out when the ship was in the ice, and they were sometimes forgotten. Captain Sturrock was fined.

Valentine, Captain William

Master of *Horn* and of *Achilles*, Captain Valentine was one of the most popular whaling masters in his day, but has been all but forgotten now. He was master of *Horn* from 1805 right through to 1820 but after that the records are a trifle confused. Ingram claims that he was master of *Achilles* from 1821 to 1828 but the customs records state he was master of *Fairy* from 1821 to 1824. It is possible there were two masters of the same name at the same time. However, there was only one Captain William Valentine mentioned in the *Dundee Directory* for 1818 and 1824, and he lived in Crichton Street.

Captain William Valentine died on Saturday 28 March 1829 aged 64. His obituary stated he had been on 45 voyages to Greenland, with 24 of them as a master working for the Dundee Whale Fishing Company. When he died, all the vessels in Dundee harbour hoisted their colours at half mast as a mark of respect.

Walker, John

Born in Peterhead, John Walker had commanded *Jean* of Bo'ness before coming to Dundee to take charge of *Wildfire* between 1863 and 1864. He was also master of *Alexander* from 1865 to 1869 and *Erik* from 1870 to 1882. While on *Erik*, he helped rescue the crew of the lost *Ravenscraig* in 1878. In 1882 he commanded *Polynia* for the sealing and took that vessel for sealing and whaling between 1883 and 1885, after which he no longer appears to have commanded a Dundee whaling vessel. The Geographical and Meteorological Societies of London employed him in surveying work of Scott's Inlet and Eclipse Sound in the Davis Straits. He died at home at Rock Villa, West Ferry, in the early years of the twentieth century, leaving a widow and family.

Captain West

Captain West was distinguished because he was the only Dundee whaling master who was suspected to have committed suicide. Born in Kirkcaldy in 1836, he gained a great deal of experience as a mate before being promoted master with certificate number 86798. He was master of *Ravenscraig* in 1879, but she returned to the Tay after a disastrous voyage when the crew refused to sail in a leaking vessel. Captain West disappeared overboard and it was suspected he committed suicide.

Yule, Charles

Captain Charles Yule was something of a Dundee legend and probably the only Dundee whaling master to live to 100. As with many successful whaling masters, he had a colourful seagoing career. Born in Montrose in 1835, he began his maritime career at the age of 14 in the local brig *Agenonia*. By 1850 he was third mate in the emigrant ship *Sea King* sailing to Australia. He was a seaman on the brig *Onkaparinga* which was driven ashore at Wanganui in New Zealand, worked on the Australian gold fields for three years, and signed on *Columbia* as a seaman.

When he was 28, Yule gained command of the Montrose brig *Gazelle*, followed by the Alexander Stephen and Sons-owned *Isabella*. In this last ship he took a cargo of timber from Prussia just before the Danes clamped down their naval blockade. This timber was used to build *Esquimaux*, the first Dundee whaling vessel that Yule commanded. He was with her from 1866 to 1879, followed by command of *Resolute* and finally *Polynia* from 1881 to 1883. During his whaling career, Captain Yule was religious, and neither swore nor touched alcohol. Retiring from the sea, he became the harbour-master at Dundee until 1920 when he retired. He survived to see his one hundredth birthday in August 1935 but died the following month, leaving an estate of £8,177 12s 2d.[3] Captain Yule was married to Jane Edith Helen Kilvert who survived him. They lived at Braeside, Grove Road, Broughty Ferry.

Appendix 3

Dundee Whaling Men

Name	Position	Ship	Year	Notes
Abbot, Dick		*Erik*	1876	Dick Abbot was a member of a boat's crew when they harpooned a whale. The boat overturned and Abbot was lost; one of the many casualties of the whaling trade.
Abbot, James	Line Manager	*Dorothy*	1836	James Abbot was mentioned in *Dorothy*'s Pay Book, held at the McManus Gallery and Museum in Dundee. This may be the same James Abbot who lived in Hawkhill, Dundee but who drowned when his whaleboat capsized, leaving a widow and child.
Abbot, John	Fireman	*Narwhal*	1881	Aged 50, John Abbot was born in Dundee
Able, Martin	Seaman	*Dorothy*	1835	Martin Able was mentioned in *Dorothy*'s Pay Book, held at the McManus Gallery and Museum in Dundee. He signed for his wages with an X, which is an indication that he was illiterate.
Adam, David	Seaman or Common Mariner	*Mary Ann*	1810	David Adam is mentioned in a list of mariners protected from the Impress Service
Adam, David	Blacksmith	*Intrepid*	1882	Aged 30, Adam was born in Dundee, His previous ship was *Victor.*
Adam, George	Able-bodied Seaman	*Narwhal*	1883	Aged 20, George Adam was born in Dundee
Adam, George	Cook	*Nova Zembla*	1883	Aged 55, George Adam had previously served in *Resolute*

Name	Position	Ship	Year	Notes
Adam, William	Line Manager	*Estridge*	1815	William Adam was named on the Customs list as having a Protection against being Impressed by the Royal Navy.
Adamson, Andrew	Common Seaman	*Jane*	1809	Andrew Adamson was named in the Protection List that year.
Adamson, Andrew	Line Manager	*Calypso*	1810	This Andrew Adamson was named in a Protection List; he may be the same man as the previous entry, but if so has been promoted.
Adamson, George	Boatsteerer	*Advice*	1810	Named in a Protection List, George Adamson had the responsible task of steering the whale boat to the best position to harpoon the whale.
Adamson, Henry	Boatsteerer	*Active*	1892–93	Aged 36 and born in Perth, Henry Adamson was part of the Dundee Antarctic Whaling Expedition.
Adamson, John	Seaman	*Friendship*	1832	There are details of John Adamson's pay in *Friendship's* pay book held in Dundee Museum.
Adamson, Robert	Harpooner	*Dorothy*	1829	There are details of Robert Adamson's pay in *Dorothy's* pay book held in Dundee Museum. As a harpooner he was an important man on the ship.
Adamson, Robert	Specktioneer	*Dorothy*	1836	There are details of Robert Adamson's pay in *Dorothy's* pay book held in Dundee Museum. As specktioneer he was one of the leading specialists and an experienced man.
Adamson, William	Chief mate	*Fairy*	1845	William Adamson died on board *Fairy* in the Davis Straits, April 1845, aged 40. He had also sailed on *Dorothy* in 1836 and *Advice*, 1837 and 1839, and *Princess Charlotte* in 1843.
Aitken, Alexander	Various	*Enterprise; Resolute; Balaena; Esquimaux; Diana.*		Born 1830, Alexander Aitken made his first voyage as a 15 year old apprentice in 1845. He spent 50 years as a whaling seaman, sailing in various vessels. He spoke with Franklin and survived shipwreck with *Resolute*. His final voyage was in 1901.

Name	Position	Ship	Year	Notes
Aitken, Thomas		*Princess Charlotte*	1828	Born in St Monance in Fife, Thomas Aitken was fastening the anchor at the ship's bows when he fell into the Tay and drowned; he was unmarried.
Alexander, James	Harpooner	*Jan Mayen*	1881	James Alexander had served on this vessel the previous year.
Allan, Alexander	Sail maker and boats-teerer	*Diana*	1892–93	Aged 25; sailed to Antarctica on this voyage. Alexander Allan was born in Peterhead.
Allan, James	Able seaman or boats-teerer	*Chieftain*		James Allan was involved in the attempted capture of the Tay Whale.
Allan, James W.	Surgeon	*Aurora*	1893	The journal of Surgeon Allan is held in the Scott Polar Research Institute, Cambridge.
Allan, John		*Thomas*	1836	John Allan was one of the survivors when *Thomas* was wrecked in the ice. He was rescued by *Norfolk*, but later died on board that vessel.
Allan, Thomas	Seaman	*Dorothy*	1834	Thomas Allan was part of a boat's crew that struck a whale.
Allan, Thomas	Sailor	*Mary Ann*	1813	In common with many of the crew, Thomas Allan deserted *Mary Ann* in Aberdeen to avoid the Press Gang.
Allan, William	Third mate	*Diana*	1900	William Allan was taken to court for bartering with the Inuit in Ponds Bay, Eastern Canada. Ponds Bay is now Ponds Inlet and is home to an Inuit community.
Allan, William	Harpooner	*Esquimaux*	1890	Aged 37, his previous ship was *Red Sea*.
Anderson, Alexander	Seaman	*Friendship*	1831	Alexander Anderson signed for his wages with an X, which suggests he could not write.
Anderson, Alexander	Harpooner	*Eclipse*	1905	Harpooned a whale 7 July 1905.
Anderson, D.	Able-bodied seaman (AB)	*Victor*	1879	Aged 22 in 1879, Mr Anderson was born in Dundee.
Anderson, D. R.	Engineer	*Seduisante*	1911	Aged 51, Mr Anderson lived at 15 Mid Street, Dundee.

Name	Position	Ship	Year	Notes
Anderson, David	Ordinary seaman (OS)	*Narwhal*	1883	Aged 14, David Anderson had been born in Dundee. As an Ordinary Seamen he would be expected to do the unskilled but essential tasks on board.
Anderson, George	Sailor	*Dundee* of Dundee	1753	Came back from Greenland 25 July 1753.
Anderson, George	Line Manager	*Calypso*	1810	Lived at North Ferry.
Anderson, Robert		*Ravenscraig*	1869	Mr Anderson was left behind when the wind changed while they were sealing. A Norwegian vessel later rescued him. He was a Dundee man.
Anderson, William	Line Manager	*Morning*	1910	Aged 20, sailed with Captain Adams in 1908, lived at 278 Brook Street, Broughty Ferry.
Angus, James	Line Manager	*Mary Ann*	1808	Named on a Protection list in Customs Records.
Archibald, John	Boatsteerer	*Advice*	1815	When the harpooner Robert Nicoll fell sick, Robert Pattie was promoted in his place and John Archibald moved up to Boatsteerer.
Archibald, William	Harpooner	*Friendship*	1839	Mentioned in the Wages book of *Friendship* held by McManus Gallery and Museum, Dundee. It would be nice to think this harpooner was the later Captain William Archibald from Kirkcaldy.
Archison, James	Blacksmith	*Nova Zembla*	1883	Born Kirriemuir, aged 29, this was James Archison's first voyage.
Baird, James	OS	*Ravenscraig*	1874	Aged 16, James Baird had sailed in the same ship the previous year.
Baker, Edward	Seaman	*Alexander*	1862	*Alexander* was lost in Melville Bay that year. The ship *Emma* brought him home, but while he was celebrating his survival in Stromness, he fell and broke his leg.
Bannerman, Jim	Harpooner	*Erik*	1876	The ship's log mentions Jim Bannerman catching a whale.
Barclay, George	Line Manager	*Advice*	1838	Aged 27, born in Dundee, his previous ship was *Pacific*.

Name	Position	Ship	Year	Notes
Bard, James		*Fairy*	1838	Mentioned in the logbook kept by Thomas Dowie and held in Local History Department, Central Library, Dundee.
Barnie, Thomas	Seaman	*Advice*	1838	Aged 29, Thomas Barnie was born in Dundee.
Barrie, David	Harpooner	*Fairy*	1838	On 30 July 1838 David Barrie harpooned a whale.
Barry William		*Advice*	1836	William Barrie caught scurvy in this year, when *Advice* was trapped in the ice over winter.
Baxter, John	Seaman	*Advice*	1840	December 1840, in the Graving Dock in Dundee, John Baxter fell into the hold and cut himself but recovered.
Beaton, David	OS	*Esquimaux*	1890	Born in Dundee, aged 19.
Beattie, William	Sailor	*Dundee* of Dundee	1753	Arrived in Dundee 25 July 1753.
Begbie, Andrew	AB	*Intrepid*	1866	Born in Edinburgh, aged 24, he earned £2 10s a month for basic wage.
Bell, James	Seaman	*Friendship*	1815	Named on protection list so he could not get press ganged by the Royal Navy.
Bell, Patrick	Chief Engineer	*Resolute*	1887	Patrick Bell found a plug of tobacco on Beechy Island; possibly it had been left by the missing Franklin Expedition.
Bennet, James	Sailor	*Dundee* of Dundee	1753	James Bennett had previously served on the whaling ship *Peggy* of Glasgow, which arrived at Bo'ness from the Greenland Sea.
Berry, Thomas	Seaman	*Snowdrop*	1905	Born in Dundee.
Bishop, George	Common seaman	*Estridge*	1809	In protection list against impressments.
Black, David	Line Manager	*Estridge*	1816	Named in a list of men protected against impressments.
Blair, John	Carpenter	*Friendship*	1831	Mentioned in a wages book held in Dundee Museum.
Blair, Robert	Greenman	*Three Brothers*	1819	Sailed to Davis Straits. As he was a Greenman, this would be his first voyage.

Name	Position	Ship	Year	Notes
Blyth, Archie	Harpooner	*Erik*	1876	On 16 July, Archie Blyth harpooned a whale.
Blyth, David	Harpooner	*Dorothy*	1828	On 20 March, this seaman from Dubbyside in Fife was fastening the hoisting tackle for the stern boat. He must have slipped, for he fell into the Tay. It was a dark, stormy night and he drowned. He was married with seven children.
Bonar, Robert	Harpooner	*Balaena*	1892–93	Aged 49 and born in Dundee, Robert Bonar sailed on *Balaena* as part of the Dundee Antarctic Expedition of 1892.
Bowman, Andrew	AB	*Narwhal*	1883	Aged 21, and born in Dundee, Andrew Bowman's previous ship was *Clarissa*.
Bowman, John		*Thomas*	1836–37	Unlike many of his shipmates, John Bowman survived the wreck of *Thomas*
Bowman, Robert		*Princess Charlotte*	1836	Fell off a yardarm on the homeward voyage and drowned.
Boyd, George	OS	*Intrepid*	1866	Born in Dundee and earned £1 15s a month plus oil money. There was a carpenter named George Boyd in *Active* in 1892 who may have been the same man.
Brand, James	Boatsteerer	*Calypso*	1814	Took over boatsteerer's role in place of Mark Christopher, who had died.
Brown, George		*Polar Star*	1896	Mentioned in the Dundee *Courier* as hunting whales with 'rocket and lance'.
Brown, James	Mate	*Diana*	1892	James Brown went to sea aged 15 and served on many whaling and sealing vessels. He spoke at least one Inuit language and lived in Forester Street, Dundee. In 1907 became Master of *Snowdrop*.
Brown, John	Harpooner	*Esquimaux*	1890	Aged 43, John Brown was also in the Naval Reserve.
Brown, Peter		*Advice*	1836	Rescued from the scurvy-ridden *Advice* but died on board *Grace* 6 June 1837.

Name	Position	Ship	Year	Notes
Brown, Philip		*Dorothy*	1834	Part of a boat's crew that struck a whale, 01 July 1834.
Brown, William	Seaman	*Esquimaux*	1866	William Brown died on board in September 1866.
Bruce, Alexander		*Chieftain*	1890–91	There are certificates of discharge for this seaman in Dundee Museum.
Buchan, David		*Chieftain*	1883	David Buchan's boat became separated from *Chieftain* in a mist. He fell overboard and drowned.
Burnett, G.	Steward	*Advice*	1893	Mr Burnett was prosecuted for smuggling tobacco on his return to Dundee.
Burnett, Mr	3rd Mate	*Resolute*	1882	Suffered from delirium tremors on this voyage.
Burnett, Thomas	2nd Mate	*Thetis* or *Aurora*	Not known	Thomas Burnett was on the ice, filling his pipe when a whale surfaced below him. He and the pipe were thrown into the sea, but only he was rescued. The pipe was never seen again.
Butters, Joseph	Harpooner	*Dorothy*	1834	Harpooned a whale, 5 July 1834.
Cameron, Frederick	Harpooner	*Eclipse*	1905	Harpooned a whale 23 July 1905.
Cameron, John	Apprentice	*Ebor*	1837	While *Ebor* was still in Dundee harbour, John Cameron fell from the deck to the bottom of the hold. He recovered in the infirmary.
Cant, Alexander	AB	*Balaena*	1892–93	Aged 35 and born in Broughty Ferry, Alexander Cant accompanied *Balaena* to the Antarctic.
Cargill, Andrew	Mariner	*Estridge*	1815	Received a Protection against Impressment for this voyage but failed to arrive. The Customs officials checked to see if he was in the Navy, without success. Andrew Cargill vanished from the whaling records.
Carson, James	Seaman	*Thomas*	1836	Rescued when *Thomas* foundered in the ice but later died aboard *Grenville Bay*.

Name	Position	Ship	Year	Notes
Cassie, David	Line Manager	*Narwhal*	1883	Aged 23; served on *Narwhal* in 1882 and 1883.
Chambers, James	Boat steerer	*Nova Zembla*	1883	Born in Dundee, 29 year old James Chambers had previously sailed on *Esquimaux*.
Chaplain, or Chaplin, Stewart	Boat steerer	*Thetis*	1883	Mr Chaplain drowned in the Davis Straits. He was in a boat that had harpooned a bottlenose whale but the whale overturned the boat and Mr Chaplain drowned.
Chapman, John	Line Manager	*Dundee* of Dundee	1754	A veteran of the Leith whaling ship *Tryal,* John Chapman was one of the earliest known Dundee whaling men.
Cheyn, Andrew	Boatsteerer	*Thetis*	1881	Aged 29, Mr Cheyn was one of the very many whaling seamen who sailed from Dundee but who were born in Peterhead.
Cheyne, Andrew	Seaman in 1753 and line manager in 1754	*Dundee* of Dundee	1753 and 1754	Andrew Cheyne was one of the many Greenlandmenwho advanced through the ranks.
Christie, David	Assistant Engineer	*Eclipse*	1905–06	Born in Perth in 1881, David Christie was five foot three with grey eyes and dark brown hair and had tattooed initials on the back of each hand. That voyage he was fined for passing some smuggled tobacco to his 12 year old brother.
Christie, Robert	Line Manager	*Nova Zembla*	1883	Aged 21, Robert Christie was one of the hundreds of Shetlanders without whom the Dundee whaling industry could not have operated.
Christopher, Mark [Junior]	Boatsteerer	*Calypso*	1814	Died on voyage without having received a protection from the press gang.
Christopher, William	Possibly mate		Before 1866	William Christopher died in Dundee Poorhouse on 16 August 1866. He was a whaling man and the son of a whaling man. The Dundee children called him Captain Christopher.
Collins, John	Seaman?	*Thetis*	1881	Peterhead born, Mr Collins fell from aloft from the rigging of *Thetis* and broke his leg.

Name	Position	Ship	Year	Notes
Copland, William	Harpooner	*Jan Mayen*	1881	Aged 40; had sailed on same ship on previous voyage.
Cornelius, Symon	Harpooner	*Dundee* of Dundee	1753 and 1754	Mr Cornelius was possibly one of the Dutch specialists who trained the early Scottish whaling men.
Cosgrove, Thomas		*Terra Nova*	1904	Aged 28 in 1904. Thomas Cosgrove may have been born as Thomas Flynn, but that is uncertain. He was a boy on board *Mars*, and at age 15 went to sea on a Norwegian steamboat, then transferred to a schooner and finally to the whaling when he served on *Active* and on *Terra Nova* during the rescue of Captain Scott. Also sailed in coasters, the D.P. & L and the Tay Ferries. *Lived at* 52 Kemback Street, Dundee.
Cossans, John	Boatsteerer	*Estridge*	1815	When Robert Davidson was promoted to harpooner, John Cossans took his place as boatsteerer.
Coupar, James	Boatswain	*Esquimaux*	1890	James Coupar was also in the Royal Navy Reserve.
Coutts, George		*Camperdown*	1874	Died of a severe cold when on board *Camperdown*.
Cowie, Peter	Shipkeeper	*Victor*	1880	Aged 46 and born in Buckie.
Cowie, William	OS	*Intrepid*	1866	Aged 21 and born in Broughty Ferry.
Craig, Gordon	Second mate	*Polar Star*	1896	Acted as a harpooner when hunting for whales.
Crammond, Peter		*Alexander*	1853	Peter Crammond was lost when a narwhal upset a whaling boat he was in. He left a widow and a large family at Westhaven.
Cummings, James		*Terra Nova*	1887	Aged 76. James Cummings died while hauling a seal aboard the ship. He had been on 57 voyages to the Arctic.
Cunningham, Thomas	Harpooner	*Mary Ann*	1808	Named on a Protection List so the Royal Navy could not press him.
Dacre, John	Second Engineer	*Camperdown*	1861	John Dacre was so prone to sea sickness he had to resign his position.

Name	Position	Ship	Year	Notes
Davidson, David	Seaman and line manager	*Dundee* of Dundee	1753 and 1754	Sailed in same ship on at least two consecutive voyages.
Davidson, Robert	Harpooner	*Estridge*	1815	Robert Davidson was named on a Protection List so he could not be pressed into the Royal Navy. He was promoted from boatsteerer to harpooner.
Davidson, Thomas	Mate [second?]	*Dorothy*	1829	Thomas Davidson was prosecuted for smuggling rum into Dundee.
Davie, Thomas	Harpooner?	*Advice*	1810	Named on Protection list in place of James Brown who sailed on *Raith* of Leith instead.
Davis	Harpooner	*Diana*	1903	Mr Davis was at the masthead on the 9th July and sighted a whale.
Dawson, William	Seaman	*Princess Charlotte*	1835	While loading the vessel, William Dawson was jammed between a cask and the cart. He was taken home in a sedan chair but died later of internal injuries.
Deuchars, David	Harpooner	*Victor* and *Arctic*	1874?	First went to sea in 1861; David Deuchars was born in Dundee. He was a Presbyterian, married with two children and was chosen as an Ice quartermaster for the 1875 Polar Expedition. Lived off Blackness Road, Dundee.
Doig, Alexander	Carpenter	*Advice*	1844	Born around 1810. First voyage was in 1834, aged 24. Alexander Doig was five foot nine and a quarter with dark brown hair, fresh complexion and grey eyes. He had two moles on his left cheek.
Dougal, William	Harpooner	Vessels included *Polar Star; Polynia; Erik*	1875	Aged 40 in 1875. Born in Peterhead; Presbyterian, 24 voyages by 1875, married with one child, he could drive a dog sleigh and lived in the Hilltown.
Duncan, John	Harpooner	*Dorothy*	1834	Struck a whale on 31 July 1834.
Duncan, John	Steward	*Eclipse*	1898	Caught smuggling tobacco.
Dunn, William	Line manager	*Esquimaux*	1890	Born in Newfoundland, his previous ship was *Dart*.

Name	Position	Ship	Year	Notes
Easson, David	Boatsteerer	*Thomas*	1829	Mr Easson became involved in a legal dispute as to the ownership of a harpooned whale: *Thomas* of Dundee or *Traveller* of Peterhead.
Edward or Edwards, George	sail maker	*Friendship*	1837 and 1838	Mr Edward (s) was paid 5s to buy sail maker's needles before the start of the voyage.
Elder, Thomas	Harpooner	*Polar Star*	1896	Known as 'Tom' : in charge of a whale boat that got fast to a whale on 13 May 1896.
Fenton, Alexander	Harpooner	*Estridge*	1810	When he mislaid his Certificate of Protection in early 1810, the Royal Navy pressed him for service.
Fenton, John	Line Manager	*Estridge*	1808?	John Fenton obtained a Protection so he could sail on *Estridge*, but illegally sailed on *Lady Forbes* to Jamaica instead.
Finlay, Robert	Sailor, steersman	*Dundee* of Dundee	1753 and 1754	Mr Finlay had also been a seaman on the Leith whaling ship *Tryal*.
Fraser, Adam	Line Manager	*Nova Zembla*	1876	Aged 43; came from Shetland. Mr Fraser was washed overboard and drowned, leaving a widow and family.
Fyall, James	Boatsteerer	*Friendship*	1832	Paid 2s 6d for a Bible while on board.
Ganson, Thomas	Line Manager	*Esquimaux*	1890	A Shetlander aged 24, Thomas Ganson was also in the Royal Naval Reserve.
Gellatly, David	Mate	*Friendship*	1837 and 1838	In the 1838 voyage he earned £4 10s plus £4 4s oil money.
Graham, James	Second Engineer	*Thetis*		Aged 23 and born in Kirriemuir, James Graham's previous ship was Intrepid.
Great, John	Seaman	*Friendship*	1823?	Buried in the Howff Graveyard, Dundee.
Greig, Andrew	Line Manager	*Horn*	1809–10	Had a Protection against Impressment but in 1810 was dismissed from *Horn* for improper conduct.

Name	Position	Ship	Year	Notes
Grieve, Alexander	Loose harpooner	*Friendship*	1831	A loose harpooner was a man not yet fully qualified for the position. He was on probation. A man of the same name was noted as a harpooner in *Friendship* in 1835, which suggests Alexander Grieve was promoted. He signed with an X so presumably could not write.
Grogan, Henry	Boatsteerer	*Active*	1881	Aged 32 and born in Dundee.
Guthrie, John	Harpooner	*Princess Charlotte*	1843	John Guthrie harpooned a whale 23 May 1843. Mentioned in the Log of *Princess Charlotte* held by Dundee Museum.
Guthrie, Thomas	Mariner	*Three Brothers*	1815	Received a Protection for the voyage but did not turn up for the voyage.
Halcrow, James	AB	*Esquimaux*	1890	A 23 year old man from Shetland who was also in the Royal Navy Reserve.
Hamilton, William		*Thomas* and *Advice*	1836	A St Andrews man, William Hamilton died of scurvy aboard *Advice* after being rescued from the sunken *Thomas*
Harp, James		*Ravenscraig*	1869	James Harp was stranded on the ice when the wind shifted during a seal hunt. A Norwegian vessel later rescued him. He came from Peterhead.
Henderson, Mr	Carpenter	*Thetis*	1883	Mr Henderson was drowned on the voyage. He was in a whaleboat that harpooned a bottlenose whale; the lines tangled and capsized the boat.
Henderson, Robert	Fast harpooner	*Dorothy*	1837	Robert Henderson complained to the Master of *Dorothy* he had only been paid as a loose harpooner, losing £5 in wages
Henry, John	AB	*Jan Mayen*	1881	Aged 21, born Sandsting, Shetland
Hill, Charles	Boatsteerer	*Ravenscraig*	1874	Aged 23 and born in Dundee, Charles Hill's previous ship was *Ravenscraig*.
Howie, James	Line Manager	*Polynia*	1891	Aged 34, Edinburgh born James Howie had also served in *Polynia* the previous year.

Name	Position	Ship	Year	Notes
Hutton, Thomas	AB	*Chieftain*		Mr Hutton was involved in the capture of the Tay Whale.
Ireland, James	Various	*Rodney*	1812	First went to sea on *Rodney* in 1812, with his father as Master; transferred to *Friendship*, became mate in 1824, then moved to the Baltic trade. Lived at Link Cottage, Broughty Ferry and died aged 81.
.Irons, Robert	Boatsteerer	*Polar Star*	1889	Aged 38, born in Shetland, previous ship was *Chieftain*.
Ironside, Colin	2nd Carpenter	*Intrepid*	1882	Aged 25, born Peterhead, his previous ship was *Intrepid* and before that, *Jan Mayen*.
Irvine, J.	AB	*Jan Mayen*	1881	Aged 29; born Nesting, Shetland
Jamieson, James	Mate	*Active*	1913	Once worked on an Aberdeen trawler. Born in Shetland but lived in Aberdeen.
Johnston, James	AB	*Intrepid*	1866	Born Fraserburgh, aged 21 in 1866; earned £2 a month basic pay.
Kay, William Norrie	2nd Engineer	*Narwhal*	1863	Born 1840, known career: *Narwhal* (2nd Engineer) 1863; *Alexander* (2nd Engineer) 1864, 1865; *Nimrod* (1st engineer) 1867; *Narwhal* (1st engineer) 1868; *Scotia* (2nd engineer) 1869–10 August 1870. Drowned aged 33.
Keith, Robert	Seaman	*Ebor*	1838	In March 1838 Robert Keith fell into King William's Dock while drunk. He was rescued but swore at his rescuers. Five years later and again drunk, he began his night by assaulting an innocent passerby and continued by attempting to knife a policeman, but only managed to stab himself in the hand.
Kelly, Barry	Harpooner	*Erik*	1876	Caught at least one whale during the 1876 voyage.
Kenelly, John	Mate	*Terror*	1850?	According to the Courier of 28 September 1859, John Kenelly left the whaling to become-quartermaster of *Terror* on the doomed Franklin expedition. He left a widow and an invalid son.

Name	Position	Ship	Year	Notes
Kennedy, Mr	2nd Engineer	*Active*	1881	In the journal written by Surgeon J. Melville Keith, when he returned to Dundee after the voyage, Mr Kennedy was 'half beside himself with gladness' to be back home with his wife.
Kerr, George	Boatsteerer	*Horn*	1809 and 1810	Had a Protection against Impressment by the Royal Navy.
Kerr, James	AB	*Esquimaux*	1890	Aged 25, James Kerr was also in the Royal Navy Reserve.
Kettleson, Frederick	Seaman	*Friendship*	1832	During this voyage, Frederick Kettleson bought a Bible for 2s 6d.
Kidd, Alexander	Seaman	*Achilles*	1830	Alexander Kidd was a member of the crew of *Achilles* when she was lost in the ice that year.
Kidd, Robert	Ship's Boy	*Thomas*	1836	This child was a member of the crew of Thomas. He was rescued when *Thomas* sank in the ice but later died of scurvy on board *Advice*.
Kilgour, Alexander	Harpooner	*Thomas*	1829	Mr Kilgour harpooned a whale that had already been claimed by the crew of *Traveller* of Peterhead. The dispute reached the High Court in Edinburgh and *Traveller* won their case.
Lagget, James	Surgeon	*Friendship*	1837	In this voyage Surgeon Lagget was paid £4 13s 9d plus a bonus of 10s 6d fish money.
Latto, William	Harpooner	*Dorothy*	1834	According to the unpublished log of Thomas Dowie, on the 21 September 1834, William Latto 'got fast to a fish'.
Lees, Thomas	Seaman	*Estridge*	1815	Thomas Lees was from St Monance, one of many Dundee whaling men from that town. He had a Protection from the Royal Navy on this voyage.

Name	Position	Ship	Year	Notes
Leggat, Richard	Seaman	*Terra Nova*	1897	An experienced Arctic mariner, in 1888 Richard Leggatt, while sailing on *Nova Zembla* became sick with 'inflammation of the lungs and dropsy' and came home in a Danish vessel. In 1897 he became very jealous of his wife and murdered her in their John Street home.
Lonie, James	Boatsteerer	*Eclipse*	1896	James Lonie was testing the harpoon gun but was injured by the gun charge.
Lonie, Robert	Mate	*Alexander*	1859	Fined for smuggling duty free tobacco back to Dundee.
Lorimer, David	Line Manager	*Estridge*	1809	Protected against impressment from September 1808. In 1810, while serving aboard *Calypso* he was badly injured while firing the customary salute when entering the Tay and a power horn exploded in his hand.
Lurk, Thomas		*Resolute*	1882	In the journal of Surgeon Peters, Thomas Lurk is mentioned as having a swollen hand on the 24 February 1882.
Lyon, James	Harpooner	*Polar Star*		Supposed to have made the first successful harpoon strike on the Tay Whale (the skeleton of which is in Dundee Museum).
MacDonald, Alexander	Surgeon	*Narwhal*	1872	Successfully treated an outbreak of smallpox on board during the voyage.
Mail, Andrew	Boatsteerer	*Horn*	1810	Andrew Mail was on the Customs list of mariners protected against the Impress service. He took the place of Andrew Greig who had been dismissed for 'improper conduct'.
Manson, Magnus	OS	*Ravenscraig*	1874	Aged 20, this Shetland born seaman had also served in *Ravenscraig* the previous year.

Name	Position	Ship	Year	Notes
Martin, George	Mate and harpooner	*Camper-down*	1861	Mentioned in the unpublished journal of Chief Engineer Alexander Smith, Peterhead born Mr Martin may have been the mate of the same name who was famous for his vivid use of language. He was mate of *Camperdown* in 1867 but fell into Dundee harbour as the ship made ready for Greenland.
Martin, George (cont.)	Mate and harpooner	*Camper-down*	1861	He sailed on the voyage but died a few days later. As mate of the Peterhead sealing ship *Xanthus* he had survived days alone on the ice, hunted by polar bears and wearing seal skins for warmth.
Mathieson, George	First harpooner	*Balaena*	1909	Fined for concealing smuggled goods in the foresheet of a ship's boat.
Mawer, Robert	Sailor	*Dundee* of Dundee	1753	Robert Mawer became master of the Dundee whaling ship *Grandtully* and a burgess of Dundee.
McCulloch, Francis	OS	*Narwhal*	1883	Dundee born McCulloch also served in *Narwhal* the previous year.
McDonald, James	Surgeon	*Tay*	1868	Lived in Paton's Lane in Dundee but died on the voyage home. One of the crew rowed ashore at Broughty to ask Mr Piper, the Seaman's Missionary to reach his wife and break the news, but she was waiting at the quay for her husband when the ship docked.
McDougal, Leslie	Harpooner	*Alexander*	1845	On the 10 July 1845 Leslie McDougal harpooned a whale.
McDougall, Alexander	OS	*Polar Star*	1892–93	Seventeen year old Alexander McDougall had been born in Dundee. He sailed with *Polar Star* to Antarctica.
McDougall, Alexander	Line Manager	*Mary Ann*	1814	Mr McDougall had to withdraw from this voyage due to bad health.

Name	Position	Ship	Year	Notes
McIntosh, Frank	Boatsteerer	*Balaena*		Aged 27 in 1898, Frank McIntosh was married and thought of as steady and respectable. Nevertheless he was fined £1 15s for smuggling two pounds of tobacco that year.
McIntosh, James Haddow		*Chieftain*		Born in Australia of a Dundonian father, James McIntosh made a name for himself for being the only survivor of an open whale boat that got lost in the fog. He lost the lower part of both legs through frostbite but survived and fathered ten children.
McKenzie, Alexander	Steward	*Narwhal*	1883	Fined £5 for smuggling tobacco.
Mackenzie, James		*Morning*	1910	Reputed to be the finest fiddle player in the entire whaling fleet.
Mackenzie, Robert	Seaman	*Polar Star*	1896	Part of a successful whale boat crew and earned an extra 2s 6d.
McWilliams, J.	Harpooner	*Eclipse*	1905	Captured at least one whale.
Miller, John	Sailor	*Dundee* of Dundee	1753	Had served on *Peggy* of Glasgow before signing articles on *Dundee*.
Milne, James	Harpooner	*Resolute*	1882	James Milne suffered from dysentery on the voyage. He had the same complaint while on a voyage to the East Indies.
Milne, William	Specktioneer	*Fairy*	1842	William Milne was heavily involved in the mutiny of that year.
Moncrieff, James	Seaman	*Thetis*		Rescued after falling overboard a week out of St John's Newfoundland. He later became Assistant Harbour Master in Dundee.
Morris, John	Line Manager	*Estridge*	1811	John Morris was given a Protection against the Impress service in place of Peter Mann.
Mouatt, W.	Seaman	*Diana*	1898	Caught smuggling tobacco.

Name	Position	Ship	Year	Notes
Myers, Charles	Various ranks	Various vessels	1851–78	The McManus Gallery and Museum in Dundee holds many Certificates of Discharge of Charles Myers, covering much of his career. Born in Heligoland around 1818, he served in many Dundee whaling vessels including *Princess Charlotte, Alexander, Narwhal* and *Victor*. His wife, Agnes, collected much of his pay.
Nicator, Peter	Mate	*Dundee* of Dundee	1794	When the French frigate *Brest* captured *Dundee,* Peter Nicator managed to hide. He was still on board when the Royal Navy recaptured the ship and brought her back to the Tay. The majority of the crew were taken into French captivity.
Ogston, Robert	Mate	*Narwhal*	1859	Caught smuggling tobacco.
Pattie, Robert	Harpooner	*Advice*	1815	Replaced Robert Nicoll, who was in bad health – a condition verified by a surgeon. Robert Pattie also received a Protection Certificate for this voyage and was promoted from Boatsteerer to Harpooner.
Pearson, John	Mate	*Terra Nova*		John Pearson was born in Falkirk. He sailed with Captain Adams on *Arctic*; in 1910. During the First World War a U-Boat captured his vessel *Erne* He died in 1954 leaving a son and two daughters; he had another son who was a fur trader in Hudson Bay but died in Alaska; other son a ship's master with Burmah Oil Company.
Peters, Stewart	Surgeon	*Resolute*	1882	Stewart Peters lived at 31 Union Place, Perth Road, Dundee.
Petrie, David	Cooper	*Victor*	1867	Aged 24; Mr Petrie was given a character of Very Good after the voyage to St John's Newfoundland.
Ravie, James		*Dorothy*	1831	James Ravie died of TB on the homeward voyage.

Name	Position	Ship	Year	Notes
Reid, Alexander	Line manager		1908	Aged 33; Alexander Reid died on the voyage and was buried at Lake Harbour in Cumberland Gulf.
Robertson, Alexander	Apprentice	*Dundee* of Dundee	1794	Alexander Robertson was one of two crew members who managed to evade capture when the French frigate *Brest* captured *Dundee*. Instead he appears to have joined the Royal Navy when H.M. Sloop *Kingfisher* recaptured the whaling ship.
Robertson, Alexander	Seaman	*Polar Star*	1896	Earned 2s 6d for being part of a boat's crew that got 'fast' to a whale.
Robertson, John	Seaman	*Horn*	1838	While off Peterhead, John Robertson fell overboard. There was a heavy gale at the time and he could not be rescued. He was married with a family.
Ross, Charles	OS	*Intrepid*		Aged 22, this Dundee born seaman had previously sailed in *Ravenscraig*.
Scott, Alexander	Harpooner	*Active*	1881	In the journal of Dr J. Melville Keith, a copy of which is held by the McManus Gallery and Museum, it states that Alexander Scott was 'one of the funniest fellows I ever saw in my life'.
Scott, Edward	Harpooner	*Diana*	1903	Had been sick for weeks and died 18 July 1903.
Sharp, Alexander	Engineer	*Esquimaux*	1901?	Mr Sharp served on board *Esquimaux* and as Chief Engineer on *Terra Nova*, and later on *Morning*. He was married to Anne Easson, had seven children and qualified for the Polar Medal.
Silverton, John	Seaman	*Dorothy*	1834	John Silverton was a member of a boat's crew that struck a whale on 1 July 1834.
Smith, Charles	Cooper	*Our Queen*	1879	Charles Smith was cooper when *Our Queen* sunk in Melville Sound. When he reached land he believed he found gold. A later expedition found no gold.

Name	Position	Ship	Year	Notes
Smith, James	Seaman	*Tay*	1865	After signing articles for *Tay*'s voyage, James Smith spent some of his advance pay in the Dundee pubs and missed the ship when she sailed. Arrested for breaking his contract, he was jailed for two weeks.
Smith, William	Chief Engineer	*Aurora*	1884	Mentioned in p. 20 of David Moore Lindsay's *A Voyage to the Arctic in the Whaler* Aurora.
Stenhouse, William	AB	*Polynia*	1872	Kirkcaldy born William Stenhouse served in Polynia until 1878, thereafter in other vessels. He worked his way up to Mate, was married to Susan Watson and in 1910 became harbourmaster at Kirkcaldy.
Stewart, Alexander	Harpooner	*Esquimaux*	1890	Had served on vessel *Nova Scotia*; became a Specktioneer.
Stirling, Andrew	Fireman	*Active*	1880	Dundee born Andrew Stirling broke his leg during the voyage. When *Active* arrived back in Dundee he was taken home on a stretcher.
Strachan, Robert	Mate	*Horn*	1837	A block fell on Robert Strachan's head as *Horn* was returning from the whale fishery. He was mortally injured and later died.
Sword, Alexander	Line manager	*Rodney*	1808	Alexander Sword had been on a Protection List but his name was removed as the enemy had taken him prisoner.
Tawse, David	Boatsteerer	*Columbia*	1868	David Tawse had been on at least seven previous Arctic voyages.
Taylor, John	Harpooner	*Diana*	1903	At one point on this voyage Mr Taylor harpooned a whale, but it escaped.
Thomson, Sinclair		*Ravenscraig*	1874	Sinclair Thomson was accidentally shot during a seal hunt. A bullet hit him in the thigh and he bled to death.

Name	Position	Ship	Year	Notes
Vannet, James.	Boatsteerer	*Diana*	1904	Boatsteerer for the Second Mate, James Vannet sighted a whale on 7 July 1904. He had the reputation of being very sharp-eyed.
Wales, John Callendar	Cook	*Diana*	1901–03 and 1905	Born in Dundee in 1882, John Wales lived in Carmichael Street and Moncur Crescent in Dundee. The McManus Gallery and Museum holds a splendid picture of him with his wife.
Walker, Alexander	Boatsteerer	*Columbia*	1868	When *Columbia* was sunk in the ice, Alexander Walker took the owners to court for loss of earnings, blaming an incompetent shipmaster. He lost the case.
Walker, David		*River Tay*	1868	As this iron ship was sinking, David Walker drank from what he thought was a bottle of whisky. Unfortunately it was carbolic acid and he died within 20 minutes. He was buried in the ice.
Wallace, Thomas	Harpooner	*Aurora*		At least once in his career, Thomas Wallace hunted a polar bear.
Warden, John	Linemanager	*Estridge*	1809–10	Had a Protection in 1809 but he deserted in 1810.
Watson, James	First harpooner	*Nova Zembla*	1888	Aged 45; he was a member of the Royal Navy Reserve but accidentally shot himself while sealing, leaving a widow in Rosebank Street, Dundee.
Williamson, Thomas		*Nova Zembla*	1876	During the outward voyage to Newfoundland a wave washed Thomas Williamson overboard. He was feared lost but the next wave brought him back, injured but alive.

Appendix 4
Dundee Whaling Ships Lost

Ship	When lost	Where lost
Dundee	1782	Greenland Sea
Jane	1809	Tay Banks
Rodney	1810	
Mary Ann	1819	'Crushed in ice'
Tay	1819	'Crushed in ice'
Calypso	1822	'in the ice'
Estridge	1825	Unknown
Three Brothers	1830	Melville Bay
Achilles	1830	Davis Straits
Thomas	1836	Davis Straits
Horn	1852	Fife Ness
Heroine	1858	Davis Straits
Advice	1859	Davis Straits
Princess Charlotte	1859	Davis Straits
Alexander	1862	Davis Straits
Dundee	1863	Davis Straits
Jumna	1863	Melville Bay
Emma	1864	Greenland Sea
River Tay	1868	Greenland Sea
Wildfire	1868	Davis Straits
Alexander	1869	Melville Bay
Arctic	1874	Davis Straits
Tay	1874	Melville Bay

Ship	When lost	Where lost
Camperdown	1878	Davis Straits
Our Queen	1879	Davis Straits
Ravenscraig	1879	Davis Straits
Victor	1881	Davis Straits
Jan Mayen	1882	Davis Straits
Mazinthien	1883	Peterhead Bay
Narwhal	1884	Davis Straits
Cornwallis	1885	Davis Straits
Intrepid	1885	Greenland Sea
Jan Mayen (II)	1886	Greenland sea
Resolute	1886	Labrador
Star	1886	Cumberland Gulf
Triune	1886	Davis Straits
Arctic (II)	1887	Melville Sound
Polynia	1891	Lancaster Sound
Chieftain	1892	Greenland Sea
Maud	1892	Davis Straits
Polar Star	1899	Cumberland Gulf
Nova Zembla	1902	Dexterity Fiord
Vega	1903	Davis Straits
Windward	1907	Davis Straits
Seduisante	1911	Hudson Bay
Earnest William	1913	Cumberland Gulf

Appendix 5

Dundee Whaling Ship Companies

Company name	Dates	Address	Owner or manager	Vessels
Union Whale Fishing Company	c1751		Sir John Halyburton, afterward Provost of Dundee	
Dundee Whale Fishing Co	Current 1754, 1756 and 1774; in operation 1783		John Rankine, merchant in Dundee, agent in 1783; owners included William Alison, John Guthrie and James Jobson[1]	
Ship Jane Company	Current 1809		David Jobson, senior, agent. Committee: Gersham Courtney, Wm Bisset, Jas Gray, A. Pitcairn, David Auchterlony	*Jane*
Ship Rodney Co	Current 1809		David Jobson, senior, agent. Committee: John Peter, Gersham Courtney, Wm Bisset, Jas Gray	*Rodney*
Ship Advice Company	Current 1809		David Jobson, agent. The Committee was John Jobson, Samuel Bell, Thomas Webster and James Campbell	*Advice*
Ship Estridge Company	Current 1809		W Bisset, agent. Committee: David Jobson, senior; David Cock; John Duff Jnr.	*Estridge*
Rodney Greenland Ship Company	Current 1818			*Rodney*

Company name	Dates	Address	Owner or manager	Vessels
Powrie and Russel	Current 1818 through to at least 1824		Thoms in 1818; by 1824 managed by John Gabriel Russel. This is presumably the same J. G. Russell, Insurance Broker of the Wellgate	1818: *Calypso* 1818–24: *Three Brothers*
Union Whale Fishing Company (Also known as the Dundee Union Whale Fishing Company)	From at least 1818 until at least 1834 and probably 1837. This might be the same company that was operating in 1751.	Seagate	In 1830 the registered owners of the company were: John Blair Miller, merchant; John Calman, shipbuilder; and John Gabriel Russel, Insurance Broker; all three were trustees. In 1818 J. G. Russell was the manager. Pat Cameron of Foundry Lane was manager in 1829 and 1830	1818: *Calypso, Three Brothers* 1824: *Thomas, Three Brothers* 1829: *Thomas,Three Brothers*
Dundee Whale Fishing Co	1818–38, when possibly amalgamated with Dundee Union Whale Fishing Company		Alexander Thomas Bailie one of the partners, with James Fairweather, shipmaster	
Dundee New Whale-Fishing Company	From at least 1818 until the company was dissolved on 30 October, 1849	Seagate	In 1825 shareholders included: George Fyffe, James Law and John Livingstone In 1824 manager was James Soot, New Entry Inn, Dundee	1834: *Fairy, Heroine.* By 1840 *Fairy* was managed by the Fairy Whale Fishing Company
Dorothy Whale Fishing Co	Approximately 1824–40	Yard and Office, Seagate. In 1828 the agent, Mr James Justice, worked from 3 Peter Street, Dundee	1827: owners were: David Ouchterlony, Mrs Elizabeth Gray, Mrs Margaret Halliburton, Misses Flora Bisset and Janet Bisset, Mrs Helen Bisset or Thomson, Miss Catherine Wright, Robert Stirling and George Milne.	*Dorothy, Friendship*

Company name	Dates	Address	Owner or manager	Vessels
Friendship Whale Fishing Company	Current 1824		David Jobson, manager,	*Friendship*
Dundee Whale Fishing Company	Until 1826			*Achilles, Alexander*
William Stephen	Current 1834	Seagate	Patrick Cameron, Foundry Lane, manager	*Ebor, Thomas*
Fairy Whale Fishing Company	From around 1840 to at least 1846	Yard and Office, Seagate	Manager: 1840– David Keith, 7 Peter Street; 1842 – James Law, Commission Merchant and Agent of Trades Lane; 1845 – George Fyffe, with a possible business address of 16 Dock Street	*Fairy*
Dundee and Union Whale Fishing Co	Current from 1843 until at least 1858	Yard and Office, Seagate	Patrick Smith, manager	*Alexander; Thomas*
Arctic Fishing Company	1858–74	18 or 19 Dock Street, Dundee	William Clark, shipowner, 19 Dock Street [house at 56 Magdalen Green] and W. O. Taylor, Ship and Insurance Brokers were the managers. W. O. Taylor of 18 Dock Street, Dundee, became interim manager around 1860–61 and thereafter manager.	*Tay*
Dundee Seal and Whale Fishing Company	From at least 1867 until 1894 when the company entered liquidation	Whale Lane, East Dock Street (Sometimes called Whale Yard)	James Yeaman and David Bruce were joint managers when the company began, but David Bruce was sole manager by 1876.	A variety of vessels: the screw ships *Narwhal, Polynia* and *Camperdown* with the sailing vessel *Columbia* in 1867, but within a few years *Esquimaux* had been purchased and *Columbia* had gone. By 1902 only *Esquimaux* was left.

Company name	Dates	Address	Owner or manager	Vessels
Anthony Gibb and Sons, London	1869–82		Manager: David Bruce	*Erik*
Dundee Polar Fishing Co	1876–1906		Managed by W. O. Taylor and Company. In 1906 the director was J. M. Hunter Mitchell	*Jan Mayen, Nova Zembla*
South Sea Whale Fishing Company	Formed 1893 to take over *Active, Balaena, Diana* and *Polar Star* but project abandoned			
Dundee Arctic Fisheries Company Limited	1895–98	3 Royal Exchange Place and later 31 Albert Square	Directors: Messrs Robert McGavin, George A. Cox, Alexander Henderson, George M. Cox, David Bruce. Managed by David Bruce and Co.	*Esquimaux, Terra Nova*
James Mitchell	Current 1897		James Mitchell (managing owner)	Bought *Eclipse* from Peterhead in 1892, owner until at least 1898.
The Balaena Fishing Company;	1902–14	39 Dock Street, Dundee	James Mitchell was manager in 1902 and 1903; In 1902 the directors were: James Mitchell; Joseph Gibson; Charles Yule. In 1908 the directors were Charles Yule, William Hunter and James Mitchell. In 1906 the secretary was John Hunter Mitchell.	*Balaena*

Appendix 6

Letter about Impressing Seamen, 1803

Gentlemen,

The Lords of His Majesty's most Honourable Privy Council having caused Letters to be written to the Lords Lieutenants of the several Counties in England and Wales, the Mayors and Chief Magistrates of sundry Cities and Towns, and to the Lord Provost of Edinburgh, and other Cities and Towns in Scotland, enjoining the Justices of the Peace &etc to cause all straggling Seamen, fit to serve on Board His Majesty's Ships, to be taken up, and sent by proper Persons from Place to Place, until they shall be brought to the Clerks of the Cheque of His Majesty's Yards, and signifying His Majesty's Pleasure, that a Reward of Twenty Shillings for each Seaman fit for His majesty's Service, and Sixpence for every Mile they respectively travel, not exceeding Twenty Miles in the Maritime Counties, and Forty Miles in the Inland Counties, be paid to the Person entrusted with the conducting such Seamen, by the Clerk of the Cheque, Naval Officer, or Officer employed in raising Men for His majesty's Fleet; but in case the Men so taken up shall be sent to any Place where no such Clerk of the Cheque, Naval Officer or Officer employed in raising Men doth reside, that the same Allowance be paid to the Conductor by the Collector or proper Officer of the Customs residing at or nearest to the Place whereunto such Seamen shall be brought: I am commanded by the Lords Commissioners of His Majesty's Treasury, therefore, to desire that you will give the necessary Orders to your Officers to make such Payments accordingly.

I am

Gentlemen

Your most humble servant

John Sargent

Treasure Chambers

1 April 1803

Appendix 7

Jute Batching Oil Advert

MACARTHUR & JACKSON

LUBRICATING OIL MANUFACTURERS

WORKS AND HEAD OFFICE

GLASGOW

We desire to call the attention of JUTE SPINNERS to our

SPECIAL JUTE-BATCHING OIL,

which is now largely used in all Jute Spinning districts, both at home and abroad

This oil is guaranteed to be a mixture of Fish Oil and Mineral Oil, prepared by a process of our own, whereby the Body of the Pure Whale Oil is retained in the compound.

Jute Spinners who have regularly and exclusively used this Oil, since the date of its introduction assure us that it causes less waste, gives the yarn a smoother 'skin' and yields full weight; while, in respect to cost, it shows a large saving compared with any mixtures prepared by Spinners themselves to produce equally good results.

As a Batching Oil, combining efficiency with economy, it holds a pre-eminent position in the trade

Branch office – 2 Meadow Place Buildings, Dundee

Appendix 8

Dorothy Whaling Company Expenditure, 1830

Reason	To whom paid	Date	Amount
Piloting James Chapman	John Lorimer, Pilot	29 October 1830	£1 10s
Shore Dues on Blubber	Customhouse, Dundee	27 October 1830	Not given
Greenwich Money for Dorothy	Customhouse, Dundee	27 October 1830	£8 15s
Northern Light Dues	Customhouse, Dundee	27 October 1830	£3 16s 8d
Tay Light Dues	Customhouse, Dundee	27 October 1830	£1 16s 9d
Tonnage, anchorage and beaconage: Dorothy	Shore Dues Officer	Not given	£2 5s 4d
Plank dues	Shore Dues Officer	Not given	5s 6d
Town Clerk's Dues	Not given	Not given	6d
Friendship: tonnage, anchorage and beaconage	Shore Dues officer	29 October 1830	£10 2s 8d
Plank dues	Shore Dues Officer	29 October 1830	6d
Freight charge and shore dues for five coils rope	Dundee Hull Shipping Company	Not given	5s 5d
Cleaning 31 hundredweight of bone	Elizabeth Hunter	26 November 1830	£3 9s 9d
Greenwich money (Friend-ship)	Custom House	25 October 1830	£9 0s 10d
Northern Light Dues	Custom House	25 October 1830	£3 3s 4d
Tay Light Dues	Custom House	25 October 1830	£1 13s 6d
Sound Dues, per Economy from Petersburgh: 6 bundles whalebone	Brown and Bund, Elsinore	30 November 1830	£2 3s 3d
Coals	Owners of schooner Jean	11 March 1831	£12 16s
Porters	Owners of schooner Jean	11 March 1831	10s 8d

Reason	To whom paid	Date	Amount
50 bolls English coals for Friendship	Owners of schooner Jean	06 March 1830	£10 10s 5d
Fine London hat and hat box for Thomas Nicoll	Walter Haldane, 2 Castle Street, Dundee	30 January 1830	£1 1s 6d
3 bushels salt for Dorothy	Not given	05 April 1830	3s 9d
Onions	William Patterson	06 January 1831	10s
Green table cloth for Dorothy	Robert Moyes	20 March 1830	11s
24.5 yards of channel laid at whale yard, including square stones and labour	Neil McDonald	30 December 1829	£4 18s 3d
Cordage: cord for whale bone	James Bell	11 November 1830	£2 17s 2d
Repairing copper boilers	John Batting copper-smith	19 October 1830	£12
Allowance to coppersmiths and passage to London	Mrs Helen Whitton	July 1830	£6 14s 2d
Passage for three persons to London	Dundee Perth and London Shipping Company	01 August 1830	£4 10s
Freight of Freight of 24 casks whale oil to Newcastle	Owners of Mary and Ann	08 October 1830	£3 13s
Freight charges: oil and whale fins	Dundee Perth and London Shipping Co	09 September 1830	£16 12s
Shore Dues on oil and bone to date		07 October 1830	£7 15s 3d
Medicines	William Bisset	05 October 1830	£2 9s
Expenses in regard to harbour bill	Cobb and Michell, Writers	04 October 1830	£3 15s
Crockery for Dorothy	Richard Wright	18 September 1830	£1 7s 8d
Masonry for Friendship Whale Yard	William Butchart	21 September 1830	£23 18s 7d
Assessment on Boiling Yard	Town of Dundee?	11 September 1830	£5 15s
Assessment for Whale Lane	Town of Dundee?	Not given	£5 15s
Scots coals for Dorothy	James Keiller	11 September 1830	£5 0s 10d
Smith work	James Miller	30 August 1830	£144

Reason	To whom paid	Date	Amount
Freight of bone and oil	Dundee, Perth and London Shipping Company	30 August 1830	£3 10s
Freight 30 casks oil to Glasgow via the Forth	DPL Shipping Co.	30 August 1830	£12 8s
25 Hundredweight salted Shetland Cod	John and James Thom	06 September 1830	£16 5s
Freight crown piece of copper bottom	DPL Co.	No date	£1 13s
Five casks butter	William Curr	21 August 1830	£11 19s 3d
Pilotage of Dorothy from Carolina Roads to harbour	Thomas Webster	02 November 1830	15s
Pilotage into the River Tay [Carolina Roads]	Alexander Cunningham	27 October 1830	£3
Copperwork	Alexander Middleton	No date	£8 3s 2d
Freight	DPL Co.	No date	£1 5s 11d
12 Casks oil	Dundee Newcastle Shipping Co.	29 December 1830	£1 15s 11d
Freight of bone to be shipped to Bremen	Hull Shipping Co.	09 August 1830	5s
Ironmongery: knee nails, Batten nails etc	Robert Adamson	31 July 1830	£6 11s 11d
Hardware	Robert Adamson	02 July 1830	£20 12s
Coal	Alexander Crichton	24 July 1830	£1 2s 6d
Freight of 16 casks oil	DPL Co.	20 July 1830	£ 9 11s
Candles etc (Dorothy)	William Bell Jnr.	16 July 1830	£4 4s 8d
Candles (Friendship)	William Bell Jnr.	No date	£1 8s 2d
Porter	J. G. Thomson and Co., Leith		£12 16s 6d
80 bundles hoops	Dundee Hull Shipping Co.		£1 12s
1 basket dried raisins	Samuel Brodie	29 June 1830	£1
Crane dues for 1829	Dundee harbour?	18 June 1830	Not given

Reason	To whom paid	Date	Amount
Joinery work to Dorothy: outside and cabin: Dec to March 1829	James Cunningham	31 May 1830	£46 3s 2d
Freight of 20 oil casks (Mersey – ship's name?)	DPL Co.	17 May 1830	£12 4s 6d
Do Anna	DPL Co.	17 May 1830	£11 4s 6d
Shore dues on oil per Anna		17 May 1830	13s 8d
Groceries	Thomas Simson	15 May 1830	£6 12s 4d
Groceries for Friendship	Thomas Simson	15 May 1830	£14 2s 7d
Wood for decks	Kinmond and Hill		£76 6s 4d [Bill partly paid by two casks of oil]
Canvas etc (Friendship)	Peter Mitchell	07 May 1830	£15 12s
Canvas (Dorothy)	Peter Mitchell	07 May 1830	£14 13s
Mast for Friendship	Kinmond and Hill	No date given	£21 12s
Fine cheeses	David Hutcheson	05 May 1830	£3 0s 6d
Wines etc for Dorothy	Alexander Bell	04 May 1830	£9 17s
Wines for Friendship	Alexander Bell	04 May 1830	£7 9s 6d
Groceries for Dorothy	James Cameron	01 May 1830	£8 13s 11d
Work on new boilers in Boiling Yard	Abram Middleton	30 April 1830	£63 11s
Work on Dorothy	Abram Middleton	30 April 1830	£9 3s 11d
Shore dues on oil : Elbe and Anna	Not given	26 April 1830	£1 13s
Joinery work at Dorothy and yard	Charles Smith	17 April 1830	£11 13s
Biscuit and Flour: Dorothy	David Jobson	17 April 1830	£76 0s
Graving Dock Dues:	Dundee Harbour Commission	16 April 1830	£36 1s 6d
Compass repairs: Dorothy	William Chadwick	16 April 1830	£2 0s
Freight charges	DPL	Not given	£1 7s 6d
Freight of 15 casks oil per Anna	DPL	Not given	£10 5s

Reason	To whom paid	Date	Amount
Painting Dorothy: black paint; white lead	James Mearns	14 April 1830	£19 11s 11d
Painting Friendship including boats	James Mearns	14 April 1830	£13 15s
Fresh beef: Dorothy	Robert Small	13 April 1830	£20 6s
Shore dues on oil: London and Glasgow	Not given	12 April 1830	£2 18s 9d
62 stone pease: Dorothy	Thomas Dow senior	13 April 1830	£6 9s 2d
Nine cheeses and 74 stone pease: Friendship	Thomas Dow senior	13 April 1830	£11 4s 2d
Pilotage Dorothy from harbour out to sea	Thomas Webster	Not given	£2
Carpenter work: Friendship, Dorothy and boiler yard	D. & A. Brown [shipbuilder]	09 April 1830	£726
36 bolls oatmeal; 48 stone barley: Dorothy and Friendship	Hugh Mitchell	10 April 1830	£40 6s
Not given	Robert Pennans	10 April 1830	14s
Blocks: Dorothy	Robert Pennan	10 April 1830	£9 5s
Cordage: Friendship	James Bell: rope and sail maker	17 April 1830	£1 3s 6d
Cordage: Dorothy	James Bell	17 April 1830	£61 16s 11s
Tablecloth: Friendship	Robert Moyes	29 March 1830	7s
12 dozen brooms	Captain Spinks	27 March 1830	£2 2s
25 dozen eggs	Captain Chapman	22 March 1830	14s 7d
24 dozen eggs	Captain Davidson	03 April 1830	14s
11 dozen bungs	Francis Newton	03 March 1830	7s 4s
Sawing plank	Charles Cochran	03 April 1830	4s 6d
Two tides of barge for lightening Dorothy	Thomas Lee	03 April 1829	£6
Repairing Compasses	William Chadwick	06 April 1830	19s 6d
Insurance: Dorothy and Friendship	William and George Hunter: Glasgow	No date given	£221

Reason	To whom paid	Date	Amount
24 hundredweight pork: Dorothy	John Guillan	No date given	£30 14s 6d
41 hundredweight pork: Friendship	John Guillan	No date given	£51 12s 6d
New 26 foot whaleboat	John Calman	No date given	£24 14s
Carpentry work: Friendship	Robert Pennan	No date given	£10 13s 6d
Medicines: Friendship	James Drummond	No date given	£2 2s
Ropes and sails: Friendship	Alexander Buik	19 April 1830	£68 17s 6d
Ropes and sails: Dorothy	Alexander Buik	19 April 1830	£18 6s 6d
Two casks sawdust	William Walton	30 March 1830	5s
Carriage of harpoons to and from Pittenweem	James Brown, carrier, Anstruther	31 March 1830	15s
Harpoons etc: Friendship	James Adamson	01 April 1830	£8 1s 6d
Harpoons etc: Dorothy	James Adamson	01 April 1830	£8 5s 3d

Glossary

articles: the contract signed by crew members before the beginning of a voyage

baleen: the plates of horn-like material used by certain species of whale to extract their food (plankton) from the sea. The plates are suspended from the whale's upper jaws. These plates were valued and were also known as whalebone.

barque: sailing vessel of three masts, with square rigged sails on the fore and main masts and fore and aft sails on the mizzen

barque-rigged: see above; the arrangement of the sails and rigging on a barque

beset: trapped in an ice field

blow: a spout emitted by a whale as it surfaces. It is composed of the moist breath of the animal and is not sea water.

blubber: the layer of fat beneath a whale's skin. This material was boiled to make the very valuable whale oil.

blubber boat: whaling ship

bran: term used to describe the action of a boat on lookout along the edge of an ice field. It was 'on the bran.'

brig: a two-masted sailing vessel, square sailed on both masts

carvel-built: a wooden built vessel where the planks of the hull are laid edge to edge to create a smooth finish

clean ship: a ship that been unsuccessful in catching whales

clinker built: wooden ship where the lower edge of one side plank overlaps the upper edge of the one below

crow's nest: also called the 'barrel'; an enclosed, barrel shaped look out position attached to the main mast while hunting was in progress. It could have a seat and be equipped with a telescope; sometimes it was lined with straw. Scoresby, the Whitby whaler, is sometimes credited with its invention, but the Americans also claim it for themselves.

doubled: a hull with extra planking so it has double the thickness to make it stronger in the ice

fall: a successful strike by a harpooner

fast boat: a boat attached 'fast' to the whale by a harpoon and line

fish: whaling term for the whale

flensing: the process of removing blubber from the carcass of a whale

floe: a sheet of ice

flukes: the tail of a whale

foreganger: the length of line, about three fathoms (eighteen feet) attached to the harpoon at one end and to the whale-line proper at the other. It 'gangs before' the line.

full ship: a whaling ship with a full cargo of whales

greener gun: for firing darts into whales. This weapon had a two-inch bore (the width of the barrel) and was mounted in the bows of whaling boats. Although the first was invented as early as 1733, they were not commonly used until the 1790s when percussion caps replaced the old flintlock mechanism. Even then, many whaling vessels used hand-thrown harpoons well into the nineteenth century.

greenheart: a south American timber that is very hard and so resists the various nautical parasites that bore into wooden vessels

Greenlandman: a whaler or whaling ship

greenlander: name for a whaling ship (current in 1782)

greenman: First Voyager; a seaman who is on his first voyage in a whaling vessel

Indiaman: a vessel which sailed to the 'Indies', either the West Indies (the Caribbean) or the East Indies (basically anywhere east of Africa)

iron bark: a type of hard wood used in shipbuilding

ketch: a two-masted sailing vessel, originally with square sails on both masts, but by the latter half of the nineteenth century, the rig had altered to fore-and-aft.

letter of marque: a document that allowed private vessels to attack vessels of hostile powers in times of war. Sometimes the term was applied to the vessel itself as an alternative to the name 'privateer'

loose harpooner: harpooner on trial

lowery tow: the length of cable used for securing the skins of dead seals as they were dragged over the ice

making off: the process of cutting blubber into small pieces for stowing in casks below deck

nipped: crushed by ice

pan: a pile of dead seals

prize crew: when one ship captured an enemy vessel in wartime, the victors placed a small number of men on board to take control of their capture or 'prize'

row raddie: a canvas belt worn by men when they were bodily towing a ship through a passage in the ice. The towing line passed around the belt so the men had some protection from friction or injury

schooner: a vessel rigged with fore-and-aft sails; she has two or more masts; she may have square topsails on her foremast

screw: propeller; the rotating device that drives a ship through the water

scrimshaw: the traditional art of the whaling man; usually a design picked out on a piece of whale bone or a sperm whale tooth. Also called bone carving

ship: in the days of sail, a ship was a vessel with three masts or more

ship rigged: see above; the arrangement of the sails and rigging on a ship

ship's husband: a ship's husband was an agent of the owners of the cargo or sometimes an owner himself. He travelled with the vessel or remained with her when she was in port and took care of all the business arrangements for the cargo. He was also sometimes known as supercargo.

skeaman: officer in charge of ship's hold; from the Dutch 'schieman' captain of the forecastle.

specktioneer: head harpooner or officer in charge of removing the blubber from the whale

square rigged: sails are at right angles to the hull of the vessel

stove-boat: a boat damaged by a whale

sweiler: sealing seaman from Newfoundland

trying-out: boiling the oil from blubber

uni, unicorn: narwhal

whaling boat, whaler: normally sharp at both ends so it could move in either direction. Six oars and no rudder - manoeuvred with a long steering oar. Livvies was the main Dundee firm that made these vessels.

white whale: narwhal or beluga

Notes

The following abbreviations are used throughout the notes.
DCL: Dundee Central Library
DCA: Dundee City Archives
DUAS: Dundee University Archives Services
DAGM: Dundee Art Galleries and Museums

1   The Progress of British Arctic Whaling

1   DCL Lamb Collection 361 (44).
2   *Read's Weekly Journal,* 9 August 1755.
3   Gordon Jackson, *The British Whaling Trade.* Research in Maritime History No 29. (St John's, Newfoundland: Memorial University of Newfoundland, 2005), p. 22.
4   DCL Lamb 361 (44).
5   DCL Lamb 361 (44).
6   *Read's,* 20 July 1754.
7   Eric Jay Dolin, *Leviathan: The History of Whaling in America* (New York: W. W. Norton, 2007), pp. 1–35.
8   Alexander Starbuck, *History of the American Whale Fishery from its Earliest Inception to the year 1878* (New York: Washington, 1879), p. 58.
9   *St James Chronicle,* 9 January 1766.
10 Jackson, *British Whaling,* p. 57.
11 *Extracts from the Records of the Convention of the Royal Burghs of Scotland,* Vol. 4 (Edinburgh: 1917), p. 517, 9 April 1711.
12 Jackson, *British Whaling,* p 48.
13 Ibid., p. 40.
14 Ibid., p. 48.
15 *Craftsman or Says Weekly Journal,* 16 May 1772.
16 *General Evening Post,* 15 May 1787.
17 Jackson, *British Whaling,* p. 51.
18 *Whitehall Evening Post,* 6 May 1786.
19 DCA CE 70.2.25, 2 September 1790.
20 DCA CE 70.2.7, 16 July 1806.
21 DCA CE 70.1.11, 20 September 1807.
22 DCA CE 70.1.11, 20 September 1807.

23 Jackson, *British Whaling*, p. 51.

24 *Whitehall*, 17 April 1750.

25 *Penny London Post*, 1 October 1750.

26 *London Advertiser*, 16 April 1751.

27 *Read's*, 23 February 1751.

28 *General Advertiser*, 13 September 1751.

29 *London Daily Advertiser and Literary Gazette*, 11 November 1751.

30 *Read's*, 18 July 1752.

31 Jackson, *British Whaling*, p. 52

32 National Archives of Scotland E508.51.8, recorded in David Dobson, *Scottish Whalers Before 1800* (St Andrews, n.d.)

33 *London Evening Post*, 13 August 1774.

34 Gordon Jackson, 'Government Bounties and the Establishment of the Scottish Whaling Trade 1750–1800', in J. Butt and J. T. Ward, eds, *Scottish Themes: Essays in Honour of Professor S. G. E. Lythe* (Edinburgh: Scottish Academic Press, 1976), p. 56.

35 *Universal Chronicle*, 8 April April 1758

36 *London Evening*, 24 March 1759

37 *London Chronicle*, 3 April 1760

38 *Public Advertiser*, 1 April 1762,.

39 *London Evening*, 5 August 1762

40 Jackson, *British Whaling*, p. 54

41 Ibid., p. 55

42 *London Chronicle*, 17 March 1764

43 *St James*, 11 August 1764

44 *St James*, 2 February 1768

45 *Public Advertiser*, 31 July 1755

46 *Read's*, 18 July 1752

47 *Gazetteer and New Daily Advertiser*, 12 December 1765

48 *Lloyd's Evening Post*, 12 March 1766.

49 *Lloyds*, 27 March 1767.

50 *General*, 13 April 1774.

51 *Public Advertiser*, 3 August 1768.

52 *London Evening*, 22 June 1756.

53 *Gazetteer and London Advertiser*, 29 July 1762.

54 Jackson, *British Whaling*, pp. 58–9.

55 Ibid., p.59.

56 Ibid., pp. 81–91.

57 *Morning Post and Daily Advertiser*, 24 August 1779.

58 Quoted in *Morning News and London Advertiser*, 27 July 1781.

59 *London Evening*, 19 February 1763..

60 *Public Advertiser*, 31 July 1782.

61 *Gazetteer*, 23 September 1782

62 *Public*, 31 July 1753.

63 *London Chronicle*, 11 September 1783.

64 *General*, 11 March 1784

65 Ibid., 29 January 1785.
66 *Whitehall*, 1 March 1787.
67 *Baldwin's London Weekly Journal*, 10 May 1788.
68 Jackson, *British Whaling*, p. 56.
69 *Public*, 27 September 1787.
70 *General*, 30 June 1787.
71 *Morning Chronicle*, 25 August 1787
72 *General*, 19 July 1787
73 *Owen's Weekly Chronicle*, 9 May 1758
74 *St James*, 17 February 1788; *Morning Post*, 21 February 1788
75 *Oracle and Public Advertiser*, 8 May 1798
76 *Observer* (London), 9 February 1800
77 *The Hull Packet*, 4 February 1800
78 *Lancaster Gazetteer*,13 February 1802
79 *Caledonian Mercury*, 3 September 1804
80 Jackson, *British Whaling*, p 107
81 www.nationalgasmuseum.org, 16 December 2011
82 *Mercury*, 15 June 1816
83 *Trewman's Exeter Flying Post*, 2 September 1819
84 *Mercury*,10 April 1823
85 *Hull Rockingham*, 14 April 1841
86 Jackson, *British Whaling*, p. 117
87 *Westminster Journal and London Political Miscellany*, 20 July 1765
88 *London Evening*, 23 June 1767
89 Ibid., 23 June 1774
90 *Lloyds Evening*, 9 August 1775
91 *Chronicle*, 19 July 1783
92 *Read's*, 20 April 1751
93 *General*, 10 March 1772
94 DUAS MS 254/1/2/17/1
95 DCL Tat p. 80
96 DUAS MS 254/1/2/17/1
97 DUAS MS 254/1/2/17/3
98 DUAS MS 254/1/1/18
99 DUAS MS 254/2/1/13, *Voyage to Davis Straits by Thomas Macklin,on board the SS Narwhal*, 11 July 1876
100 DUAS MS 254/2/1/16, Vannet Logs, 24 August 1910
101 *Macklin*, 20 March 1874; ibid., 20 March 1874 (*2 x notes 101?*)
102 *Macklin*, 20 March 1874
103 Jackson, *British Whaling*, pp. 129–32

2 The Hunting Process

1 *Diary of a Voyage to the Davis Straits Aboard the Nova Zembla of Dundee 1884 by Mathew Campbell, Surgeon*, 25 February 1884
2 *Banffshire Journal*,24 Feb 1852

3 Jackson, *British Whaling,* p. 63.

4 *St James,* 10 March 1764

5 DCA CE 53.1.17 17 July 1802

6 *Dundee Advertiser,*23 April 1872; 17 April 1874

7 Innes MacLeod, ed.,*To the Greenland Sea: Alexander Trotter's Journal of the Voyage of the Enterprise in 1856 from Fraserburgh and Lerwick* (Lerwick: The Thule Press, 1979) 26 March 1856, p. 30

8 Macleod, *Trotter,* 31 March 1856, p. 32

9 Ibid., 31 March, p. 32

3   Prizes, Privateers and the Press

1 *Public,* 2 February 1765

2 *Lancaster Gazetteer,* 13 February 1802

3 *London Daily,* 20 April 1751

4 DCA CE 70.1.10, 18 February 1804

5 DCA CE 70.1.12, 16 February 1809

6 *General Evening Post,* 23 February 1793

7 DCA CE 70.1.10, 19 February 1804

8 DCA CE 70.1.10, 11 July 1805

9 DCA CE 70.1.10, 16 February 1805

10 DCA, CE 70.1.12, 21 March 1809

11 DCA CE 70.1.12, 2 May 1809

12 *Read's,* 25 September 1756

13 Ibid.,14 May 1757

14 *Whitehall,* 25 April 1782

15 Gilbert Gourdie, ed., *The Diary of the Reverend John Mill: Minister of the parishes of Dunrossness, Sandwick and Cunningsburgh in Shetland 1740–1803* (Edinburgh: Scottish History Society, 1889) April 1781, p. 51

16 *St James,St James,* 3 May 1781

17 *Public Advertiser,* 7 May 1782

18 *St James,* 13 August 1797

19 Ibid.,17 July 1798

20 *Mercury,*19 July 1804

21 *Public,* 9 May 1758

22 *Whitehall,* 12 June 1756, 6 July 1756

23 *London Evening,* 23 September 1756

24 *Lloyd's,* 4 August 1762

25 *London Evening,* 7 August 177

26 Ibid., 12 August 1777

27 Ibid., 26 August 1777

28 *General,* 11 September 1779

29 *London Evening,* 20 September 1777

30 *Chronicle,* 8 August 1780

31 Ibid.,22 August 1780

32 *St James,* 4 April 1782

33 DCA CE 70.1.1, 13 March 1793

34 *Chronicle,* 25 February 1792

35 *Lloyd's,* 30 March 1796

36 *St James,* 11 March 1796

37 Ibid., 8 August 1797

38 *True Briton,* 31 July 1799

39 *Packet,* 3 March 1801

40 *London Evening,* 27 February 1776

41 *True Briton,* 30 August 1796

42 *Oracle,* 8 May 1798

43 *Bell's Weekly Messenger,* 19 August 1798

44 *Mirror of the Times,* 10 November 1798

45 *Morning Post,* 22 June 1803

46 *Aberdeen Journal,* 21 May 1806

47 *Mercury,* 16 June 1806

48 Ibid., 25 August 1807

49 Ibid., 3 September 1807

50 *Aberdeen Journal,* 23 July 1806 and *Morning Chronicle,* 23 July 1806

51 *Mercury,* 31 July 1806

52 *Owen's,* 22 July 1758

53 *London Evening,* 18 July 1780

54 *General Evening Post,* 5 August 1794

55 *Mercury,* 10 July 1806

56 Ibid., 19 July 1806

57 *London Packet,* 15 August 1794

58 *Extracts,* 2 August 1755

59 *Public,* 15 March 1756

60 *Whitehall,* 3 August 1756

61 Ibid., 3 August 1756

62 *Chronicle,* 7 August 1759

63 Ibid., 7 August 1759

64 *Lloyd's,* 6 August 1779

65 Ibid., 3 September 1781

66 *Chronicle,* 23 July 1782

67 *Morning Chronicle,* 10 November 1787

68 *London Evening,* 19 November 1776

69 *Advertiser,Gazetteer and New Daily Advertiser,* 24 June 1779

70 *St James,* 24 October 1780

71 Ibid., 17 April 1781

72 *Lloyd's,* 28 July 1794

73 *London Packet,* 20 August 1794

74 *Evening Mail,* 6 August 1798

75 *Advertiser,Gazetteer and New Daily Advertiser,* 24 August 1790

76 *Morning Chronicle,* 19 September 1807

77 *Packet,* 22 September 1807

78 Jackson, *British Whaling*, p. 55

79 Ibid., p. 60

80 DCA CE 53.1.22, 15 October 1813, *Mercury,* 12 August 1813

81 *Mercury,* 12 August 1813

82 Ibid., 15 December 1814

4   The Dundee Whaling Industry

 1 *Read's,* 21 April 1753

 2 *London Evening,* 1 July 1755

 3 Ibid., 22 June 1756

 4 *London Evening,* 6 August 1757

 5 *Owen's,* 8 July 1758

 6 *Chronicle,* 11 August 1759

 7 *Lloyd's,* 28 July 1769

 8 *St James,* 3 July 1787

 9 Ibid., 18 June 1791

10 *General Evening Post,* 17 August 1784

11 *St James,* 27 July 1799

12 *Packet,* 14 August 1804

13 Ibid., 14 July 1807

14 Ibid., 2 August 1808

15 Ibid., 4 May 1813

16 *News Courant,* 28 August 1819

17 *Mercury,* 16 September 1822

18 Ibid., 10 April 1823

19 *Advertiser,* 23 September 1823

20 Ibid., 15 January 1824

21 Ibid., 2 February 1826

22 Ibid., 7 December 1826

23 *Advertiser,* 27 September 1827, 4 October 1827 and 1 November 1827

24 Ibid., 29 November 1827

25 DCL John P. Ingram Papers Whaling and Sealing

26 DCA *Dundee Register of Shipping* CE 70.11.17, 23 July 1859

27 *Ingram*

28 Ibid.

29 *Ingram, Shipping Information* A-D D31111

30 *Advertiser,* 18 October 1839

31 Ibid., 25 September 1823

32 Ibid., 19 October 1821

33 Ibid., 20 October 1825

34 *Ingram*

35 *Advertiser,* 27 October 1831

36 Ibid., 3 November 1831

37 Ibid., 16 April 1874

38 Ibid., 9 October 1823

39 Ibid., 21 March 1843

40 DCA CE 70.2.9, 20 November 1811

41 *Statement concerning the whale-fishing trade at Dundee in reference to its proposed introduction into Burntisland* (Burntisland, 1830) pp. 1-2

42 *Ingram,* 1840

43 Ibid., p. 2

44 *Public,* 20 February 1789

45 Ibid., 21 February 1786

46 DUAS MS 254/3/1/11

47 *Vannet*

48 *Vannet,* 06 July 1907

5 Why They Hunted

1 *Advertiser,* 02 February 1826

2 DUAS MS 254/3/1/10 [A]

3 *Glasgow Herald,* 8 Dec 1851

4 *Packet,* 17 February 1818

5 *Advertiser,* 21 October 1821

6 Ibid., 15 December 1825

7 Ibid., 25 October 1832

8 Ibid., 8 November 1833

9 *Advertiser,* 30 January 1835

10 Ibid., 21 October 1830

11 Ibid., 4 November 1830

12 Ibid., 14 June 1839; 30 January 1835

13 *Courier,* 23 April 1872

14 DUAS MS254/1/2/5

15 University of St Andrews Special Collection MS 15914

16 DUAS MS 254/3/1/11

6 The Greenland Whaling Ships

1 Jackson, *British Whaling,* p. 24

2 DCL *Tay Whaling,* p. 155

3 *Chronicle,* 5 August 1784

4 *London Evening,* 28 May 1776

5 Macleod, *Trotter,,* 28 June 1856, p. 55

6 Tim Flannery, ed., *The Life and Adventures of John Nicol, Mariner, 1822* (Edinburgh: Canongate,2000) p. 60

7 *General,* 30 June 1787

8 Gourdie, *Mill;* 1787; page 51

9 June Starke (transcriber), *Baffin Fair: experiences of George Laing, a Scottish Surgeon in the Arctic Whaling Fleet 1830 and 1831* (Hull: Hutton Press, 2003), p. 29

10 *Advertiser,* 13 January 1837

11 Ibid., 27 January 1837

12 Ibid., 17 February 1837

13 *A Journal of a Voyage from Dundee Towards the Davis Straits on board the Dorothy in 1834* (Captain Thomas Davidson) 4 June 1834

14 *Campbell* 27 June 1884

15 *Chronicle,* 2 July 1791

16 *London Evening,* 25 June 1754

17 *Public,* 13 July 1758

18 *Owen's,* 29 July 1758

19 *Public Advertiser,* 29 July 1762

20 *Chronicle,* 9 August 1790

21 *Public,* 27 August 1788

22 *London Evening,* 18 September 1788

23 *Whitehall,* 23 August 1789

24 *Advertiser,* 4 August 1825

25 Ibid., 11 October 1832

26 Macleod, *Trotter,* 5 July 1856 p. 56

27 *London Packet,* 23 April 1787

28 *Read's,* 29 April 1758

29 *Lloyd's,* 30 July 1764

30 *Dorothy,* 18 May 1834

31 *Lloyd's,* 3 August 1761

32 *Public,* 20 February 1789

33 Douglas Mawson, *The Home of the Blizzard* (London & Kent Town: Wakefield Press, 1915, 1996), p. 3

7 The Business of Whaling

1 Jackson, *British Whaling,* p. 65

2 Jackson, *British Whaling,* p. 66

3 DCL ledger 1 MS Dundee 1815-1821,*Tay Whale fishing Company*

4 *Ingram,* 1824

5 *Ingram,* 1788

6 William Barron, *Old Whaling Days* (Hull: William Andrews,1895), p. 47

7 *Ingram,* 1841

8 *Ingram,* 1867

9 DUAS MS 254/3/4/1

10 *Tay Ledger,* p. 130, p. 167, p. 212

11 *Mercury,* 30 March 1818

12 *Advertiser,* 9 November 1826

13 Ibid., 21 December 1826

14 Ibid., 29 November 1827

15 Ibid., 10 December 1827

16 *London Evening Post,* 13 August 1774

17 *Practical Magazine,* DUAS MS 254/3/1/5

18 *Ingram,* 1811

19 DUAS MS 57/3/2

20 *Tay Ledger,* p. 52

21 John Dyson, *The Hot Arctic* (London: William Heinemann,1979) p.187

22 On the 24 November 1830 the *Aberdeen Journal* carried an advertisement stating William Chambers, Treasurer of Police, wanted six tons of best boiled whale oil 'for the public lamps of the city'.

23 *Mercury,* 8 September 1814

24 Ibid., 11 September 1817

25 *London Evening,* 23 July 1765

26 S. G. E. Lythe, 'The Dundee Whale Fishery', quoted in DUAS 254/3/1/11

27 DAGM 1975-2-2(8)

28 Cargo Book of *Dorothy,* 1832, DAGM 75-536-6

29 Cargo Book of *Dorothy,* 1833, DAGM 1975-536-6

30 DUAS Dorothy Whale Fishing Company 57/3/2, 8 September 1830

31 *Mercury,* 27 October 1823

32 Ibid., 2 February 1826

33 Ibid., 14 September 1826

34 Ibid., 5 November 1829

35 Ibid., 21 October 1830

36 Ibid., 4 November 1830

37 Ibid., 25 October 1832

38 *Ingram,* 18

8   The Whaling Masters

1 Barron, *Whaling,* p. 140

2 *Mercury,* 29 May 1815

3 DAGM 1957-423-1, *Journal of a Voyage to Baffin Bay aboard the ship Thomas commanded by Alex Cooke, signed John Wanless 1834* 10 July 1834

4 DCL *An account of a Voyage to Greenland aboard the whaler SS Camperdown in the year 1861 written and illustrated by Alexander Smith of Dundee, chief engineer,* p. 2

5 Captain A. H. Markham RN, *A Whaling Cruise to Baffin's Bay and the Gulf of Boothia and an Account of the Rescue of the Crew of the Polaris* (London: S. Low, Marston, Low and Searle, 1874) p. 290

6 DUAS MS 254/1/1/2

9   The Greenlandman's Experience

1 *Gazetteer and Daily Advertiser,* 21 February 1772

2 Sigismund Bacstrom, *Account of a Voyage to Spitzbergen in the year 1780,* published in the *Packet* 11 March 1800

3 *Nicol,* p. 60

4 DAGM *Kinnes Journal,* 24 June 1900

5 *Bacstrom*

6 *Nicol,* p 61

7 Ibid., p. 61

8 DUASMS 254/2/1/5 *Journal of Stewart Peters, Resolute 1882*

9 DUAS MS 254/3/1/10 (a)

10 *Smith,* p. 71

11 DAGM *Log of David McAdam; Surgeon, Horn 1839*

12 DUAS 254/1/2/50

13 DUAS MS 254/2/1/5

14 Certificates of discharge held in Local History Department, Central Library, Dundee

15 DUAS MS 254/3/1/5, *Journal of a Whaling Voyage from Dundee to Davis Straits 1894* in *Polar Record* Vol. 10, No. 65, May 1960

16 *Dorothy,* 06 June 1834

17 DAGM *Kinnes Journal* 11 June 1900

18 Ibid.

19 Ibid.

20 *Macklin, 2 June 1874*

21 *Campbell,* 28 February 1884

22 *Campbell,* 21March 1884

23 DAGM *Kinnes Journal* 25 June 1900

24 Ibid., 28 June 1900

25 *Macklin,* 2 June 1874

26 DUA MS 254/2/1/21, *Adamson's Log on Board Advice*; 02 May 1838; hereafter *Adamson*

27 *Adamson,* 10 May 1838

28 *Dorothy*; 30 June 1834

29 Ibid., 1 July 1834

30 DCA CE 53.1.1.15

31 *Tay Ledger,* p. 80

32 *Smith,* 17 June 1861 p. 102

33 *Campbell,* 19 July 1884

34 DUAS MS 254/1/2/5

35 DUAS MS 57/3/3

36 DAGM *Kinnes Journal* 4 July 1900

37 *Dorothy*; 1 July 1834

38 *Barque Fairy from Dundee Towards Davis Straits: David Davidson, Master 1838,* 7 June 1838

39 *Dorothy,* 18 May 1834

40 Ibid., 27 May 1834

41 Ibid., 4 June 1834

42 *Macklin,* 26 May 1874

43 DAGM *Whaling Log of Alexander J Lamb,* 28 May 1903

44 DCL Lamb 8 September 1903

45 Captain G. Clark, *The Last of the Whaling Captains* (Glasgow: Brown, Son and Ferguson, 1986) p. 56

46 Gavin Sutherland, *The Whaling Years: Peterhead (1788–1893)* (Aberdeen: Centre for Scottish Studies,1993) p. 110

47 *Mercury,* 12 October 1818

48 *Whitehall,* 5 August 1786

49 *Advertiser,* 30 November 1826

50 Ibid., 14 February 1828

51 *Wanless*

52 Ibid.

53 Ibid.

54 DAGM 1973-1946 x : *Intrepid*

55 *Campbell*, 26 February 1884

56 *Lloyds*, 06 August 1762

57 Burntisland, Whale-fishing, p. 3

58 Gourdie, *Mill*, 1787

59 W. G. Burn Murdoch, *From Edinburgh to the Antarctic* (London: Longman,1894) p. 341

10 The Last Hurrah: The Dundee Antarctic Expedition

1 *Courier*, 21 September 1892

2 *Pall Mall Budget*, 20 June 1893

3 *Courier*, 5 September 1892

4 Ibid., 26 August 1892

5 Ibid., 27 August 1892

6 Burn Murdoch, *Edinburgh to Antarctic*, p. 19

7 Ibid., p. 20

8 Ibid., pp. 39–51

9 *Courier*, 24 June 1893

10 Ibid., 1 June 1893

11 Ibid., 19 April 1893

12 Ibid., 31 May 1893

13 Ibid., 29 May 1893

14 Ibid., 16 June 1893

15 Ibid., 1 July 1893

16 Ibid., 29 May 1893

17 Ibid., 13 June 1893

18 Ibid., 21 June 1893

19 Ibid., 13 June 1893

20 Ibid., 21 June 1893

21 Ibid., 29 July 1893

22 Ibid., 24 June 1893

23 Ibid., 12 August 1893

24 St Andrews University Special Collections MS 15914 (26 January 1903) and MS 15925 (31 October 1908) letters from Frederic Augustus Lucas, Director of American Museum of Natural History, to D'Arcy Wentworth Thompson

25 Jackson, *British Whaling*, pp. 143–5

11 Farewell to the Whaling

1 Ibid., pp. 134–7

2 St Andrews University Special Collection: MS 15939

12 Twentieth Century Scottish Whaling

1 Ibid., MS 13656
2 Sigrid Alvestad, 'Whaling from the Shores of Scotland in the 20th Century', in *Whaling and the Hebrides* (South Lochs, Isle of Lewis: The Islands Bool Trust,2008) pp. 157–9
3 Ibid., pp. 160–1
4 Norman Maclennan 'The Bunabhaineadar Whaling Station in West Loch Tarbert' in *Whaling and the Hebrides* (South Lochs, Isle of Lewis: The Islands Book Trust, 2008), pp. 165–8
5 St Andrews University Special Collections: MS 13656
6 Maclennan, pp. 167
7 D'Arcy Wentworth Thompson; *On Whales Landed at the Scottish Whaling Stations during the Years 1908 – 1914 and 1920 – 1927*, (HMSO, 1928) summary.
8 Alvestad, pp.160-161
9 George Cummings, 'History of the Christian Salvesen Company', in *Whaling and the Hebrides* (South Lochs, Isle of Lewis: The Islands Bool Trust, 2008), pp. 13–16
10 Tam Gordon, *Whaling Thoughts Recalled* (St Andrews, n.d.) p. 5
11 Cummings, pp.13–16
12 Jackson, *British Whaling*, pp. 155–9
13 Ibid., pp. 200-23

Appendix 1

1 *London Chronicle*, 15 July 1786
2 DUAS; MS 254/1/2/42
3 A. Barclay Walker; *The Cruise of the Esquimaux (steam whaler) to Davis Straits and Baffin Bay April to October 1899* (1909) Liverpool DUAS MS 254/2/1/4
4 *Advertiser* 29 September 1884
5 DUA MS 254/3/2/

Appendix 2

1 DUAS; MS 254/1/2/29
2 William S. Bruce, *Polar Exploration* [1911] London, Page 53
3 DUAS; MS 254/1/1/17

Appendix 5

1 DUAS; MS 254/2/2/2 and MS 254/2/2/2

Bibliography

PRIMARY SOURCES

The McManus: Dundee's Museum

Cargo Book of *Dorothy*, 1832, 1975-536-6
Diary of a Voyage to the Davis Straits Aboard the Nova Zembla of Dundee 1884 By
  Mathew Campbell, Surgeon,
Intrepid 11973-1946
Journal of a Voyage from Dundee Towards the Davis Straits on board the Dorothy
  in 1834 (Captain Thomas Davidson) 4 June 1834
Journal of a Voyage to Baffin Bay aboard the ship Thomas commanded by Alex
  Cooke, signed John Wanless 1834
Kinnes Journal
Log of David McAdam; Surgeon, Horn 1839: DAGM: 1957-423-1
Whaling Log of Alexander J Lamb

Local History Department, Central Library Dundee

An account of a Voyage to Greenland aboard the whaler SS *Camperdown* in the year
  1861 written and illustrated by Alexander Smith of Dundee chief engineer,
Barque Fairy from Dundee Towards Davis Straits: David Davidson, Master 1838; 07
  June 1838
Dundee Directories, [various dates]
John P. Ingram, Shipping Information A-D D31111
John P. Ingram Papers Whaling and Sealing
Ledger of the Tay Whaling Company 1815–1821
Lamb Collection: Whaling 361 (44)

Dundee City Archives

Customs and Excise Records
Dundee Register of Shipping
Dundee Year Book 1880
Dundee Year Book 1883 .

Dundee University Archive Services

MS 57/3/2 Dorothy Whale Fishing Company Accounts
MS 254 David Henderson Collection, in particular:
MS 254/3/1/5 *Practical Magazine*
MS 254/2/1/5 *Journal of Stewart Peters, Resolute 1882*
MS 254/2/1/13 *Voyage to Davis Straits by Thomas Macklin,on board the SS Narwhal*
MS 254/2/1/16 *Vannet Logs*
MS 254/2/1/ Walker, A. Barclay, *The Cruise of the Esquimaux (steam whaler) to Davis Straits and Baffin Bay April to October 1899* (Liverpool, 1909)

University of St Andrews Special Collection

University of St Andrews Special Collection MS 15914

Newspapers

Aberdeen Journal
Baldwin's London Weekly Journal
Banffshire Journal
Bell's Weekly Messenger
Caledonian Mercury
Craftsman or Says Weekly Journal
Dundee Advertiser
Dundee Courier
Gazetteer and New Daily Advertiser
Gazetteer and London Advertiser
General Advertiser
General Evening Post
Hull Rockingham
Lancaster Gazetteer
Lloyd's Evening Post
London Chronicle
London Advertiser
London Chronicle
London Daily Advertiser and Literary Gazette
London Evening Post
Mirror of the Times
Morning Chronicle
Morning Post and Daily Advertiser
Morning News and London Advertiser
News Courant
Observer (London)
Oracle and Public Advertiser
Owen's Weekly Chronicle

Bibliography

Penny London Post
Public Advertiser
Reads Weekly Journal
St James's Chronicle
The Hull Packet
Trewman's Exeter Flying Post
True Briton 1793
Universal Chronicle
Westminster Journal and London Political Miscellany
Whitehall Evening Post

Books

Barron, William, *Old Whaling Days* (Hull, 1895

Bruce, William S., *Polar Exploration* (London, 1911)

Burn Murdoch, W. G., *From Edinburgh to the Antarctic* (London, 1894)

Dobson, David, *Scottish Whalers Before 1800* (St Andrews, n.d.)

Hunter, Thomas, ed., *Extracts from the Records of the Convention of the Royal Burghs of Scotland*, Vol. 4 (Edinburgh, 1917)

Flannery, Tim, ed., *The Life and Adventures of John Nicol, Mariner, 1822* (Edinburgh, 2000)

Gourdie, Gilbert, ed., *The Diary of the Reverend John Mill: Minister of the parishes of Dunrossness, Sandwick and Cunningsburgh in Shetland 1740–1803* (Edinburgh, 1889)

Gordon, Tam, *Whaling Thoughts Recalled* (St Andrews, n.d.)

MacLeod, Innes, ed., *To the Greenland Sea: Alexander Trotter's Journal of the Voyage of the Enterprise in 1856 from Fraserburgh and Lerwick* (Lerwick, 1979)

Markham RN, Captain A. H., *A Whaling Cruise to Baffin's Bay and the Gulf of Boothia and an Account of the Rescue of the Crew of the Polaris* (London, 1874)

Mawson, Douglas, *The Home of the Blizzard* (London, 1996)

Robertson, R. B., *Of Whales and Men* (London, 1956)

Starke, June, transcriber, *Baffin Fair: Experiences of George Laing, a Scottish Surgeon in the Arctic Whaling Fleet 1830 and 1831* (Hull, 2003)

Statement concerning the whale-fishing trade at Dundee in reference to its proposed introduction into Burntisland (Burntisland, 1830)

Thompson, D'Arcy Wentworth, *On Whales Landed at the Scottish Whaling Stations during the years 1908–1914 and 1920–1927* (Glasgow, 1928)

SECONDARY SOURCES

Alvestad, Sigrid, 'Whaling From the Shores of Scotland in the 20th Century', in *Whaling and the Hebrides* (South Lochs, Lewis, 2008)

Archibald, Malcolm, *Whalehunters: Dundee and the Arctic Whalers* (Edinburgh, 2004)

Baldwin, John, 'Subsistence Whaling in the Western and Northern Isles of Scotland', in *Whaling and the Hebrides* (South Lochs, Lewis, 2008)

Clark, Captain G., *The Last of the Whaling Captains* (Glasgow, 1986)

Credland, Arthur G., *Whales and Whaling: the Arctic Fishery* (Hull, 1982)

Cummings, George, 'History of the Christian Salvesen Company', in *Whaling and the Hebrides* (South Lochs, Lewis, 2008)

Dolin, Eric Jay, *Leviathan: The History of Whaling in America* (New York, 2007)

Dyson, John, *The Hot Arctic* (London, 1979)

Francis, Daniel, *Arctic Chase: A History of Whaling in Canada's North* (St John's, Newfoundland, 1984)

Henderson, David S., *Fishing for the Whale: A guide/catalogue to the collection of whaling relics in Dundee museums* (Dundee, 1976)

Jackson, Gordon, *The British Whaling Trade*, Research in Maritime History No 29 (St John's, Newfoundland, 2006)

Lubbock, Basil, *The Arctic Whalers* (Glasgow, 1937, 1955)

Maclennan, Norman, 'The Bunabhaineadar Whaling Station in West Loch Tarbert', in *Whaling and the Hebrides* (South Lochs, Lewis, 2008)

Sanger, C. W., 'The Origins of the Scottish Northern Whale Fishery', unpublished PhD Thesis, University of Dundee (1985)

Whatley, Christopher A., Swinfen, David B. and Smith, Annette M., *The Life and Times of Dundee* (Edinburgh, 1993)

Index of Whaling Ships and Other Vessels

For whaling ships, the port of registration and approximate dates of operation are given. Appropriate details are also given for other vessels.

Index of Whaling Seamen

All masters, captains and crewmen mentioned in the text and appendices are listed. Dates of operation are given for masters and captains.

General Index

Printed and bound by CPI Group (UK) Ltd, Croydon, CR0 4YY

04/02/2025

01831613-0001